ISLANDS

Bill Robinson

ISLANDS

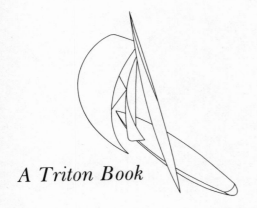

A Triton Book

DODD, MEAD & COMPANY, INC. · NEW YORK

Copyright © 1985 by William W. Robinson
All rights reserved
No part of this book may be reproduced in any form
without permission in writing from the publisher.
Published by Dodd, Mead & Company, Inc.
79 Madison Avenue, New York, N.Y. 10016
Distributed in Canada by
McClelland and Stewart Limited, Toronto
Manufactured in the United States of America
Designed by G. G. Laurens
First Edition

Library of Congress Cataloging in Publication Data

Robinson, Bill, 1918–
Islands.
1. Sailing.   2. Islands—Description and travel.
I. Title.
GV811.R53   1985   910'.09142   84-13817
ISBN 0-396-08497-4

Contents

I S L A N D S

Introduction:
The World of Islands

A lifelong fascination with islands is the background for this book, and it has taken me to hundreds of them in many years of sailing and travel. They have been as contrasting as the rocky skerries of Sweden and New Guinea's tropical luxuriance, and I have been under the spell of their enchantment whether on the low, sandy sedge bank I see from my bedroom window or the most remote atoll of the South Pacific. Though I have been to many, no one could take in all the islands on earth, or even all the best known ones, so this is a book of personal experience, relating the overall magic of the world of islands to my own adventures. Nevertheless, before getting to them, there are some general comments that should be made.

First, although all the world is made up of islands in that the land masses are surrounded by the sea, in the context of this book Eurasia or Australia are not thought of as islands, nor are the British Isles, Japan, or even Manhattan. I am concerned, rather, with the effect created in a visitor— a state of mind, a feeling of insularity, of escape, and of that certain sensibility that only comes when there is an awareness that the most important feature of a given piece of land is that it is surrounded by water.

There are islands and there are *islands.* They vary greatly beyond the basic of separation by water, and the contrast can range from the midocean isolation of Bermuda to the intricate interrelation of the rocky islets of Lake Huron's North Channel, from a tiny dot like Monhegan to a land mass as big as New Guinea, or from the primitive atmosphere of the San Blas to the teeming civilization of Hong Kong. They can be reached by a short bridge or a ferry, first glimpsed from a deck, or approached after a flight of thousands of miles, but the broad result is the same—entry into a different world, one apart, where we perhaps undergo a shift to a new mentality.

Within this general change in attitude and state of mind, each is a separate experience. Martha's Vineyard is not Nantucket, Martinique is not Antigua, Tahiti is not Moorea, and Patmos is not Mykonos. With the shifting nuances of climate, speech, architecture, life-style, and scenery, we can go from island to island in neverending wonder and fascination, and each return is a renewal of the intriguing excitement few fail to experience.

The first and most obvious difference between islands is the way in which they have been formed. Some, like the sedge-topped ones in New Jersey's Shrewsbury River in front of my house, are mere overgrown sandbars, often augmented by dredging fill from maintenance of the navigation channels. Man has made some sizable islands from fill, but nature has different ways of creating them.

During eons of geological development in which human history is a mere wink of the eye, land masses have broken off from continents or been separated by a change in the level of the oceans, which has varied by hundreds of feet through the ages, depending on the state of the polar ice caps. Large islands like New Guinea, and some close to continents, like the Whitsundays of northern Australia, owe their insular status to forces like these. There are legends, too, of whole sunken continents, like Atlantis, whose myth Plato propagated, and even of Gondwana, which might have stretched across the southern hemisphere, taking in Africa, South America, and Australia. This could account for the large land mass of New Zealand, although the scientific support for Atlantis and Gondwana is slight.

Many islands were formed volcanically, and their soaring cones and dramatic contours are among the most striking scenic effects associated with islands. Hawaii is a prime example, and volcanos there are still active, giving modern man a glimpse of the awesome forces that took millions and millions of years to shape the modern world. The Pacific Ocean has many volcanic islands, and Bora Bora's stark peak is typical. Its low ridge leading to the adjacent cone is all that is left of an immense crater rim, and the island is gradually sinking, in a geological sense. However, anyone with hotel reservations there next winter need not worry. The sinking process will take a few hundred thousand years at least, and then all that will remain will be an atoll supported by the surrounding reef. Tahiti was formed by the merging of two volcanos that erupted close to one another and eventually merged, creating a double island. Most of the Antilles in the Caribbean were formed volcanically, and Martinique and St. Vincent have had eruptions even in the twentieth century, St. Vincent as recently as 1979. In unstable areas like the sea near Iceland, the Azores, or the Aleutians, new islands have been seen to emerge from the deep, sometimes resubmerging, in recent times. This is probably an endless process. Sometimes the *tsunamis,* or tidal waves, generated by these eruptions do great damage to other islands.

Perhaps the most fascinating way that islands are formed, also in a process that never stops, is the reef-building action of the small marine animals known as corals. Corals cannot exist in water temperatures under 70 degrees Fahrenheit, so coral islands are largely confined to tropical areas. Bermuda, however, in 32°20′ N. is based on coral because the Gulf Stream warms the waters around it, making it the coral island most distant from the Equator.

Reefs are formed by the process of corals building on the skeletons of their ancestors. When the tiny animals, which take many colorful forms, die, their skeletons become a limestone deposit that compacts with mollusk shells and coralline algae. Corals cannot live deeper than 20 to 25 fathoms, because they need light to survive, so coral reefs that are deeper than that trace back through countless centuries to an era of lower water levels in the oceans. Drillings on some Pacific atolls have brought up coral deposits from several thousand feet. Corals also cannot survive in air for any length of time, so reef life stops at the low-tide level.

There are three types of reefs formed by corals: fringing, barrier, and atolls. Fringing reefs are attached to a land mass, and life on them is largely confined to the seaward edge. Barrier reefs, of which the Great Barrier Reef off Australia and those off the Florida Keys and Belize in the western

Caribbean are probably the best known, form offshore with open water in between. Atolls take a roughly circular form, also offshore, around a central lagoon. While many atolls remain reefs that are barely exposed at low tide, they also contribute to the formation of islands in many cases. Coral rubble thrown up by wave action remains out of water and eventually collects enough sand to form a solid piece of land. This will, over a long period of time, develop vegetation through winds and migratory birds carrying seeds. Bikini is probably the best known, if most unfortunate of atolls, and many of the familiar Pacific names from World War II such as Eniwetok, Tarawa, and Kwajalein are atolls. There are very few in the Atlantic Ocean and there is only one, a tiny spot called Hogsty Reef near Inagua, in the Bahamas. All three types of reefs can support dry land given the circumstances described, but the life of the reef itself never emerges above the low-tide level.

Along the east coast of North America, many of the off-lying islands, such as Nantucket and Martha's Vineyard, are the product of glacial action, actually piles of rubble marking the southern limit of glacial movement in the last ice age.

Just as islands have these varied backgrounds, they also mean many things to many people. For some, escape from the "real world" to an ambience for relaxation is all that is sought, whether in an air-conditioned, high-rise hotel or at the most primitive of beach resorts. There is, for many people, a desire to be completely alone, while some yearn for a group experience. There are those who go to an island mainly for the fishing, especially in such famous centers as Bimini, or Cat Cay in the Bahamas, while divers particularly seek the coral islands for the unique snorkeling and scuba opportunities they provide. There are some who know islands only as stamp collectors, through the often colorful, exotic imprints issued by small island countries as a means of raising income, like Grenada and Papua. My father was a stamp collector, and I remember him telling me years ago that the "Blue Penny Mauritius" was the world's most valuable stamp. That was the first time I had heard of that Indian Ocean island, and I think of the stamp now whenever Mauritius is mentioned.

Permanent residents of islands have an extra sense of community, of individuality that sets them apart from all off-islanders. Whereas Nantucketers talk about going "to America" when they visit the mainland, the reverse can be found in that sense of confinement, a form of "cabin fever," that can only be alleviated by periodic escapes off an island. The security of isolation was always of strategic military importance in less sophisticated days, and formal physical confinement, as in Alcatraz or Devil's Island, has created a different image for islands, while Elba and St. Helena live on in the imagination as symbols of exile. Today, escapists in varying forms are seeking islands as a permanent base, with many former summer residents settling in retirement on places like Martha's Vineyard, and, in this jet age, airline personnel have found that they can make a pleasant home life on an island in the Caribbean or Bahamas while commuting to their jobs in major cities in the mainland. The Channel Islands of England, long a bastion of individuality, have become tax havens for the fortunate, wealthy few who can arrange residence there.

And islands come in every political shade. There are some strange political connections, such as St. Pierre and Miquelon in the Gulf of St. Lawrence, which still belong to France, or the island of St. Martin/Sint Maarten, shared by France and the Netherlands in the Caribbean. Evidences of colonialism still remain in such areas as Tahiti, the Society Islands, and New Caledonia, French possessions in the Pacific, or the vestiges of the Dutch and British empires in the Caribbean and South Pacific. The United States has Guam and American Samoa, as well as Puerto Rico, but the overseas empires of older colonial powers like Spain and Germany have been eliminated by their changes of fortune in the cauldron of European conflicts.

The trend of the late twentieth century, however, has been toward self-determination and independence by islands whose European rulers have usually been all too happy to turn them loose because they had become burdens in a changing economy. In the days of slavery and the worldwide importance of the sugar trade, the islands of the Caribbean were some of the richest, most highly prized and therefore most highly contested possessions in the world. Today, with many of them caught in a deficit economy due to changing world conditions, they have become a liability, and the swing to independence has been encouraged, especially by Britain.

Tiny islands, at least in relation to the size of most countries, like Grenada, Dominica, and St. Lucia, have achieved independence as members of the British Commonwealth, and the transition, Grenada's particularly, has not been easy. In some cases, racial conflicts have created tensions, as in the Bahamas and Jamaica, but it is just as common to have purely internal struggles between newly self-governing blacks develop into violence and revolution.

Many have been unable to support themselves through a combination of lack of resources and inexperienced (or graft-ridden) management, and the natural inclination to depend on the magic cure of tourism to take up the slack has led to additional tensions. Newly independent island natives, proud of their status and with many more educated young people joining the work force due to improvements in schooling, do not take kindly to discovering that service jobs, catering to the affluent white tourist, are the only career openings. There is also the problem of just how much tourism to encourage, in an effort to keep a balance between improving the economy and preserving the attractions that bring tourists. Some tourists add charm, color, and panache to an island by entering into its life with sympathy and understanding, but untold damage has also been done by the insensitive tourist.

Controlling one's destiny on a small island no longer coveted by a bigger power for economic or military reasons is far from an easy task, as many of the young, emerging island nations have discovered. For the visitor there is the uncertainty of how the political wind is blowing at the moment, and often an expectation of trouble leads to an attitude that becomes a self-fulfilling prophesy.

But many islands have no political problems, and they do not have to be in an exotic clime to exert a sway. Even insignificant, unexotic islands can create that special feeling of release and separation. My family has lived since World War II on the shores of the Shrewsbury River, a pleasant little tidal flat tucked south of Sandy Hook and the Lower Bay of New York Harbor on the New Jersey coast, and three generations of the family have taken special delight in its small, sandy islands. The nearest one, called Gunning Island, a hundred yards away across a shallow channel, has several white beaches, is uninhabited, and is covered with a nice mix of sedge, salt grass, bayberry, sumac, and one stately poplar. It is a wonderful miniwilderness that my wife, Jane, and I view, fostering an illusion of being much more isolated from civilization than we are, and in the fall it lives up to its name with several duck blinds. Beyond it, the beaches and coves of the other islands that string out like stepping stones to the far shore are part of the family's private geography, with special names that never appear on a chart, and happy associations. For picnics and exploration, for digging in the sand, and for scrounging through driftwood and flotsam for untold treasures, they form a tiny world of their own as isolated in spirit as a cay in the Bahamas or a crag of rock off the Maine coast.

The big poplar tree on Gunning Island is a special landmark for us, a reference point that can be seen from all points in the river's spread of two by three miles, a localized version of the way seamen have used islands and their individual shapes as identification for navigational purposes for centuries, long before the invention of aids to navigation. All sailors know that land masses collect fair-weather clouds, and this fact has long been a staple of primitive piloting. In the Bahamas and Caicos, where islands string in definite patterns along the edge of reefs and banks, the lay of land beyond the horizon can often be followed by the pattern of clouds centered on the cays as they warm in the sun during the day.

While most seamen in primitive times depended on visual sightings to get from point to point, epic voyages of Polynesian navigators covering great distances in the Pacific are the most likely answer to the riddle of the spread of their civilization across those vast areas. Without instruments of any kind in giant multihull canoes that are the ancestors of today's popular one-design catamaran classes, they used the signs of nature to guide them. They knew the stars and used them as signposts, and they also could tell where land lay many miles over the horizon by the presence of cloud formations, the flights of birds, and the behavior of wave patterns that changed direction when diverted by land masses. An interesting book, *The Voyaging Stars* by Dr. David Lewis, who has made a lifelong study of this subject and has used the methods himself in extensive South Seas voyaging, describes these ancient practices.

This fascinating island lore is based on fact, not imagination, but the island has also long been a staple of literary invention. In its evocation of the mystique of a desert island, is there a more enduring myth than the tale of Robinson Crusoe? Who is there who has not, at some time, fantasized living as Crusoe, and who has not, at the sight of footprints on a lonely beach, harked back to Crusoe's man, Friday? *Treasure Island*'s tremendous appeal lies in its perfect blend of adventure, mystery, and the fascination of pirate treasure, all revolving around a secret island. James Michener's *Tales of the South Pacific* caught the unique flavor of war in that improbable setting, and his image of Bali Hai has become part of the language. His *Hawaii* also traded on an island milieu for its popularity. Hemingway's preoccupation with fishing and with island bases for pursuing it, Bimini, Key West, and Cuba, was strongly evoked in *Islands in the Stream, The Old Man and the Sea,* and *To Have and Have Not. The Lord of the Flies* and *The Admirable Crichton* had to have an island location, and Mark Twain used an island setting to great effect when Huck Finn went into hiding. Thor Heyerdahl has written well about the strange mystery of Easter Island in *Aku Aku,* and in *Fatu-Hiva* he told of his own adventures living primitively in the Marquesas. His *Kon-Tiki* contributed greatly to increased understanding of some of the questions surrounding the island civilization of the Pacific.

Islands have been the thematic generator in such diverse works as Shakespeare's *The Tempest,* Nathaniel Benchley's *The Off Islanders* (which was filmed as *The Russians Are Coming, The Russians Are Coming*) and his son Peter's best-selling melodramas, *The Deep* and *The Island. The Bounty Trilogy* revolves around islands, *South Wind* is an island classic, *Island in the Sun* is a fictionalization of Grenada, and many a Gothic romance has a mysterious island for its setting. Jules Verne actually used that—*Mysterious Island*—for a title. In literature and life, the lure of islands exerts a profound sway.

Now we turn from the general to that particular story of my own life-long fascination, starting in the ancient citadel of the world of islands, the Aegean Sea. From here the journey will trace a course that is roughly westward around the world, across the Atlantic and Caribbean to the far reaches of the Pacific.

The taverna on the Ios waterfront.

1 · The Greek Islands

*F*rom the battlements atop the monastery of St. Christodoulos, shadows from the shifting patterns of sunset could be seen moving across a great panorama of Aegean land and seascapes far below. A shimmer of light plated the darkening sea in the west, and the hills of Patmos, brown and dusty olive during the day, now glowed with a patina of gold. Scala Harbor at the base of this highest of the three peaks of Patmos was purpling into deep shadow, and a cruise ship at anchor looked like a white toy on its dimming mirror. The village houses, pale cubes clustered at the base of the towering gray walls of the monastery, shone briefly in panels of gold, orange, and crimson until they too fell into shadow, and a soft, mauve twilight spread over mountain and sea.

Next to us at the chest-high, crenellated wall, a monk in gray robes was scanning the harbor through binoculars. His hair was gathered at the back of his head in a small pigtail and his salt-and-pepper beard, riffled by the soft breeze of evening, had a cigar stub protruding from it. As twilight faded into darkness, he led us down a steep, narrow staircase into the chapel, rich with the smell of incense, where the relic of St. Christodoulos, who built the fortified monastery in 1088, was encased in a silver shrine. The walls were ornately and intricately carved and decorated with inlaid crosses, icons, censers, and candles. Cases lining the walls held jeweled presentation pieces, many of them gifts of the Russian imperial family. From the hushed, aromatic chapel we were ushered through a labyrinth of corridors, high-walled courtyards, and a massive gate, across a moat, and out into the dim streets of Chora.

It was on this same mountaintop that an altar of Artemis, sister of Apollo, stood in antiquity. Halfway down the slope a cave where St. John the Divine is said to have dictated the Apocalypse to his disciple, Prochoros, is now a chapel. A hollowed indentation in rock shelving is pointed out as the place where his head lay when he slept, meditated, and had his vision.

Far below, as we followed the curving road in windy darkness, the rigging of yachts at the quay in Scala formed a tracery in the lights of the town; and bouzouki music echoed in the night from a taverna. At an open-air table under the feathery green of tamarisk trees, we had a standard Aegean dinner of eggplant, tomatoes, and *barbounya*—a small reddish fish—after an aperitif of ouzo, served with small black olives, octopus, and feta cheese. *Retsina,* the heavily aromatic, resinated wine often described as "an acquired taste that some never acquire," came with dinner, followed by the sweet, muddy Turkish coffee known as *metrio.*

During dinner, men at the tables responded to the thumping rhythm of the bouzouki, played by an impassive, wrinkled old man. They danced first by themselves, drifting dreamily in circles, a handkerchief or napkin swaying limply in one hand. As the tempo increased they whirled faster, joining others by grabbing an end of a flying handkerchief. Finally they broke free and launched into leaps and midair heel clickings. Throughout, their expressions were enigmatic, unchanging, and remote, no matter how feverish the effort.

· *THE AEGEAN* ·

This was Patmos, but it was also the entire spirit of the Aegean islands in microcosm, a world that has stirred the imagination of man since earliest time by its physical images, mythology, and history. Nowhere else on earth are these elements combined with such an impact on the intellect, emotions, and senses. The monk, cultivated and worldly in a detached way, fluent in English, graciously hospitable, and proud of his calling, was a link with a strange, remote life, and the dancers in the taverna brought us back to the colorful vitality of modern Greece. The yachts across the quay, ghostly shapes in the light flickering through the tamarisks, fit well with the scene but were also reminders of the world we had left, and of the special excitement of sailing through this most storied of all seas.

Since *The Iliad* and *The Odyssey* and Homer's description of it—"gray-eyed Athena sent them a favorable breeze, a fresh wind, singing over the wine-dark sea"—the Aegean has held a fascination beyond normal reason for all who come to its shores, especially sailors. We had seen it that day, not wine-dark, but a hard, vivid blue, brighter than the richness of tropical waters, setting off the dun hills of Cos, Lemnos, and Calymnos, as we threaded our way through the narrow cuts and channels of the Dodecanese. Against the brown of the hillsides, here and there relieved by a dusty grove of olive trees gnarled and bent with the wind or the spire of a lonely cypress, the white of village houses and monasteries, often high on a mountaintop like a misplaced cloud or improbable snowdrift, gleamed supernaturally.

History and legend crowded in on us every inch of the way, from reminders of nighttime battles fought in the narrow channels by British and Italian destroyers in World War II, to the ruins of the Aesclipion, the world's first hospital, and Hippocrates teaching his medical students under a great plane tree, in legend the same ancient of days that spreads over the square near the harbor in Cos, although in reality this one is only 500 years old. The Dodecanese have been handed back and forth between nations through the centuries. Ancient Greeks and Romans, Persians, Turks, Italians, and modern Greeks again have asserted ownership in a tangled sequence of invasions, subjections, and liberations. The vacant buildings of a mammoth Italian naval base can still be seen in the spacious harbor of Leros, a reminder of Italian control between the two World Wars. Mykonos, in the Cyclades, was once the private preserve of an elite Venetian family—the deserving rich, evidently—later controlled by Russia, and always a haven for pirates exercising squatter's rights.

There are towns and villages at the harbors, but the major settlements, like the village on Patmos, usually have been located on the highest point of an island for purposes of defense, with seafront buildings considered expendable. The inconvenience of hill travel was outweighed by considerations of security. Also dotting island hillsides, often on lonely points of land or even on off-lying islets, are hundreds of little chapels. Every town has its church standing high above the huddle of square, white houses, and the monasteries are often large and sprawling, following the contours of the hills, but these chapels are private affairs, and usually very small. They have been built by families, or by seamen who, caught in perils at sea, have vowed to build a shrine in gratitude for their survival. One like this stands on a rocky crag off the west end of Cos. The ruins of a Byzantine church look out at the chapel from a point marking the end of a deserted curve of beach. The bone-white little building, just one tiny room, was an offering to St. Nicholas by a grateful seaman who made it safely home, and once a year priests row out to place lighted candles on its miniature altar.

Greeks have always been seamen. The Aegean was a principal highway in antiquity, and control of the seas meant control of the known world. It was through domination of Aegean waters that Athens flourished. Between 490 and 400 B.C., a century including the age of Pericles, the civilization of Athens and the foundations of modern humanism were spread throughout the Mediterranean. The ships they used would not have seemed too archaic to Columbus, or even to Lord Nelson, insofar as the basic techniques of handling the big square sails that gave them their power were concerned.

Islands played a major role in the maritime-oriented ancient world. Delos, where Leto took refuge from the pursuit of Hera, jealous wife of Zeus, and gave birth to the twins Apollo and Artemis, later became a major shipping center and a crossroad of commerce. At one time it was also a religious center that women were not allowed to visit. Today, one wonders at its importance as a port, as it is a relatively small, barren island without water supply, uninhabited, and living with the ghosts of the past—and a daily invasion of tourists. They must all make the short passage across from Mykonos by ferry or launch to see the ruins of the sacred island, dominated by the heavily eroded but still striking row of lions, made of marble from Naxos and dating from the seventh century B.C. They guarded the approach to the sacred palm tree in whose shade Apollo, god of the sun, and Artemis, goddess of the moon and the hunt, were born.

While bare, ruined Delos is a relic of antiquity, Mykonos is a disturbing example of how the twentieth century has caught up with at least part of the timeless ambience of the Aegean. In recent years, Mykonos has become the most heavily visited of all the central islands. As one of the most picturesque, and as the gateway to Delos, it has succumbed to most of the trappings: shops selling gimcrack souvenirs and cheap clothing, bars, tavernas, and fast-food outlets, and an atmosphere of frantic, forced gaiety. This goes on along the waterfront, where the trippers stream off the ferries from Piraeus, but the hundreds of windmills on the hills behind the town flail away against the pure blue sky, and the winding alleys and back streets removed from the water have kept their original charm. There are many who enjoy Mykonos enough to be satisfied with it as their complete Aegean experience.

Mykonos is also the focal point for that phenomenon that so dominates an Aegean summer, the wind known as the *meltemi*. This is a giant thermal action, generated far to the north on the great plains of Russia (so Greeks will tell you) that gathers force as it funnels through the central Aegean. It blows from early July to late August, with variations between the days, and a slackening at night, a fair-weather wind in a cloudless sky, with temperatures in the middle 70 degrees Fahrenheit and all the appearances of perfect conditions, except that its blasts are as high as 40 to 50 knots. As the Aegean widens south of Mykonos, the meltemi fans out from its north-south axis to slant southeast and southwest, moderating a bit, but yachts are often weathered in for days in the crowded harbor of Mykonos, while the windmills spin, and spray dashes high over the windward side of the seawall.

Fortunately, the Aegean experience has included more than the gift shops of Mykonos for us. We came there through a wild meltemi from Patmos, slicing through the foam-streaked whitecaps of the central Aegean, steep, short, brilliantly clear and blue, and surprisingly cold in the sting of their spray, at the end of two weeks of racing and cruising in the 46-foot cutter *Toxotis* (the archer–Orion). I had raced with a crew led by sailors who had been gold medalists in the Olympics when the then-Prince Constantine won the Dragon Class at Naples in 1960. This was in the Aegean Rally, the major sailing event in Greece, in a two-part race from Piraeus to Ios and Ios to Rhodes, which we won. Jane had followed the fleet in a "tall ship," a training vessel used as committee boat, and we then cruised back from Rhodes to Mykonos with the owner of *Toxotis,* John Sikiarides, a cultured Harvard graduate and delightful host, and his professional captain, Markos.

It was one of the highlights of a lifetime of sailing to be shipmates with these Greek sailors. Markos was one of the finest seamen I have ever met, a joy to watch as he went effortlessly about his tasks. He was a native of lonely Orthonoi, the northernmost point of Greece in the Adriatic northwest of Corfu, where men are born to the sea. Heavily muscled, he was bigger and taller than most Greeks, with strong features and a flashing grin that was shy when he tried English words, but bold and beaming when I noticed some good touch of seamanship. Although he spoke almost no English, and my Greek is effectively confined to *parakalo* (please) and *efkharisto* (thank you), we managed to communicate with appropriate laughs and shrugs by sign language, gestures, and the special nautical lingua franca of the Mediterranean that uses a mixture of Greek, Italian, French, Spanish, Arabic, and English words. I had learned some of them, such as *panni* (mainsail), *flocca* (jib), *baloni* (spinnaker), *lasca* (let out), *ferma* (take in) and even *boom vang,* which is English for a strap that helps trim the boom, and is used without translation.

The racing crew was one of the most skilled, and noisiest, I have ever shipped with, captained by the appropriately named Odysseas (the modern spelling—or Ulysses, if you prefer). They were my first introduction to the Greek custom of settling even the most trivial questions in loud, prolonged argument. Whatever the minor detail, the decibels and gestures increase, and everyone talks at once in a great hubbub of shouts. Eyes flash, feet stamp, and knives or fists would seem to be the next step, but suddenly someone gives in, and the loser, no matter what he is doing, makes the ultimate gesture of concession, a great shrug, with hands thrown wide, palms out at waist level, and a grunt that sounds like "ennnh!" If he happens to be holding a halyard or steering, the results can be unnerving, but then everyone laughs and all go smiling about their business.

No matter how serious the racing, we had our "happy hour" every afternoon, with bouzouki music on a portable, hand-wound victrola, ouzo, and even a quick variation on the Greek male dance in the limited confines of the cockpit. When we won the regatta, the celebrations were long, noisy, and abandoned, and I almost became used to being kissed (on both cheeks) by my shipmates.

On the first leg from Piraeus to Ios, the course took us by Cape Sounion at the southeast tip of Attica, where the ruined pillars of the great Temple of Poseidon stand high atop the promontory looking out over the blue reaches of his realm. It was here, so one version of the story goes, that the Aegean got its name, when King Aegeus, keeping watch for the return of his son Theseus from battling the Minotaur in Crete, sighted his ship approaching under black sails. When he had left for Crete, Theseus had promised to use white sails if he was returning in victory, but he had forgotten the pledge, and Aegeus, thinking his son vanquished and dead, threw himself into the sea that now bears his name.

Although there are legends like this on almost every headland and island, we were concentrating on the racing, and we broke away from the fleet, assuring our eventual victory, through the very special local knowledge of Odysseas. We were almost becalmed in a fitful southerly, the afternoon breeze that blows into the Bay of Phaleron at Piraeus, when he spied a cloud of butterflies not far away in the direction of the land. He knew this signaled the edge of a new breeze, the beginning of a tentative meltemi that had blown the butterflies off the flower-covered hillsides of Sounion, and we managed to work our way into it, the only boat to do so. As the pale wings fluttered across our deck and *Toxotis* heeled over and trimmed to the new breeze, we swept away from the becalmed fleet around Sounion and on past Kithnos and Seriphos in the Cyclades to victory at Ios.

Ios, as much as Patmos, is the perfect model of an Aegean island. It is hilly and barren, with agricultural terracing on brown slopes rising sheer from the sea, blindingly white chapels dotting the hillsides, a drift of village houses across the summit of the highest peak, and a cluster of buildings around the harbor quay. We moored fore-and-aft to the quay amid brightly painted caiques festooned with drying nets, and the whole populace was there to greet the racing fleet with cheers and shouting as each boat tied up. In the evening the waterfront plaza was a blaze of lights, with music from tavernas as a background to the cheers of the villagers along the sea wall. Jane and I spent the night in a tower room of a small hotel at harbor's edge, the cleanest, neatest, sparest room I have ever been in, with the hardest bed and pillows. In the morning, after breakfast at the taverna downstairs with post-celebrants from the fleet, I went up to the hilltop village for a magnificent view of the whole island. It was a whitewashed town of houses packed closely in geometric patterns over narrow, arched alleys, clean and quiet in morning sunlight. The experience would have been a perfect one except for the mode of transportation—a recalcitrant donkey.

Ios is one of the places where Homer is supposed to be buried. Perhaps. Supposedly, his mother was an Ios woman. I hope it is the true place. It seems just right.

• *RHODES, CYPRUS, SANTORINI,* *AND SYMI* •

Rhodes, in the southeast at the lower corner of the Aegean, is a long, ridged island with olive groves and cedar forests on its windblown slopes, windmills turning to the last fingers of the meltemi, a valley that is home to thousands of butterflies, and a fascinating mix of cultures from ruins of antiquity to blue-mirrored disco clubs. We swept in on the end of a meltemi to finish the Aegean Rally off Mandraki Harbor, leading to a round of receptions, folk-dance festivals, fireworks, and all-out celebration through the night-clubs of one of the most heavily visited spots in the Mediterranean. There is a strip of hotels in Miami Beach—modern along the strand that runs west from Mandraki, looking across the windy blue strait 15 miles to the dark mountains of Turkey; but Rhodes is big enough to absorb all this without submerging the pervasive evidences of its long, long history.

At the entrance to Mandraki, bronze deer, symbols of Rhodes, stand on jetties at each side. Legend has them marking where the feet of the Colossus once stood as one of the seven wonders of the ancient world, but the actual site was farther inland. Behind Mandraki's quays, crenellated fortresses from the Crusades rise in forbidding grandeur. Thirty miles away on the south shore, the ancient capital of Lindos forms a fascinating layer cake of history and archaeology. On its acropolis, standing boldly above the Mediterranean, there are ruins of Greek, Roman, and Byzantine civilizations, with a modern village skirting the lower slopes of the golden hill in a frieze of white. Below all this is a semicircle of beach fringing a small, symmetrical harbor, and on the other side, a tiny, landlocked cove is called St. Paul's Harbor, as it is here that he is supposed to have landed on his visit to Rhodes.

In Rhodes there is a constant reminder of the age-old conflict between Greece and Turkey, a "blood feud" that goes back to prehistory. There is just that narrow strait of water between it and Turkey on the Asian mainland, visible through the Aegean haze. Until recently Rhodes had a sizable resident population of Turks, who lived in harmony with local Greeks. While individual Greeks and Turks manage to get along very well when there are no political problems hanging over them, and they have long lived and worked side by side in peace in many of the Greek islands near the Turkish coast, they become helpless pawns in a political struggle when the old animosities flare up.

Cyprus, east of Rhodes and physically similar to it, has been a focal point of the conflict for centuries, divided as it has been between the two ethnic groups. The struggle for political control of it in the early 1970s, which erupted into armed confrontations and heightened emotional reaction in both countries, was another episode in the long history. The situation was so tense that the Turkish residents on Rhodes were forced to leave after centuries of peaceful coexistence. Cyprus, physically beautiful and a fascinating melting pot of cultural strains, remained in a limbo of tension and uncertainty, a problem that centuries of effort have failed to solve. The Greek-Turkish political enmity, brought to a head in Cyprus, has developed ramifications far beyond a local rivalry due to the strategic location of both of them, in that uneasy area where the communist and Western worlds touch each other physically. Cyprus, serene physically, has become a symbol of world tensions.

Santorini, northwest of Rhodes in the center of the Aegean, takes one back, because of its physical reminders, to that ancient era when the earth was undergoing the cataclysmic volcanic alterations that helped to form its present topography. In some prehistoric geologic age there was probably a land bridge from Europe to Asia across the Aegean from the Peloponnesus to Anatolia, or Asia Minor, with Crete and Rhodes a part of it, as well as the islands of the central Aegean. Eruptions and subsidences eventually brought about the present conformation of sea and islands. Santorini, or Thera as the Greeks called it, was a large island and a thriving center of commerce and art when one of the greatest eruptions since man has been civilized, probably in about 1500 B.C., blew out its center section, leaving a ring of islands of about 20 miles in circumference around a sunken crater over 390 yards deep. Occasionally a center island of black lava still shows signs of volcanic action. The walls of the crater rise perpendicularly for 1,000 feet from the water and are topped by modern villages that have become a major tourist attraction. Their white houses are strung along the cliff tops like laundry spread out to dry.

The fate of Santorini and its civilization, which is still being rediscovered in an archaeological dig at Akrotiri, at the eastern end of the island, could have given rise to the legend of Atlantis, that mythical land said to have sunk into the sea, far-fetched as the connection might seem today.

The Aegean experience can be repeated in island after island, and each has a special hold on its natives. Men go off to sea or mainland cities to make more money than the spare living most islands can provide, but they never shake the memory of the place where they were born. Some come back broken and tired to doze in the sun, some return for brief visits with family and friends and move on again, perhaps building a small chapel in thanks for some special piece of good fortune. Others only send money as they rise in the world. But there is a strong, mystic bond to their home island that can never be broken.

Although the heritage of the Aegean is shared by all the islands, there are dramatic contrasts in the way they have developed. Symi, our first stop as we cruised northwest from Rhodes, is set in a bay between Turkish capes, a short sail from Mandraki, and a lifetime away. Here there is almost no tourism, and no firm basis for local economy. Symi has been, depending on the century, a trading center, a shipbuilding port, and a farming and fishing community, but none of these endeavors has been economically successful. It is one of those lonely, forgotten islands, which the young people all leave if they possibly can, seeing better opportunities elsewhere.

We sailed into Paniero Harbor and moored at a small pier in front of an impressively long, white, red-roofed building, capped by a bell tower at the center. It was the monastery, called Panormiti. In the general downward drift of life on Symi, the monastery had been left with just an abbot and two monks to maintain the order and the building itself. Their solution had been to rent the unused cubicles as low-cost hotel rooms for vacationing families, and evidently this was more of a success than Symi was accustomed to.

The abbot invited us to visit the monastery, and he proudly showed us his chapel, with its ornate carvings and hundreds of offerings in gold and silver that had been left by worshipers. In this sea-minded community there was also a ship-model museum, a touchingly crude collection of native craft, and he was particularly proud of one toy boat that had sailed into the harbor by itself from an unknown point. The tour ended with ceremonial wine and candy in the monastery's plushly furnished, formal sitting room, whose main use was in the twice-yearly visits of the Bishop of Rhodes. As the abbot, in halting but clear English, played gracious host and was telling us some of the history of Panormiti, an American from another yacht came into the room and was included in the pleasant ritual by the abbot, who greeted the visitor with "Welcome to our island."

The new arrival answered, as though he were talking about an oblivious two-year-old, "My goodness! He speaks English." We could only cringe.

There could be no more completely different an environment than Hydra, 30 miles from Piraeus off the Peloponnesus. Its history is as long and colorful as any of the islands, but today, served by hydrofoils—great, roaring water bugs—and excursion steamers that come from Piraeus every few minutes, this rocky collection of soaring crags, along with nearby Poros and Aegina, is a day tripper's delight. Its compact harbor is alive with activity, although the heights of the rest of the island have a lonely grandeur untouched by the revelry below.

We came there on a pleasant sail from Piraeus and squeezed our way into the jam of yachts moored stern-to-the-quay in Mediterranean style on a Saturday afternoon in May, and long before dark, there was not room for a canoe in the harbor. Groups moved from boat to boat, laughing and calling out, as the clink of ice-filled glasses echoed from the cockpits of sailboats and fantails of glossy motor yachts. Music, both Greek and rock 'n' roll, drifted from tavernas to clash in the evening air, enlivening the crowd parading along the waterfront. Lights from boutiques and gift shops shone across the stones of the quay, and tables in the outdoor tavernas were filled with people drinking beer, ouzo, and brandy, or sipping metrio. Restaurants along the quay and up the narrow side streets were filled, and a hum of joyous abandon seemed to permeate the warm spring night. After dinner, many of the yachting people made their way down a narrow path to a discotheque at the water's edge, where the party carried on for most of the night amid whirling lights and the throbbing, repetitive beat of the music. It was Saturday night fever, but it could have been Monaco, Miami, Chicago, or Marstrand. It was not very Greek.

Sunday morning along the quay seemed more typically Greek. The taverna tables were filled with coffee drinkers reading newspapers in pale sunlight and languidly discussing the doings of the night before. Along the quay, boat crews began to stir, making motions about leaving, and there was one bit of action that caught the attention of all the taverna patrons. Two large motor yachts tangled their anchor lines and had to proceed out of the harbor locked in unwanted intimacy before the problem could be solved, a typical Sunday morning sight in a harbor like Hydra's.

· CRETE ·

Crete stands athwart the southern approaches to the Aegean, and its massive peaks, topped by the 8,000 feet of Mount Ida, seem to stand guard over the whole Greek archipelago to the north. Crete was the home of the ancient Minoan civilization and through the centuries it has been in contention as a point to control, for whoever held Crete dominated the eastern

Mediterranean. It had periods of Turkish rule and was not politically joined to Greece until 1913. This was largely the work of Eleutherios Venizelos, the Cretan-born statesman who was prime minister of Greece during World War I, but who had first entered political activity by leading a revolt against Turkish rule on Crete at the turn of the century.

An Aegean odyssey is not complete without a visit to Crete, and we flew there on a day of wind and rain squalls in March. Jane, who has read extensively on archaeology, had long wanted to see the Minoan palace at Knossos, and we took a day away from engagements in Athens for the trip.

The great ruins of Knossos are an impressive sight. The ruins were restored from 1898 to 1935 by Sir Arthur Evans, and the restoration evoked one of the greatest controversies ever when the authenticity of the work was questioned. One area of questionable restoration revolves around the use of bright-colored pillars, murals, and room decorations. In most unrestored ruins, centuries of weather have washed away all colors except that of the stones themselves, whereas restored Knossus is a many-hued divergence. It was also interesting to me that this fabulous labyrinth, now well inland in a green and peaceful valley, had been a seaport in ancient times.

In Heraklion, the major town of Crete, there is an archaeological museum, and we also visited the house of Nikos Kazantzakis, the author best known for *Zorba the Greek*. His study has been set up as though he were working in it. It was affecting, then, to be taken to his grave on a bleak, lonely hill not far from town. Because of his position on religious matters, he had been denied a church funeral and burial in consecrated ground, and, when we first saw it in 1967, his grave was a simple mound of earth on an open, grassless plot, marked only by a cross made from rough, unfinished boughs. While we stood there, rain squalls swept in from the mountains of the interior and clashing towers of blue-black clouds formed a somber backdrop. El Greco, to whom Kazantzakis addressed his autobiography, *Report to Greco,* had been born near Heraklion, and the mood of this setting was very much in his style. On a visit twelve years later, in bright, warm sunshine, it was anticlimactic to find the plot prettied with flower beds, extensive plantings, and a frame of masonry over the mound of earth, and, although the rude cross remained, an inscription had been added. It was his own existentialist epitaph, the philosophy that kept him in conflict with the church: "I hope for nothing; I fear nothing; I am free."

We were to take a late-afternoon plane back to Athens for a dinner party, and the plane was landing on its flight from the mainland when we checked in at the tiny waiting room. The rain had continued, and darkness had already fallen as we took seats on hard wooden benches to await the flight announcement. The stuffy room was full, mostly of men in dark suits, and we seemed to be the only non-Greeks. Flight time came and passed with no announcement, and I looked out the window and saw men with flashlights crawling underneath the plane, evidence of some mechanical problem. Soon afterward the loudspeaker crackled to life, and I did not have to wait for the English translation to know what was said. As soon as the words came into the waiting room, every man there took out his *komboloia*, the string of "worry beads" all Greek men carry, simultaneously. When the English announcement said that the flight was delayed for mechanical reasons, I could hardly hear it for the click-click-click of komboloia on all sides.

When we did get off the ground and back to Athens, a bit late, the millions of lights on the great plain of the city, the floodlit Parthenon, and an elaborate banquet at the Athens Hilton all seemed a million miles from the islands stretching out, not so far away, from Poseidon's temple at Sounion.

· CORFU ·

Corfu—Kerkyra to the Greeks—on the edge of the Ionian Sea, has none of the look of the dun and arid Dodecanese and Cyclades. The aspect is Italianate, green and rich in trees and vegetation on the lofty, graceful hills. The buildings, French or Italian in style, have more ornamentation, far different from the simplicity of the white cubes of the Aegean. Corfu is one of the most popular resorts in the Mediterranean, drawing tourists from all over Europe. There is direct jet service from France, and waiters speak French as a second language rather than the usual attempts at English. There are big hotels, nightclubs, fancy restaurants, and umbrella-filled beaches, but it is big enough (40 by 20 miles) to absorb the flood of tourism and retain a lovely rural air throughout most of the countryside. Through the centuries, Corfu, in its strategic position on the Strait of Otranto, has been occupied by various Greek city-states, Sicilians, Genoese, Venetians, French, Serbians, and English, before being ceded to Greece on the basis of a plebiscite in 1864. In World War II it was bombed by the Italians and occupied by the Germans. The result is a cosmopolitan atmosphere that is pan-European in cultural mix.

We stayed in a modern luxury hotel near the city of Corfu on the east coast, with a view across riotously blooming flower gardens to the five-mile-wide strait separating us from the mainland. Beyond were the forbidding mountains of isolated, antisocial Albania, the "loner" nation of the Balkans, where no visitor may enter. The hotel's clientele was largely English, and gazing around the dining room we could have been in Brighton or Weston-Super-Mare for all the Beefeater complexions and stolid, "good-old-mum" faces that ranged across the spotless napery.

The countryside is far from British, however, as we discovered as we explored inland. Endless groves of olive trees, silvery pale and green in the filtered sunlight, are a staple of the island's economy. Thickly clustered bay and ilex break the monotony of olive, with stands of evergreen, darker against the steep, soaring hillsides. Corfu's central mountains rise close to 3,000 feet, and there are sudden breathtaking views as the road rounds a shoulder, with glimpses of the distant sea gleaming between the trees.

Crossing the island, we came to a small, completely protected harbor, approached by the hairpin turns of a sharply descending road. From the heights above it, its water paled from the deep blue of the harbor entrance to pastel shades of green shading to white at the innermost beach. Gay umbrellas dotted the sand, and indecisive wakes of pedal boats formed traceries across inshore waters. In a grove of trees behind the beach stood a large taverna, red-roofed and bordered by open-air terraces filled with tables. This was Paleokastritsa, a popular cruising harbor and a perfect target for a one-day excursion from Corfu. We had a cool, relaxing swim, then straightened out with a waiter that what we wanted was "la douche" for a shower, and followed that with a magnificent lobster at the taverna—a clawed, boiled red, Maine-looking one, not a crayfish.

I had been told that the Xenia Hotel was the best place to stay in Corfu, but we could not get a reservation and thus ended up in our bastion of the British. *Xenia* means foreigner in Greek and all the hotels called Xenia throughout Greece are run by the government as a boost to the tourist trade. Before we ended our brief weekend on Corfu, I wanted to see this Xenia, so we drove there, parked in its curving driveway, and walked through the lobby to a terrace on the far side. The hotel was on the high outer end of a point in a grove of trees, and the terrace was actually a big balcony, standing away from the hotel building and thrust into space, with trees hovering over it. At the far end an opening in the trees gave a view of the coast stretching off to the south. It was quiet there, and we had the balcony to ourselves as we took easy chairs by the rail and settled down to drink in the scene.

Across the bay the mountains of Corfu receded into dim distance along the coast, and just below us a long causeway led to a monastery that completely covered the tiny islet of Vlacherna. The curved roofs and turreted walls of the monastery, marked here and there by dark cedars, formed a perfect symmetry, and the whole scene was as graceful, and as relaxingly pleasant, as any I had ever taken in. In the trees, insects hummed and buzzed in a midsummer symphony, and a gentle breeze riffled through the boughs overhead. There was a sense, as we sat there, that nothing in life could be pleasanter than to feel the breeze, listen to the sounds of summer, and feast the eye on the lovely scene stretching off in the blue distance. I could have stayed there forever, but an hour later came sunset, dinnertime, and the end of our stay in the Greek islands.

Setting sail from Porto Cervo.

2 · The Mediterranean

*I*n leaving the Aegean behind, Corfu marks a profound change in the
Mediterranean basin with its green and graceful countryside. No longer
is the world of classical Greece evident with every arid peak and promontory. There is, of course, the history of Rome and Carthage, which has
its influence, and the Greeks did range quite far to the west, starting with
the wanderings of Odysseus. But the medieval years and the Renaissance
have left their mark more strongly than classical times, so modern Europe
is much more in evidence in these islands. Also, the mainland shores, rather
than the islands, play a dominant role, and islands cease to be as powerful
a magnet as those in Greece.

Not that there is a scarcity. The Dalmatian coast of the Adriatic is freckled
with hundreds of islands, while Sicily and its satellites split the Mediter-

ranean in two, dominating its center. From Sicily north the Tyrrhennian
Sea has small and large islands, from Stromboli and the Liparis to Capri,
Ischia, Elba, Sardinia, and Corsica. Every schoolchild knows of Elba, and
its proximity to the Italian coast now makes it seem an unlikely spot for
true exile, symbolic though it may be. After all, nearby Corsica was home
to Napoleon.

West of the major barrier that Sardinia and Corsica form with their land
masses and imposing mountains, the Mediterranean is more open. Along
the French coast, in the Gulf of Toulon, where the dreaded *mistral,* the
cold, strong wind that sweeps down from the Alps, can change the climate
in a few minutes, there are a few small islands. The Iles d'Hyeres attract
yachtsmen from Marseilles and the Riviera, in quiet relief from the frantic
gaiety and overcrowding of Riviera resorts. Off Cannes, in the Iles de Lerin,
the little island of Ste. Marguerite is the site of the fortress where the "man
in the iron mask" was imprisoned from 1697 until 1698.

Spain's Balearic Islands, the westernmost group in the Mediterranean,
have long been famous for mild climate and sunshine. In a time of more
difficult transportation, they were the most accessible retreat from the
winter cold and summer heat of the Continent, but the jet age has opened
much wider horizons to the travelers who once made them a symbol of
romantic escape. Mallorca and Minorca, with Ibiza and Formentor off to
the west, have changed in modern times from being the "in" place for a
favored few to popular resorts for masses of visitors who flock there in
tremendous numbers during the summer.

While there is a cohesive impact in the way the unified Greek islands
are clustered in the Aegean, where you are seldom if ever out of sight of
at least one or two islands, and subgroups like the Cyclades, Dodecanese,
and Sporades almost tumble on top of each other, the islands of the
Mediterranean tend to be more isolated, with more distinctly individual characteristics both physically and politically. While one island alone,
like Patmos, seems to encompass the whole Aegean experience, the islands
of the Mediterranean stand by themselves, and a visit to one cannot
be taken as a microcosm of the Mediterranean experience. Slavs, Italians, French (the very special breed of Frenchmen that are Corsican), and
Spanish islanders act, talk, and live differently. As Mediterranean people
they are generally romantic, excitable, and outgoing, quick to show every
emotion, prone to argue, and quick to laugh and cry, but their national
characteristics do vary, making each island or group of islands a special
experience.

· SICILY ·

While Sicilians are considered very special Italians by themselves and by all other Italians, Sicily in and of itself does not impart a great sense of isolation and insularity. Its rugged landscape has a continental look to it, topped by Etna's snowy volcano, and in driving into the Sicilian interior one has a feeling of being on very solid ground, far from the sea. The Straits of Messina that make Sicily an island are less than two miles wide, and one wonders why a bridge has not been built across them. As it is, there is practically a bridge of ferryboats and hydrofoils plying those waters made famous in myth as the site of Scylla and Charybdis. These were the monsters inhabiting a rock and a whirlpool that were among the many perils Odysseus survived in what was a land of mystery and myth to the Greeks of Homer's time. There is no sign of them now as marine traffic swarms through the narrow waters at Italy's toe, maintaining contact with the mainland for five million Sicilians.

While Odysseus came to Sicily against his will at the whim of the gods and had to contend with such dangers as Polyphemus, the Cyclops, and the Sirens, as well as Scylla and Charybdis, ancient Greeks followed in his wake voluntarily as early as 735 and 734 B.C. when Naxos and Syracuse were founded on the east coast of Sicily. Searching for more fertile lands, the Greeks were colonizing both eastward and westward in that era and most probably accomplished the long sea journey to Sicily by hugging the shoreline on a roundabout route. A direct voyage from the Peloponnesus to Sicily is over 400 miles and it is not likely that they went offshore over those distances.

Greek mythology placed some of its major figures in the area of Sicily. Aeolus, god of the winds, was supposedly from the Lipari or Aeolian islands, and Hephaestus, the god of fire, lived on Isola Vulcano in the Liparis. South of Sicily, in the Maltese Islands, Odysseus is supposed to have encountered the nymph Calypso, daughter of Oceanus, who promised him immortality if he would marry her. Sicily was Greek for several centuries and cities like Agrigento had as many as 200,000 inhabitants at the height of the Grecian era. Rome and Carthage moved in, sacking Greek cities and fighting their own battles for control of Sicily in the third century B.C., and Rome finally succeeded in gaining control, making Sicily the first Roman colony in 241 B.C.

Ever since, Sicily has been pivotal in control of the Mediterranean, and from the Roman era through the Crusades and into modern times, the tides of history have washed over Sicily as contending powers have held sway and been forced to move on. As a result there are Spanish and French forts, as well as Greek, Roman, and Byzantine ruins, as Sicilian landmarks. And World War II left its mark on Sicily's beaches and in its harbors.

Today these reminders of history rise above modern highways and cities, and one can see the Temple of Concord at Agrigento, one of the best preserved of all Greek temples, loom serenely on its hilltop, dusty golden in pale sunlight, above the industrial jumble of Porto Empedocle. Driving inland in mid-October to the immense Roman villa at Piazza Amerino, with its labyrinthian spread of mosaics and courtyards high in the Heraei Mountains, one passes acre upon acre of vineyards covered in sheets of plastic, which delay the ripening of the table grapes until the Christmas season— a method the ancients never could use.

From Porto Empedocle, small steamers make regular runs to the nearby islands of Malta, Lampedusa, and Pantelleria. Malta, long under British rule, and for centuries a key to control of the Mediterranean, has had a colorful, stormy history right up to its heavy involvement in World War II, when it served as a base for British escort vessels that kept convoys moving despite the intense opposition of the Luftwaffe. The Maltese have considered themselves a race apart throughout history as they have played host to crusaders and wave after wave of military invaders, ever since the islands were settled by the Phoenicians in about 1000 B.C. St. Paul was supposedly shipwrecked there as well. Now they are embarked on independence as one of the smallest nations in the world, and controversy and conflict have continued with political assassinations and riots in the streets.

Pantelleria, halfway between Sicily and Tunisia, which was used during the Roman Empire as an island of banishment, gained unwelcome fame in World War II as the most heavily bombed spot in the world, since its airfield was important as a base for short-range fighter planes. Whether it was in Axis or Allied hands, it was bombed unmercifully by the opposition.

On Sicily, ancient and modern times join gracefully in Taormina, situated spectacularly between Etna and the sea just south of the Straits of Messina. It is a jet-set favorite with its cafés, hotels, and bathing pavilions, a popular tourist spot in season, and of interest too to students of antiquity, as its Roman theater is one of the best preserved and most beautifully situated of all that still exist. Taormina climbs the seaside mountains in tightly terraced tiers, and the theater is at the top, with the roofs, cypress trees, and the purple bougainvillea of the town dropping away from it to the sea far below. All of Taormina is an explosion of blooms, with bougainvillea cascading into the narrow streets, and flowers fringing the terraces and piazzas.

The most spectacular of all gardens is at Santo Domenico, a former monastery that has been converted to a hotel. The medieval building, clinging to the edge of a cliff high above the Mediterranean, juts out from the town at one end of the main thoroughfare, entered by a tree-filled courtyard that centers on a fountain. The rooms are high-ceilinged and panelled in dark, heavy wood, with furniture to match, and the hush is so profound that the noise of a brass band would no doubt be absorbed in the stately halls. Outside, with the cliff dropping away vertically from its outer wall, is a formal garden filled to the last inch with a controlled riot of blossoms that could only exist in the climate of the Mediterranean. When one looks up from its medieval atmosphere to a Roman theater, and down at cabanas, beach umbrellas, and discos along the shore, modern Sicily is personified.

· *THE DALMATIAN COAST* ·

Anyone obsessed by islands could probably find surfeit along the Dalmatian coast of Yugoslavia on the eastern side of the Adriatic Sea. At the southern end, near Albania's inhospitable shores, the coastline is straight and island-free. The magnificent Gulf of Kotor, a mountain-girt fjord of incredibly beautiful perspectives, has islands in the middle, tiny cays housing a nunnery or a monastery, and the medieval city of Dubrovnik is almost enisled on a round peninsula that was once actually an island. But it is northwest of Dubrovnik that the islands take over, all the way to the northeast corner of the Adriatic. There, Fiume, or Rijeka, depending on the latest assignment of its nationality, and the Istrian Peninsula put a punctuation mark to one of the most glamorous strings of islands anywhere in the world.

When island dreamers talk about the places they want to go, the Greek islands usually come first; followed by a rather vaguely defined South Pacific; and the Dalmatian coast is not far behind. After seeing these islands it is not hard to imagine why they stand so high on a romantic dreamer's list. I cruised them with my son in his 25-foot sloop, *Shere Khan*, his family as shipmates for a week of mild, warm July weather that was almost windless under a pale, hazy sky.

I joined them at Zadar, well to the north on the 250-mile stretch of coast running to Dubrovnik that is protected by offshore chains of islands, sometimes tiered four deep into the Adriatic. The Slavic names have an exotic ring to westerners that add to the fascination: Dugi Otok, Mali Losinj, Unije, Korcula, Hvar, Mljet, and others, often with medieval towns tucked away on small anchorages. Korcula, supposedly the birthplace of Marco Polo, has a perfectly preserved fifteenth-century town. (In pronouncing Yugoslavian words, *j* is pronounced *y* and is a vowel, which eases the problem somewhat.)

The mainland is mountainous and green, and one of the most heavily visited areas in Europe. Huge modern hotels, rising in balconied tiers on the hillsides, stand guard over beaches densely dotted with umbrellas, and the towns are filled with restless, swarming hordes of visitors. Many of them wear T-shirts of United States colleges, with Ohio State and the University of California at Los Angeles seemingly the most popular.

Weaving through the island channels, or *kanals*, soon brings a tremendous change. Outside Zadar the islands are in the Kornat archipelago, and the lush greens of the mainland are lost here in a world of gray rock and low scrub. Rainfall must pass over them until it hits the higher mountains inland, because they are as arid as the most barren islands in the Aegean, without the brownish-gold hues. The rocks are austere and weirdly sculptured in eccentric pinnacles and towers that can sometimes take the shape of man-made monuments or lighthouses. Occasionally a hillside will be terraced for agriculture, improbable as it would seem in the forbidding surroundings, and here and there a valley will reveal a stand of trees. Not all the islands are this barren, as some of them seem to get a bit more moisture, especially those nearer the coastal mountains. There were no big hotels here, but we did see camping grounds, and funny, lopsided little steamers made the rounds of the isolated harbors. There were a few cruising sailboats, but not many, with German, French, Swiss, Italian, and Austrian ensigns predominant. A great many rubber inflatable sport boats zipped by us on their way to camping grounds. Except for outboards, there were almost no motorboats.

There were lonely coves that gave complete isolation for a luncheon swim, but we sought towns for our overnight stops because *Shere Khan* was operated European style, without ice, which is virtually unavailable, and fresh food had to be purchased each morning. Carol, my daughter-in-law, would be off at daybreak, headed for the local market for bread, milk, and meat to be used that day, while fruits and vegetables were bought every few days when a market looked particularly good. She became adept at shopping by gestures, and not always sure just what the meat was that she was buying, as little English was spoken in the island towns. The mainland shops and marketplaces were much more elaborate and were better stocked, particularly with fresh produce.

One of our overnight stops was at an island called Zlarin in the Kornats, a town that seemed untouched by time until an occasional car or truck would rattle over the cobbled streets around the quay where we moored amid a fleet of local fishing skiffs and utility boats. The houses huddled around the narrow harbor were gray stone, colored by red roofs and the green of isolated trees. Nets were drying along the bulkheads, and women in shawls and shapeless print dresses gossiped in small groups in front of the shops, or made their way along the road with buckets, bundles, or piles of twigs balanced on their heads. Ashore, we had a pleasant dinner of local fish in an unpretentious restaurant looking out over the harbor entrance. Somehow it seemed a complete anomaly that men sitting in the bar in sleeveless undershirts, smoking and drinking beer, were also watching a television program.

• CAPRI •

We came to Capri in warm February sun that held all the promise of spring. The Bay of Naples was a placid mirror as the little steamer headed for Capri's uneven profile. Vesuvius was a dim cone astern in the mainland haze, Ischia's rolling peaks stood on the seaward horizon to starboard, and the Amalfi peninsula bulked over us to port. In contrast to full summer, the landing area at the tiny harbor was almost empty of visitors when the passengers filed down the gangway to the sunny quay, and we were beseiged by boatmen promoting a trip to the Blue Grotto. We had been told it could only be entered in flat sea conditions, so we decided to do that first, while the morning calm held.

A launch took us along the precipitous shore, where a mild surge creamed over the rocks, until we came to a cluster of waiting rowboats. They came alongside the launch by turns, taking four people in each, and Jane and I clambered in with a very dignified, very British couple, tweedy and sedately middle-aged, who had barely nodded a greeting although we were in the same small group from the hotel in Sorrento.

We started to sit on the boat's thwarts, but the boatman, standing over his sweeps in the stern, said, "No. No. Down. Down."

We lowered our heads, but he still gestured and shouted, "Down. Down."

He meant the bottom of the boat, so Jane and I squatted down there, feeling silly, but the Englishman resisted, crouching on his knees.

Still came the persistent, peremptory, "Down. Down!"

"What? Down there on the floorboards? I say!" the Englishman burst out, crouching a little lower, but the boatman would not be satisfied until all of us were seated on the bottom of the boat.

With a groan of dismay, the Englishman settled down, muttering, "How bloody undignified. Never expected this."

But his wife was laughing at him, and somehow the ice broke when he finally gave in and was seated, and we all started to laugh and talk animatedly. The entrance to the grotto is through a low, small cave that is literally just higher than a rowboat, and we all had to have our heads below the gunwale to make it into the odd light of the interior. Even a slight chop would have made it impossible, and it would have been a shame to miss the grotto and its vaulted walls and ceiling. The pale, bluish luminosity reflected up from the water, lit underneath by light coming in underwater from outside. In the eerie, crystal-clear depths odd shapes of boulders and pinnacles wavered in watery distortion far below us.

By the time we came out into the sun again, all the more brilliant in contrast to the diffused light of the grotto, we were all great friends, and the boatman was smiling in triumph. The English couple was from Bath, and we had a delightful day sharing rides with them over Capri's narrow, dizzying roads that soar out over sheer drops to the sea and wind in a snake's trail to the gorgeous views from the hilltops. Lunch was a pleasant interlude on a sunlit terrace, and the final ceremony was tea on the steamer on the way back to Sorrento. The next day, winds of over 40 knots churned the bay into a foam-streaked cauldron, and there would have been no trip to Capri.

• *S A R D I N I A   A N D   C O R S I C A* •

Sharply differing from the timeless aura of the Kornats, and as an example of the variety that can be found in the islands of the Mediterranean, we had a brief fling with the jet set at Sardinia's Costa Smeralda. Jane and I had been invited by the publicity people for this very special resort, developed by the young Aga Khan on the northeast coast of this big, mountainous, Italian island, to inspect the marine facilities as a possible base for major yachting events.

After a morning of zooming through the waters between Sardinia and Corsica on an inspection trip in the Aga Khan's high-speed express cruiser, he had invited us for lunch on his motor yacht, anchored in a secluded cove of the Costa Smeralda. Affably hospitable and obviously enjoying the power of his boat's twin 1,300-horsepower diesels, he had shown us the spread of small islands at the north end of Sardinia, and the 30-mile-wide Strait of Bonifacio separating it from Corsica, and we had had an interesting, high-speed time of it. Now, I wondered idly, what would lunch be like? First of all, would there be alcohol? We had worked up a thirst in the bright August sun of the Mediterranean. I was not sure about strictures on this, but, as we ascended the boarding ladder of the yacht, his wife, the Begum, dispelled that doubt as she greeted us in a cheery, lilting, English voice with, "Would you like a Bloody Mary?"

A former model, she is a true beauty and the most relaxing sort of hostess, although she happened to be, at the moment, two weeks away from producing the Aga Khan's first male heir. There were perhaps a dozen guests for a lunch of iced soup, salad, and cold fish and meats, served on the covered afterdeck of the yacht. The conversation was trilingual, skipping between English, French, and Italian without a pause or break. Despite my weak French and lack of Italian I could follow most of it, and its chatter about royalty ("Margaret would simply love it here!"), movie stars, and other assorted jet setters.

On shore, across the pale green water of the cove, the rolling hills of the Costa Smeralda swept up from strange, eroded rock formations along the coast toward mountain peaks rising steeply in the dim distance to a crown of clouds. Sardinia's peaks are jagged and uneven, with thin pinnacles and bold facades forming a dramatic profile that rises over 4,000 feet in the north, where we were, and more than 6,000 feet farther south. It is a big land mass, 160 by 68 miles, and the least densely populated area in Italy. Ethnic strains have remained relatively pure and local dialects retain many words of classic Latin. The dialects of north and south are so different that modern Italian often has to be used for communication between natives of the two sections. The interior is wild and almost unexplored in some areas, and banditry and kidnapping are still practiced by the mountain people.

The gracefully civilized Costa Smeralda is far different. The Aga Khan gained control of almost 30 miles of coastline, containing several good harbors, and the resort has been developed from scratch by careful planning and control. There is an overall master plan that establishes the use of each area—such as hotels, private villas, golf courses, open land, shops, and marinas. All architecture must be of an approved style, congruent with the landscape, and there are some hills where nothing can be built above the skyline, while others are designated for construction on top. There are several hotels, either luxury or first class, and a mammoth marina, perhaps the most elaborate in the Mediterranean, has been built in Porto Cervo, the main yachting harbor. In the summer there is a steady round of sporting events, receptions, and entertainments, and the waterfront plaza at Porto Cervo hums with life as vacationers sit in the open-air cafés or stroll along the water looking at the glossy collection of yachts.

It is a gay, glamorous world, but an interesting little touch of what island life can sometimes mean came in conversation with the attractive Italian woman who handled important guests for the Costa Smeralda. In recounting where we had stopped thus far on our trip, I mentioned that we had attended an all-Brahms symphony concert, Markovich conducting, in the courtyard of the palace in Monaco. Suddenly her eyes misted, and with a faraway look in them and her voice wistful, she said, "Oh, how I miss such things, being out here on an island. We have many interesting happenings here, but it's not quite the same."

On this visit we had been impressed with the cruising potential of the islands in the Strait of Bonifacio, and it was interesting to come back several years later to find a sailboat charter service in the vastly expanded harbor of Porto Cervo. Row after row of concrete piers filled the northern end of the harbor and a service yard capable of handling the biggest yachts stood next to the marina on an acre or two of concrete, complete with railways, lifts, and the most complete repair shops imaginable. There was even an ice machine, the first in the Mediterranean we were told, and an elaborate yacht club. More houses had been built throughout the Costa Smeralda, but they had all conformed to the plan and blended with the countryside as though they had been there for years. The architecture is a mix of Mediterranean influences, with smooth masonry walls in whites and pastels and lines following the contours of the site.

We took off by ourselves in a 29-foot sloop of American design to cruise for a week in the waters we had zoomed through in one hour in the Aga Khan's speed machine, and confirmed our initial, passing impression. These islands are ideal for cruising, and there are dozens of them on the Sardinia side of the Strait of Bonifacio. They seem completely unspoiled and isolated, and many of them are, until you round a point out of a narrow channel and find the good-sized city of La Maddelena sprawled along a sizable harbor. Set off on a small island, it is a combination resort and naval base and seems strangely out of place.

Actually the impression of isolation is false, as north of the Costa Smeralda, on the succession of bays that indent the coast, many big new resort hotels have been built—towering blocks of tiered concrete, with balconies on each floor set back from those below like the ones along the Dalmatian coast. They make a strange sight amid the jagged peaks and odd tumbles of rock, but the islands themselves, except La Maddelena, are lightly or not at all developed. They are hilly and modestly forested, somewhat reminiscent of the Virgin Islands, and blessed with dozens of good, out-of-the-way anchorages.

We were there in early June, and a three-month drought had broken in our honor, delighting the natives but hampering our sailing. The wind was in the east most of the time, eliminating many of the recommended anchorages, but a choice of harbors remained for any wind direction. On the day we headed across the Strait to Corsica, low clouds scudded in from the east spitting rain, but the breeze was right for a reach, and seas were moderate. I knew from our previous run in the powerboat that the great mountains of Corsica's interior could be seen from far offshore, although there was a gray void there as we skimmed along. We were surrounded by islands, and ship traffic paraded through the Strait in a steady stream. Then, out of the murk, we began to see the distinctive white corrugations of the Corsican coast next to Cape Pertusato at its southern end.

Centuries of wind and wave action have marked the sheer cliffs, which drop to the sea without a beach or line of rocks, with deep gashes, cavelike hollows, and streaks of contrasting white and gray. Five miles west of Pertusato is the town of Bonifacio, one of the most dramatically situated collections of buildings I have ever seen and one of the most fascinating cruising ports I have ever entered. From the sea, the houses perched at the top of the cliffs seem to hang beyond the edge, suspended over the water in a strange jumble of angled rooflines and gaping doorways and windows.

As we neared the hidden entrance to the harbor, the bold inland mountains began to loom into view, almost disembodied above the faces of the cliffs. Along the cliffs dark caverns cut into them at the water's edge, and oddly shaped towers of rock, eaten away at the base by the sea, sit close to shore as though they had simultaneously fallen from the tops.

The long ribbon of harbor behind the peninsula runs parallel to the outer shore for two miles, a narrow chasm between more cliffs. Its entrance, marked by a tiny lighthouse, cannot be seen until you are inside the shore-line of the peninsula that forms its seaward side. One large cave looks almost big enough to be the actual entrance right next to the real one, which appears to be a dead end at first. A short way in, however, there is a slight bend and the long slit of the harbor bursts into view, with the town perched at the inner end. Forts, walls, and ruined castles tower on the heights to starboard above the fields of bright yellow flowers on the lower hills, and then the almost perpendicular town closes around the water and rises up to the houses that could be seen on the seaward side. Yachts at the quay mix with gaily colored fishing boats, and shops and cafés line the street that follows the quay. It is a colorful setting, dedicated to tourism, and the views from the top of the cliff over the Strait and back down to the harbor are well worth the climb. Rain gave way to a pale, filtered sun as we followed a path to an old fort high on the cliff. Shafts of late, slanting sunlight shot through the clouds over the mountains, and a soft, lemony glow settled over the toylike boats and huddled houses of the port far below.

Memories of Bonifacio would be even brighter if we had not been over-charged at dinner that night in the nicest looking café on the waterfront. I chose it because it had tablecloths and without reading the prices on the menu posted in the window. They were high to begin with and astronomical when the restaurant finished exchanging traveler's checks at a three-to-one rather than five-to-one rate. My poor spoken French failed me in direct proportion to my growing anger as I tried to argue with the stony-faced *garçon*. Ah well, I had heard, of course, of Corsican bandits. Now I knew.

But this unpleasantness, if not forgotten, faded into perspective as we drifted out of the harbor the next morning, still amazed at the cliff-hanging houses, and watched the distinctive cliffs gradually blend with the whole blur of receding coastline while the boat winged her way south to Sardinia.

Russia's Kruzhenstern *in OpSail '78 off Gothenberg.*

3 · Northern Europe

The island world of northern Europe is distinct from that of the Mediterranean or North America. There are not the legends and myths attached to these islands that abound between Gibraltar and the Dardanelles, nor is there escape to the south in winter comparable to that offered Americans by the Bahamas and West Indies. To some extent, Madeira, the Azores, and the Canaries, far out in the Atlantic, offer a mild climate and do attract winter tourists, but in nowhere near the same way as do the Caribbean and its environs.

Close to the European coast there are many islands, from the Bay of Biscay on into the Baltic Sea, and while none of them is world-famous for glamour and legends, they do attract hordes of visitors in summer. It is true that Britain's insular location has had a profound influence on its history for untold centuries. The Spanish Armada, Napoleon, and Hitler are the most obvious examples of the importance of the English Channel in maintaining the security of Britain, but these "narrow seas" have all but lost their role as a defensive barrier in the modern world. And seldom has a visitor to London had any feeling of being on an island city any more than does a visitor to New York, despite Manhattan's surrounding waters.

Within the British Isles there are smaller islands that do create that insular atmosphere, and with great individuality. They are the Isle of Man and the Aran Islands, symbols of a simple, spartan life, and the Hebrides, Orkneys, and Shetlands off the shores of Scotland, in the most austere of climates. The Scilly Isles off Land's End at the southwest tip of England are almost tropical in contrast, with palm trees and a warm, benign climate for much of the year. The Channel Islands, such as Jersey, Guernsey, and Sark, are unique in Great Britain for their location—just off the French coast—their tremendous tides, the rugged individuality of the islanders in peace and in war, and, more recently, as the ultimate symbol of rugged individualism—the tax haven.

France has its own offshore isles in the Bay of Biscay, where Americans used to the New England islands might find something familiar about such sandy outposts as Belle Ile, Ile d'Yeu, Ile de Ré, and Ile d'Oléron. Even though Mont St. Michel, on the border of Normandy and Brittany, has had a causeway built out to it across the tidal flats of the Gulf of St. Malo, there is still very much the feel of being on an island in climbing around its steep alleys and the steps of its soaring, spire-topped abbey. Sometimes the Channel tides sweeping in across the flats can even inundate the causeway, returning Mont St. Michel to its original status as an island.

The Frisian Islands along the southern edge of the North Sea are also in a world of great tidal ranges, surrounded at low water by flats that quickly become submerged as the tide makes. It is in Scandinavia that Europe provides the greatest spread of islands. Denmark is almost entirely made up of islands, except for the Jutland peninsula, and Sweden and Finland have literally thousands of islands.

Out of all this my own experience has been selective, starting with one island in the south of England that is a very special one in the yachting world and in the social life of Britain. Queen Victoria gave it a cachet by summering at Osborne House near Ryde, and it was at Cowes in 1815 that the sport as we know it got its start through the formation of the Royal Yacht Squadron, whose gabled, turreted, stone clubhouse is still near the same location and is still an important, active force in yachting.

· *THE ISLE OF WIGHT* ·

Today the R.Y.S. manages to carry on the somewhat undemocratic traditions under which it was founded. No one who has been "in trade" may join it, and some of England's most influential industrialists, active and successful as yachtsmen, are denied membership. An American yachtsman who was headed for England, and naïvely perhaps, hoped to be a guest at R.Y.S., wrote to a friend who was editor of the top yachting magazine in England, asking how to get an introduction. He received the reply: "My dear chap, I don't know what to tell you except to report that I, as the editor of our leading yachting journal, have never been inside its doors."

And I, as the former editor of a leading American yachting journal, have to admit that not only have I never been inside the doors of R.Y.S.; I have never been to Cowes at all. When I mention this to sailors they cannot believe it, but it happens that I always assigned some other writer to races we wanted to cover there, and my own travels never happened to coincide with a major event. I have been to the Isle of Wight, though.

On a driving vacation tour of the south of England we wanted to see it, and, as naïvely as the man who wanted an introduction to R.Y.S., drove up to the Isle of Wight ferry at Portsmouth on a midweek day in September and joined the waiting queue of cars. When it came time to buy a ticket the agent asked if we had a return reservation, and I had to admit that we did not. We had planned a one-day drive around the island, with a look at Cowes, even though nothing was scheduled there at the moment. He informed us that no ferry reservations off the island were available for "a fortnight or more," so we parked the car on the mainland and took the hovercraft to Ryde.

A hovercraft rides on a cushion of air between it and whatever surface is underneath—land or water—and is driven by air propellers at auto-like speeds. They come in all sizes, and the cross-Solent one was like a bus, with distinct overtones of mildewy, duckblind-like dampness in its interior as we lurched across the two-mile ride to Ryde, which took only a few minutes. Without our own car, we simply took a taxi through the rolling countryside to a resort hotel at Ventnor on the south coast of Wight, and spent the afternoon wandering through a park atop bluffs overlooking a placidly mirror-like Channel. This was where the schooner yacht *America*, representing the seven-year-old New York Yacht Club, the first one in the United States, won the cup that eventually became yachting's best-known trophy.

In 1851 she beat a fleet of the fastest yachts England could assemble in a 53-mile race around the Isle of Wight, Cowes to Cowes. The trophy she brought home was named for her and was successfully held against all challengers by New York Yacht Club defenders until 1983.

Looking down on the pale Channel waters I could imagine the racing fleet, the gaff-rigged cutters and schooners of the day, beating past the cliffs in *America*'s wake, as it was on a windward leg along this south coast that she really opened up a lead on the less close-winded British boats. In the peaceful sunlight of a warm September afternoon I could also imagine the boom of cannon from one of the major battles against the Spanish armada echoing across the water to the steep bluffs, and the engine roar of thousands of vessels of every description heading across for Normandy on D-Day. History is in the air as it is in so many places in England.

· *THE FYN ARCHIPELAGO* ·

It is in Scandinavia that the European island experience is supremely rewarding. Denmark is one-half islands, including Zealand, where Copenhagen is located; the Swedish and Norwegian coasts are a continuous maze of small islands, almost uncountable in their profusion; and so is the archipelago that stretches across the Baltic from Stockholm to Helsinki. One could spend a lifetime island-hopping in Scandinavia and not take in half of them, with the added problem that the outdoor season is so short. Then, while daylight is almost continuous, Scandinavians make up for their long winter of darkness in a frenzied spasm of sailing, camping, hiking, and enjoying nature in every way possible. Whole countries take either July or August off as a holiday.

The Fyn archipelago is in the heart of Denmark, separated from the big island of Zealand by a channel known as the Store (Big) Belt and from Denmark's mainland area, the Jutland peninsula, by the Lille Belt. One big island, Fyn, or Funen, takes up much of the space, and is surrounded by many smaller ones such as Langeland, Täsinge, Drejø, and Aerø. It encompasses an area of about 100 square miles, and for Danes, Germans, Swedes, and to a lesser extent other Europeans, it is like Americans going to Nantucket or Martha's Vineyard to vacation in this rural area of farms, forests, and quaint seaports known as skipper towns. Ferries thread through the archipelago in every direction, linking all the islands. Contrary to a popular impression of Scandinavia, there are no mountains or deep fjords.

The highest spot in Denmark has an altitude of 300 feet, and I was reminded more of Chesapeake Bay than anywhere else by the look of the land as Jane and I cruised through the archipelago for a week in a 27-foot chartered sloop.

From a distance the golden grain fields also looked like the sand bluffs of New England, and the forests were so clearly defined that many of them were marked on the charts and could be used as reference points. There was a peaceful, relaxed air in the August sun, and, luckily, we had a spell of mild, pleasant weather, shirtsleeve sailing with good breezes and not much rain. In other visits to Denmark I have seen a great deal of blustery, changeable weather.

This was by no means "away-from-it-all" cruising. In these islands at the height of the season it would seem that everyone from Hamburg to Helsingborg is out in a small cruising sailboat, along with their families. Every boat has tow-headed youngsters in orange lifejackets peering over the cockpit weather cloths, toddling around the piers of the yacht harbors, or rowing around the anchorages in the evening in little dinghies and rubber boats. No one anchors out in these waters. The coasts of the islands are remarkably straight, and the current runs at a good clip in many places although there is no rise and fall of tide, and almost all the harbors are tidy little manmade ones. Those for pleasure boats are called *lystbodhavns* (say it in phonetic English and you can come up with a meaning—if you equate lust with pleasure—as can happen with many Danish words, although there is no fathoming how Danes say them in their guttural, throat-constricting accents). There is a harbormaster in charge of each port, and he assigns mooring berths as boats arrive in the afternoon, charging a very nominal fee and shoehorning them in by the dozens. There is a wash house at the piers for people from the boats, and it was fascinating to see German families marching to them, each member from father to smallest child with a towel over the arm and practically in formation, saying "Guten tag" in unison to those they passed.

The wash house is the social center of the harbor, rather like the yacht club bar in an American port. Women do their laundry and compare notes and the men discuss nautical matters in their half of the building. We found the Danes very friendly, at least after they realized that we were not German, and eager to talk about America, where most of them seemed to have relatives. With the Germans, the Danes are usually formally polite but distant. Memories of the Occupation still exist, but nobody minds having German tourist business. The Germans tend not to mix. The friendliest encounter we had was with a young Dutch couple who sat at the next table in a restaurant in Svendborg, the metropolis of the Fyn archipelago. They had sailed all the way from Holland in a 22-foot sloop and were on their way to the Baltic.

Each couple thought the other was German for a while until enough talk was overheard and they fortunately spoke English. After dinner we invited them back to the boat for a drink and then had a look at their trim little craft. They were very interested in sailing in America and asked many questions about it.

Eating ashore was one of the real pleasures of the cruise. Jane managed breakfasts and her own version of that Scandinavian specialty, the open sandwich, for lunch while we were underway, but we had dinner on land each night as part of the adventure. It was always pleasant to come ashore in the long, lingering summer twilight and amble through the narrow streets of the towns. There is a doll-house quality to the architecture right out of a Hans Christian Andersen tale in many of them, ranging from little country villages, like the town on Drejø, to Svendborg, which is really a city.

We had our best meal in Troense, a skipper town near Svendborg. Skipper towns are called that because they were the home of seafarers and a base for commercial sailing vessels in the old days, and Troense has retained a full measure of charm in its row of cottages, set in neat gardens and hedges on a rise overlooking the harbor and the channel into Svendborg. An inn converted from one of the old houses along the harbor was beautifully furnished with antiques, or what would be antiques in America at least, and dinner was as good as the setting was attractive.

In other, simpler country restaurants we could get what we wanted with three magic words: *schnapps*, *øl*, and *fisk*. Ordering gin or whisky would be murderously expensive, but the schnapps or *akavit* started things nicely, and beer (øl) went well with the fish platter that would appear. Somehow this sort of thing was the most fun, and only once did we fail to get what we thought we would, when meat and potatoes mysteriously managed to be the main course.

There was a change from all this in one night at a disco in Svendborg where we were taken as guests by a boatbuilder at whose yard we tied up. We never go to discos on our own, but we seem to end up being taken to them by well-meaning souls in places like Hydra or the Fyn archipelago, where nothing could be further from our minds. I am not much of a judge of discos, but this one seemed to be swinging. To see another side of life in the Fyn archipelago, the next day our friend drove us to Tranekaer Castle on Langeland (Long Island), said to be the oldest inhabited house in Denmark. Of soft red, ivy-covered brick, with its towers and turrets hidden among tall trees and lovely gardens surrounding it, it held an air of perfect peace and tranquility, set off among the rolling fields of the island.

Although time has caught up with the Fyn archipelago in the form of discos and modern stores and markets, and the world floods to it in midsummer, there is still a timelessness to its gentle landscape of farms and forests that has resisted these onslaughts.

· THE WEST COAST OF SWEDEN ·

"There's Smögen. See; it's such a good party town that the water tower is even shaped like a schnapps glass."

The speaker was Lars Ahren, a tall, handsome Swedish bachelor in his mid-thirties, and we were cruising the skerries of the west coast of Sweden in his 34-foot sloop *Mover*. This was a stag cruise designed to show American yachting journalists what the cruising opportunities are in Sweden, and we were standing in from the open waters of the Skaggerak to a rocky island with not a tree in sight, topped by a peculiarly flaring water tower. It did indeed look like a schnapps glass, and around its base was a huddle of houses that almost covered the center of the island. The sailing had been good in the Kattegat, that arm of the North Sea that runs north and south between Sweden and Denmark, leading to Copenhagen and the entrance to the Baltic Sea. Now we were ready for the land.

"Everybody comes to Smögen," Lars enthused. "This is where the action is, and when the girls see *Mover* coming into the harbor . . ."—he paused for effect—"they *move*."

As we threaded a narrow channel between rocks on the seaward side of Smögen and rounded a point into the harbor entrance, we could see into the long, narrow finger of a harbor. It was lined with a single row of buildings along quays on each side of it, and rocky cliffs rose behind them to higher levels, where the main town clustered around the tower. It was three o'clock in the afternoon of an early August midweek and the harbor seemed absolutely jammed with yachts. They lined the quays, starting right at the entrance, and, where the harbor opened out by another 50 yards at the first bend on the inside, they were moored fore-and-aft to the quay instead of alongside it. It looked as though there would not be room for another sailing dinghy to squeeze in, but Lars started confidently up the channel.

"It's lucky this is August and not July," he said. "Then it would be very crowded, because most Swedes take their holiday in July."

I thought he was kidding, but he was not.

"In July, though," he went on, "there would be more girls here. But we shall see . . ."

Halfway into the harbor, Lars saw a narrow gap between two boats bow-to the quay to starboard, and he pushed *Mover*'s bow in without hesitation. Far from resenting the intrusion, the crews of both boats put out fenders, helped take in our lines, and moved theirs enough for us to get our bow all the way in, with everyone smiling and shouting greetings. There we were, snugly established as part of the group. For the rest of the afternoon, as the sun made its long slow slide to the horizon in the northwest, boat after boat followed us in and managed the same sort of mooring we had, until the whole harbor was an incredible forest of masts.

A wooden boardwalk ran along the quay we were tied to, with shops, bars, restaurants, and boutiques lining the other side, and the pedestrian traffic was a continuous stream past our bow, clattering cheerfully along the boards. Perhaps everyone had taken a vacation in July, but there seemed to be a great many people with August holidays too. There were families with children tugging at their parents' hands and enjoying ice cream cones, young lovers arm in arm, elderly couples strolling comfortably, yachtsmen visiting back and forth between the boats, and girls, girls, girls. Swedish women have to be, collectively, about as good-looking as any in the world, and they were on parade here, an eye-popping sampling of statuesque blonds in T-shirts, sweat shirts, bikinis, foul-weather jackets, jeans, skirts, pedal pushers, and just about everything but a wedding dress. Lars seemed quite unhappy that only half a dozen or so stopped to check in with him, with great cries, kisses, and embraces.

"Most of the girls who were here in July have gone," he mourned.

I walked along the boardwalk toward the inner end of the harbor, part of the happy stream of paraders, looking at the boats between swivel-headed glances at the girls. Most of the yachts were cruising sailboats under 30 feet with families aboard, although there was not quite as high a percentage of tots as in the Fyn archipelago. They made a colorful array in the clear, slanting sun as ensigns flapped in the dying breeze. The Swedish national colors, yellow and blue, were predominant of course, but Denmark and

Norway, with their similar reds and whites, and the red, yellow, and black of West Germany were very much in evidence, along with a few British, Dutch, and French colors. There were parties in almost every cockpit, and the air was filled with the pulse of a disco beat thumping out of one of the bars, the tinkle of ice, shouts of laughter, and a general sense of unconfined gaiety. The Scandinavian midsummer is a time to play.

At the head of the harbor, I climbed a hill that looked down on the whole panorama in the lovely late light of the lingering sunset. The boats in the foreground were jammed together in a riot of color, and the bright blue thread of what was still visible of the harbor led out to the deep cobalt of the sound outside, lined on its far shore with grayish brown islands. Between them, blue fingers of water threaded inland toward hills on the horizon that showed more green than the sea-washed rocks close at hand.

The skerries run for over 100 miles from Gothenburg, Sweden's second largest city and major seaport, north to the Norwegian border along the Skaggerak. If anyone has ever counted all the islands, islets, and hunks of rock in this intricate archipelago, they must add up to thousands. Many of them are barren and uninhabited, while some, like Smögen, which is the most seaward of the island towns in the skerries, become heavily populated during the summer tourist season. For the rest of the year commercial fishing is the major activity. It was at Gothenburg that I saw the great spectacle of the tall ships in OpSail '78 at the start of our cruise.

There are so many skerries, and so many coves, cuts, channels, and small bays, that it is possible to find isolation as well as the frenetic gaiety of the Smögen scene, although most of the population of Scandinavia seems to be out there simultaneously. As in Denmark, no one ever anchors. It is possible to poke into a cove and tie up to a tree or to iron rings placed by commercial seamen, and when the sun shines many of these secluded coves have nude sunworshipers stretched out on the rocks next to their boats.

We had no such quiet stops, although Smögen was the liveliest of all the places we visited. In the evening we climbed the hill to a large restaurant for dinner and dancing. Because none of Lars' girls brought their mother for me, I lost track of the later activities, but Lars said the next day that July was really the better month to be there, even if the harbor was more crowded.

On another night we were at Malö, farther inland up narrow, winding channels. Here the land was greener and there were trees, while a delicately shaded purple heather carpeted the open hillsides. This was a mere village, but it is the site of a country store and restaurant called Flinck's that is known to all Swedes as the subject of a popular song by the poet-singer Evert Taube. The store, a big yellow clapboard building, sits on a rise above the town dock on an arm of the skerries, and a party had been arranged for us in its main hall. There was a lavish smorgasbord spread, with the proper accompaniment of schnapps and øl, and we went through the skoaling ritual time after time and sang a Swedish drinking song, "Helan Gaar" ("Bottoms Up") until the Americans could almost pretend they knew the words. One group of Swedes had driven up from Gothenburg, 40 miles to the south, to join the party, and it was revealing to see that one of them had "the duty" to be the driver. Swedish laws about driving and drinking are so strict that being stopped after even one drink can lead to a jail sentence and loss of license with no appeal, so this one patient chap sat through the evening cold sober, while his car mates schnappsed themselves into happy oblivion.

The Swedish skerries have none of that lonely sense of being off by themselves like so many of the storied islands. Many of them, like Malö, are connected by bridges or short ferry rides, but the state of mind they engender, the rapture of the boardwalk at Smögen, or the skoaling and singing at Flinck's country store, are very much a part of the island experience.

Great Salt Pond, Block Island, crowded with boats as usual.

4 · East of New York

*F*rom Brownsville, Texas, to Montauk Point, at the eastern end of New York's Long Island, the North American coastline is made up primarily of barrier beaches with waterways behind them—in effect, sand-dune-and-salt-grass islands. The 20-odd miles from Manasquan Inlet to Sandy Hook on the north Jersey coast are an exception; so, too, the area south of Cape Henry in Virginia, and the highly developed Myrtle Beach, South Carolina. These oppose the sea with a solid front. But otherwise the coast is one long string of islands.

Yet there isn't that feeling of escape to an offshore speck of land in visiting these sandy fingers. They are linked to the mainland, and often to each other, by causeways, and they still have a sense of community with the land mass behind them. Sometimes, as in a few spots in Chesapeake Bay like Tangier or Smith Islands, or on the Outer Banks of North Carolina, insularity does prevail, but it is not until east of New York that islands—truly isolated bodies of land, off by themselves—dominate the local geography.

Of course, there is Long Island. At its western end, attached to Manhattan by bridges and tunnels, it does not seem like an island at all. There is no sense of being on one, except when caught in a bottleneck getting off. Farther out, however, there are more reminders that water is on all sides, and satellites like Fire, Shelter, and Gardiner's Islands have interesting characteristics of their own.

And one of Long Island's better attributes is that it helps form the Sound named for it, giving yachtsmen the most popular and populous body of water in the world, with an interesting set of islands of its own along the Connecticut coast: the Norwalk Islands, Thimble Islands, and Duck Island. Then there is that geographic orphan of New York State, Fisher's Island. This enclave of discreetly displayed wealth is tied to Connecticut every way but politically, situated only a short distance from New London, with all communications tending that way. Except for license plates on the cars and the letters *N.Y.* on the highway signs, there is no reason to connect this hilly finger of land with the last outposts of New York State, ten miles away across the tide-roiled currents of the strait known as The Race at the eastern end of Long Island Sound. (It is not even shown on the Exxon road map of New York.) This is one of those strange anomalies of arbitrary political division, like the Polish Corridor, or Trieste, Fiume, and the Istrian Peninsula.

Beyond The Race is where island country really starts, an area that is decisively divided by Cape Cod and Massachusetts Bay. South of the Cape are the sandy offshore outposts of Block Island, the Elizabeth Islands, Martha's Vineyard, and Nantucket, with island-studded Narragansett Bay as a neighbor to the north. Smaller islands such as Muskeget, No Man's Land, and Tuckernuck are part of this world, too. Then, beyond the shores of Massachusetts Bay and the highly civilized centers clustering around Boston, offshore Maine offers a feast of islands of a very different sort. Here the shores are rocky. There are very few beaches or dunes, and in contrast to the bayberry and scrub, yellow bluffs, galloping dunes, and salt grass south of the Cape, the trees are evergreen and much of the scenery is backed by honest-to-God mountains, or at least respectable hills. The very air is sharper, different, and the water temperature in the low 50 degrees Fahrenheit is definitely different. The Gulf of Maine is fed by reverse currents from the north sliding down past Nova Scotia, while the southern islands, surrounded by sun-warmed shallow water, are also far enough at sea to feel the influence of the Gulf Stream. The two areas do have a common denominator—fog. In Maine it is an almost daily fact of life somewhere along the coast, while south of the Cape it is always a possibility but not quite as prevalent and all-pervasive.

Fog is a fact of life in these waters because of the flow of weather across the continent and the lay of the land, and the water near it, in New England. Especially in late spring and early summer, when even south of the Cape the sea water is still cool, masses of air are warmed as they move across North America, moving more slowly than in the rapid frontal systems of other seasons. Summer pressure gradients are less extreme between weather systems, and, with the sun at its northernmost location, the air has more chance to heat up. When these heat waves move in their continuous west-to-east passage, they eventually hit the cool waters offshore, and the violent temperature contrasts create instant fog. The moisture solidifies into a blanket of wool in the damp maritime climate. In the southern islands there is likely to be less fog as the water warms and the season continues, but the Gulf of Maine is always cold, and fog is an ever-present possibility all summer. It all depends on the frequency and virulence of the heat waves moving across the continent.

When there is not fog—or an occasional nor'easter or even hurricane— summer weather is delightful in the island-studded waters east of New York. The prevailing breeze is southwest, and it pumps around the massive high-pressure system that sits offshore, near Bermuda, in normal conditions. On Buzzards Bay and the south shore of Long Island, the south-wester, augmented by warm-day thermals caused when inland areas heat up quickly and make the air rise and suck the sea breeze in underneath, whoops in with white-capped authority, whistling across the salt grass and filtering the sunlight through a soft, smoky haze. This is not quite fog, though sometimes it can suddenly produce long, swiftly moving fingers of it out of nowhere. Elsewhere the breeze is a bit tamer, but this is the cooling "trade wind" weather that lures summer cottagers, yachtsmen, fishermen, and wave upon wave of tourists, making these islands one of the world's most popular resort areas. Easily accessible for the most part, situated on the perimeter of the greatest concentration of population in the country, and fostering, more and more consciously, their quaint charm for the benefit of off-islanders, they offer near-instant release from mainland entanglements. Just because they are near at hand, in contrast to Bali or Barbados, there is no reason to belittle what they have to offer. Amid increasing problems of overcrowding, the basic attraction is there.

Aside from physical charms, history and tradition add an aura that can take up the slack of a rainy day. Sometimes the quaintness develops into overwhelming, cutesy tourist attractions, but there are authentic old houses, public buildings, restored antiquities, museums, and monuments of varying sorts that tell the story of early life of the area.

A natural common denominator for the whole New England seacoast and its islands is the life on, in, and under the sea; the fish, lobsters, clams, quahogs, oysters, mussels, and scallops that abound in all areas and that have been so important a factor to the daily living and the economy of the islands since the Vikings brought back dried cod. Before the white man, Indians obtained much of their subsistence from the sea.

What would Block Island be without swordfish, Martha's Vineyard without stripers, Nantucket without bluefish, Massachusetts Bay without cod, and Maine without lobsters? Commercial fishing for them has long been a major industry. Although the sailing ships have gone, many of the traditions remain, and they have been fostered and glamorized as part of the present-day attraction for tourists. Sport fishing has also become big business throughout the islands and accounts for a good part of the nautical activity in summer. Casting for stripers into the surf of Squibnocket Beach on the south shore of the Vineyard on a windy, foggy night is an angling experience that brings experts from afar in great numbers.

Each of the islands has its own distinct characteristics. When combined, they amount to a tremendous variety of choice for anyone venturing offshore in this island country.

· LONG ISLAND ·

One does not have to venture far offshore to reach Long Island. The Queensborough Bridge, or one of its several sisters, will get one there from Manhattan across the narrow ribbon of the East River. For mile after square mile of Brooklyn, Queens, and western Nassau County, one has no more the sense of being on an island than of being in the western suburbs of Chicago. Eastward of the middle of the 100-mile-long oblong, however, the atmosphere changes. First there is Great South Bay and its barrier beach of Fire Island. There is probably no island anywhere where more of an effort is made to create an instant away-from-it-all life-style simply by stepping off the ferry.

Whether in its middle-class family communities, its enclaves of elitism, or the happy hunting grounds of homosexuals, Fire Island demands total surrender to a "wheee—here we are, let's cut loose" ambience. Fire Island is one of the most clear-cut demonstrations anywhere in the world of what transportation to an island can do to behavior patterns.

Fire Island is so definitely an isolated spit of sand, even though it does have a toll bridge leading to its eastern end, that it lends itself especially well to this phenomenon, and farther east, on the more solidly anchored sections of Long Island itself, there is less of that feeling of insular escapism. In the bustling Hamptons, the quality of life and of social intercourse has much less relationship to being on an island than on Fire Island. The sea and the inland bays are there, but this is really just an extension of city life with many of the same pressures and interrelationships transported to a more sunburned setting. Somehow the East River does not have the stature to effect a complete disassociation with the mainland.

It is not until the far beaches of Montauk that there is a definite awareness of the sea on all sides and that the islands that lie between the fishtail of the big island are really set off by themselves. There a sense of an insular world returns. Shelter Island, gracefully hilly, with several nice harbors along its shores and bold bluffs at its corners, has a life of its own despite the nearness of Greenport and Sag Harbor, an air of quietly existing at its own pace while the rest of the world, a five-minute ferry ride away, whirls around it at a faster tempo. A day's boat trip around Shelter Island is a lovely excursion. Beyond it, Gardiner's Island is something special. Long and sandy, with yellow bluffs along much of its shores, it has been a private island since colonial times, one of the few such rarities anywhere along the coast. Its unspoiled meadows, marshes and beaches, its plants, trees, birds and small animals all exist in the same manner and environment as they did when the Indians were the sole inhabitants. Visitors consist only of guests of the heirs of the Gardiner family, who gained title to the island by royal grant.

Even today, with swarms of pleasure boats churning by and with civilization's developments encroaching on all sides, Gardiner's Island enjoys unique isolation. In the nineteenth century it was truly a world apart, and in 1893, when President Grover Cleveland wanted to confer with J. P. Morgan about a national financial crisis, they were able to meet here in perfect privacy, with the press and the rest of the world unaware of this significant conference, by rendezvousing by yacht in a Gardiner's Island cove. Cleveland came from his summer home on Buzzards Bay as a guest on the yacht *Oneida,* flagship of Commodore Benedict of Seawanhaka Corinthian Yacht Club, and Morgan steamed out of the Sound on his own graceful, black *Corsair.* The two yachts anchored side by side and Morgan went aboard *Oneida* for a long private chat with the President.

· *BLOCK ISLAND* ·

Some 12 miles east of Montauk, Block Island is the first outpost of the real offshore islands spread over the coastal waters south of Cape Cod. Block is not named for its shape, but for Adrian Block, the Dutch explorer who discovered it in 1613. He had been using a vessel called *Tiger* in his explorations, but she burned, and Block built a trim sloop called *Onrust* on Manhattan Island, practically the first vessel constructed by white men in North America, to continue his explorations. It was in her that he came upon this lonely hunk of sand and salt grass at the eastern limits of his passage. Shaped like a pork chop, it has high bluffs at its southern end, and its gently rolling hills slope away for seven miles to a long, low, sandy point at the northern tip. In the summer, Block is invaded by swarms of tourists looking for bargains in its ancient hotels. Great Salt Pond, opened to the sea in 1897 by a man-made cut, is chock-a-block with yachts at the height of the boating season. All these transients bring the outside world with them, but sometimes, when the fog envelops Block, as it often does, isolation sets in. The light planes that fly back and forth over the 15 miles to the Rhode Island mainland are grounded, yachts stay in port, and even the ferry has to stop, or at least curtail its schedule and grope its way with radar. In the damp, gray embrace of the fog, visitors feel a loneliness and a sense of separation that makes them acutely aware of Block's location. A foggy day there is a disorienting experience.

Block was settled in 1661 by political prisoners, Highlanders of a Royalist bent who were seized during Oliver Cromwell's invasion of Scotland and transported to the iron foundries of Massachusetts. They gained their freedom when the foundries failed, and made their way to Block, then heavily wooded and known to the Indian as Manisses, where they established a rugged, independent life-style based on fishing and farming. Over the years the population has numbered as many as a thousand, but it is now back to a permanent level of several hundred. Also over the years, the trees were gradually eliminated by usage for fuel and house construction, and gales and hurricanes added to the toll, leaving the bare, windswept moors of today. From the almost total self-sufficiency of colonial times to contemporary dependence on tourism and the products of civilization, the islanders have maintained their distinct individuality. The twang of island speech is different from the Massachusetts and Maine brands, with a heavy emphasis on taciturnity and rural idiom, and anyone dealing with a Block Islander is left in no doubt about being a "furriner."

Block Island Scrapbook, a fascinating book on Block Island life published in 1957, was written by "Maizie," the business name and nom de plume of Mrs. Melvin Rose, for many years a Block Island fixture as a cab driver. An ample, hearty woman, she knew all the islanders and many of the permanent summer visitors, and a trip to the island was not complete without a ride in her cab, with her running commentary, given in a husky voice, on the weather and on island events and history.

One of her tales concerns a Block Island fisherman well along in years who had fished all of his life by himself in a small packet. One day he was anchored off the south shore, tending his lines and minding his business, and puffing on his ever-present pipe. Pleasure boats began to surround him, some coming close enough for their wakes to knock him around and throw spray into the boat, but he kept on placidly at his work without reacting. One of the boats, a particularly glossy one with a noisy, over-dressed crew of revelers, came by several times, really washing him down with their spray.

He ignored them, however, until the boat stopped alongside in a final flurry of spray that wet him down again, and the nattily togged skipper called down imperiously from the flying bridge, "Say, Old Salt, what's the course for Gannet?"

The fisherman kept his back turned to the yacht and continued at his work, wreathed in pipe smoke, until the question was asked for the fourth or fifth time in peremptory tones.

Taking his time, the fisherman finally turned around, tapped his pipe, and then calmly asked, "How did you know my name?"

"Guessed it," the yachtsman answered with a smirk, as his crew giggled.

"Well," the fisherman suddenly exploded, cords standing out on his reddening neck, "Then guess the course to Gannet."

And he turned back to his lines.

Many of the old buildings, at least those dating back to the eighteenth century, survive, often set off in some lonely, inaccessible field well away from any road or other house. Some have been taken over by summer residents, and almost every building on the island has a story of different uses behind it, often having been a school, a shop, an inn, and a residence at various times. In hard times, which always have an extra impact in a tenuous economy like Block's, summer residents have been able to purchase old houses simply by paying the back taxes, or even a portion of them. The summer colony is not a fashionable one, although more and more mainland suburbanites have been discovering Block's charms. There is not the high-pressure social life of the Hamptons, Newport, Edgartown, or Nantucket, despite a growing in-group of cottagers, and visitors are a mix of New England factory workers, schoolteachers, the elderly, and other econom-ically minded people who patronize the venerable, wide-porched Block Island hotels.

The yachtsmen who swarm in with the summer breezes are a carefree element that supports a number of restaurants and night spots, and every other June the island is overwhelmed by the Block Island regatta, which runs for one week. Started in 1965 by the Storm Trysail Club, an orga-nization of Long Island Sound ocean-racing and cruising men, it rapidly gained acceptance as an American version of England's famous Cowes Week. Now hundreds of ocean-racing sailboats descend on Great Salt Pond for a week of concentrated racing, and concentrated merrymaking ashore, one of the top events on the nation's yachting calendar. The major race is one that encircles the island. When the fleet is in, Great Salt Pond is a colorful spectacle, and the races along its shores fill the sea with sails. At first natives were wary of the influx, but they soon grew to like the early-season infusion of cash, and now, in June of even-numbered years, *Yachting* magazine sponsors its own race week there. In all these ways, Block wraps up the island experience in one wind-swept, fog-blown package.

· *NEWPORT* ·

Newport is not primarily thought of as an island, but it is on one. A yachts-man friend who lives in the tiny upstate New York end-of-the-road hamlet of Beaver Falls, has said of his hometown: "You can get to it, but you can't go through it," and Newport was like that before bridges were built to it from west, north, and east. Now it is not so much a dead end physically, despite being perched on the southern tip of Aquidneck Island, facing the open sea, and there is no feeling of being in offshore isolation as there is on Block or the islands to the east. Aquidneck, incidentally, was called the Isle of Rhodes by its early settlers, harking back to Greek history, and this was eventually reversed to Rhode Island and applied to the whole state.

Newport plays a number of roles, and the best known is as a capital of Society with a capital "S," and Society's "cottages," a ridiculously and consciously understated term for the huge, ostentatious imitations of European palaces and chateaux. These flourished as summer retreats for the Vanderbilts, Goelets, Rhinelanders, and other Society figures in the laissez-faire years from the nineteenth century to the start of the Great Depression of 1929, and are now sightseeing attractions.

The mansions decorate the waterfront along Brenton Cove and the entrance to Narragansett Bay, the ocean on the south side of Aquidneck, and tree-lined Bellevue Avenue, which runs southward on the ridge of the island. For a distance of roughly two miles, Bellevue Avenue has to be the most unusual "residential" street in the United States with its succession of iron railings and gates, and vistas across velvet lawns to the great stone facades of the houses, set way back among the trees. Roaming through their vaulted marble halls—for an entrance fee for the benefit of the Newport Historical Society that oversees their preservation and maintenance—is a disorienting experience in an American setting, as one could be at Versailles, Windsor, Blenheim, or Chaumont.

The society names attached to the "cottages" have become an American legend of sorts, and I remember once, on a tour of Bellevue Avenue with my parents many years ago, having the name "Mrs. Harrison McK. Twombly" pop into mind, from a sometime reading of the society pages, as a perfect symbol of Newport. Jokingly I made a few remarks about wondering whether we would see her in her natural setting. Later, Mother was telling the story to a friend who happened to be well connected socially, and her reaction was a perfectly literal, "Oh, too bad you didn't see Mrs. Twombly. She's a grand, lovely person. You'd have enjoyed her." So, despite the museum-like atmosphere, people did, and a few still do, live in these incredible showplaces.

There is a very different side to Newport down by the harbor, below the interesting restoration of block after block of old colonial houses packed together along the narrow streets of the town, that is perhaps even more an attraction for visitors than the dreamlike world of the cottages. For years, the U.S. Navy was Newport's major industry, and the waterfront was typical of a Navy town, with down-to-earth bars and gin mills lining Thames Street (pronounced with the *th* of *the*, not the hard *t* of the English pronunciation). There was even one little offshoot of Thames known as "Puke Alley" in recognition of its role on Navy liberty nights.

Now the Navy has gone, at least as a major factor, and Thames Street is part of the restoration project, along with the waterfront itself. The nautical emphasis has switched from the Navy to yachts, and as a result, marinas, ship chandleries and restaurants, far different from the Navy gin mills, line the waterfront in a picturesque sprawl, along with a few commercial fishing piers that help with the local color.

Newport has become a very popular cruising stop for yachts. What was a utilitarian Navy installation, Goat Island, which forms the inner harbor, now has a hotel, and a large marina and apartment complex, connected by a causeway. The harbor itself is absolutely full of yachts at moorings and at anchor all summer long. With the bridge from Jamestown coming in from the west, no longer do bulky ferries have to push their way through this obstacle course.

In addition to attracting cruising boats, Newport is the base for some of the top competitive events in the yachting world. The New York Yacht Club cruise usually forms up here, the Bermuda Race starts here every even-numbered year, and the sport's premier event worldwide, the America's Cup, was based here until the debacle of *Australia II*'s victory in 1983. It was held no more often than every three years to permit members of the N.Y.Y.C., which had held the Cup since the schooner *America* brought it back from England in 1851, to group their forces against challengers from abroad. A defense summer meant at least $5,000,000 out of the pockets of N.Y.Y.C. members for building and campaigning the 12-meter sloops used in the competition, plus all the activities of attending the trials and the Cup races themselves.

During a Cup summer, Newport, normally busy every season with jazz concerts, tennis tournaments, tourist activity, and society doings, would burst at the seams with the added impact of the America's Cup. There was a summer-long influx of extra visitors who were either connected with one of the candidates for the defense or the challenge, or had come to watch the trials and rubberneck at the glossiest collection of yachts this side of Monte Carlo. It all reached a climax during the four-out-of-seven Cup race series in September, when the press came in droves and huge spectator fleets wended in and out of the harbor each race day.

The waterfront was almost swamped with attendant festivities. Restaurants had long waiting lines, and bars were standing room only, with customers pushed out into the streets. These are far different from the old

Navy hangouts, with a marine decor, rock or Dixieland music; they have the hustle-and-bustle atmosphere of a New York singles bar, and prices to match. Every berth and slip was occupied, usually double, by yachts in for the show, and clots of the curious always gathered around the piers where the 12-meter yachts were blocked off from the public by guarded gates.

It was a gay and frenzied scene that exploded to a climax when the races were over and the winning yacht was towed into the harbor to a welcome of thousands of horns, fire hoses, band music, and shouts and screams of spectators lining every inch of waterfront right to the rooftops. Until the Aussies' victory party in 1983 this was always to celebrate an American victory, but, until then, probably the most historic night of celebration in America's Cup history came in 1962, when *Gretel,* the first challenger ever to come from Australia, won a race from the defender (and eventual winner of the series) *Weatherly.* It was the first time a challenger had won a race since 1934, one of the few times in the history of the Cup that any challenger had taken a race, and the first win ever by the underdog Aussies.

They had added a raffish note of color to the Newport scene all summer with their strange "Strine" slang, Down Under accents, robust good humor, cocky competitiveness and, above all, ability to put drink away when the occasion demanded (which it often did). And did this occasion demand it! Their unofficial headquarters all summer was a small, grubby pub down good old Puke Alley called the Cameo Bar and Grill, typical of the Navy-town bars that were still very much in evidence then. It was at the head of the pier where *Gretel* berthed, and the crew had gotten into the habit of repairing there after their daily workouts for "a grog," as they would put it. It gradually became known as the Royal Cameo Yacht Squadron, and many a good session had been held there all summer.

Then came victory night. After *Gretel* had had a welcome in the harbor that matched what most series winners get, and she was safely tucked away at her berth, the cry was "On to the Cameo!" and her crew stormed up the pier. In anticipation, there was already a good crowd, and the word spread rapidly along the waterfront that the Aussies were really going at it in the Cameo. Soon there was not a square inch of floor space, and still visitors, shouting congratulations, kept shoving in, waving beer cans and worming their way through a crush that made a rush hour subway platform look like the Gobi Desert.

A friend and I wormed and pushed and wriggled our way into a far inside corner, where we were shoved back in the recess of a doorway, bumped against, mauled, yelled at, and greeted like old friends by sweaty, grinning hordes. Beer was as much in the air as down throats, and it was absorbed through the forehead, ears, and shirt, whether you had one in hand or not. *Gretel's* crew was soon atop the bar, singing, giving toasts, and letting out aborigine yells while pouring beer on the multitude below, as the bartender all but gave up and let them take over his domain. Even Sir Frank Packer, the domineering, autocratic owner of *Gretel,* got up on the bar for a while and the crowd cheered him, too.

Through all this, as absolute bedlam reigned, came three members of an American television crew, wearing red nylon jackets with their call letters, baseball caps on backward, a microphone clutched by one of them, and bowing under heavy portable cameras. Somehow, gnomelike, they were making a sort of progress through the mob, cold sober and intent on their mission, and, as they managed to get the attention of someone, the man with the mike would push it against his face and say, "Sing 'Waltzing Matilda'." The response was a bit muddled.

Norm Wright, a stocky Queenslander with a wide-toothed grin, the expression of a cherub up to no good, and dark eyes glinting with excitement, was master of revels atop the bar, leading songs and cheers and dispensing beer over people's heads by the gallon. In complete command of the situation, he even told Sir Frank he had been up on the bar long enough and ushered him down, and the ceremony could very well have still been going on but for one teetotalling member of the crew. Since there was more racing to do—and *Gretel* did not win again in the series—he finally corralled his mates one by one, dumped them in the back of a waiting station wagon, and hustled them off to their headquarters, while the Cameo slowly emptied, never to be the same again. It has long since closed and been bulldozed away.

Up on Bellevue Avenue, there had never been a night quite like the Royal Cameo bash, but both atmospheres are part of the Newport story.

· *THE ELIZABETH ISLANDS* ·

In 1602 when Bartholomew Gosnold was dispatched to North America in the ship *Concord,* chartered by a group headed by Sir Walter Raleigh, he ranged the coast from Maine to Buzzards Bay, named Cape Cod and the 15-mile-long chain of the Elizabeth Islands, and discovered Martha's Vineyard (which he also named, although no one seems to know who Martha was) and Nantucket. A monument to him now stands on Gosnold Island, a tiny islet in Gosnold Pond on Cuttyhunk, the outermost of the Elizabeth Islands. During that era an island was considered the best place to settle because it could be easily defended and was approachable by sea. Gosnold picked lonely, barren Cuttyhunk for settlement five years before Jamestown, Virginia, was founded, but it did not last. Both Martha's Vineyard and Nantucket were settled, well established, and quite civilized when the nearby mainland was mostly wilderness.

The interesting thing about the Elizabeth Islands, with their gently rolling hills, sandy bluffs, and scrubby vegetation, is that nowhere else along the Atlantic coast is there a better place today, except perhaps on the Outer Banks of North Carolina, to get an idea of what the area looked like to the Vikings, Gosnold, Block, and other explorers. Cuttyhunk has a small village, mostly built around summer visitors who come for the fishing, but the rest of the Elizabeths have always been privately owned and remain virtually unspoiled. There are some weatherbeaten, gray-shingled summer cottages along the shores of Hadley Harbor, a deep indentation in Naushon, the largest Elizabeth Island, but they seem to blend with the landscape, and they do not detract from the primitive beauty of the islands. Except for the fact that there are usually dozens of other boats in Cuttyhunk Harbor, Quicks Hole, Hadley, or Tarpaulin Cove, the favorite anchorages in the Elizabeths, a sailor sweeping down on this chain before a smoky afternoon sou'wester, as the fuzzed, lemony ball of the sun slants toward the west, could well imagine how the islands appeared from the deck of the *Concord*. The Elizabeth Islands are something of a miracle, situated as they are a scant few miles from the teeming corridors of the east coast megalopolis.

One of their physical features that impresses sailors mightily is the strength of the tidal currents that swirl through the narrow cuts—here called "Holes"—that separate the major islands. Quicks and Robinsons are tricky enough, but the most notorious is Woods Hole, the easternmost cut between the Cape Cod mainland and the Elizabeths. Uncatena and Nonamesset, appendages of Naushon, which is the largest in the chain, form the western side of this narrow, rocky channel that always brings a note of respect into seamen's voices when talking about it.

The current charts admit to more than four knots at the peak of tidal flow, but there are times when spring tides or wind conditions add to this by at least another knot, and the result is an awesome display of nature's power. All the nun and can buoys in Woods Hole are extra-large, jumbo models, because normal-sized ones used in these waters get sucked under by the current and disappear. Most yachts, and many commercial fishing boats, have to consider what the current is doing before attempting a passage of Woods Hole. Its drag is so powerful that it can be almost as difficult, and perhaps even more dangerous, to negotiate with a following current under the keel. Also, when the wind is against the tide at either entrance to Woods Hole, the sea condition kicked up is one more challenge for the small boat.

The difficulties of passage with a fair current were never more dramatically illustrated than on a warm August morning in 1977. The New York Yacht Club cruise had spent the night at a rendezvous in Hadley Harbor, the snug, winding haven on Naushon's eastern end. The next leg of the cruise was to be to Nantucket. This meant a mass exit through Woods Hole for a racing start in Vineyard Sound. The N.Y.Y.C. annual cruise is a tradition dating to 1844, in which members' sailing yachts race port-to-port in New England waters for eight or nine days in midsummer, accompanied by a flotilla of tenders and motor yachts. The assemblage makes a fleet of well over a hundred yachts, a colorful display as it fills such harbors as Newport, Hadley, Nantucket, Edgartown, and Marion, and a scintillating spread of sail when the races start. Everything is conducted with pomp and circumstance as the Commodore's flagship leads the fleet out of each harbor early in the morning with a display of signal flags and the booming salutes of a brass cannon. No finer group of yachts is assembled anywhere under similar circumstances.

On the morning in question the tide was flooding from Buzzards Bay toward Vineyard Sound and had reached its maximum velocity as the fleet weighed anchor and fell into column astern of the flagship for the passage under power through Woods Hole. In passing through the Hole there is a choice of two routes. One is to go straight through to the eastward, almost to the ferry dock at Woods Hole, and then make a 90-degree turn to starboard for another direct passage out to Vineyard Sound. Short-cutting this route is a diagonal channel known as Broadway, along the Nonamesset shore.

The Commodore chose to make the short-cut turn into Broadway, and the fleet followed astern of his 68-foot yawl. The spot to turn 45 degrees to starboard was marked by a big can buoy, to be left to starboard, and then by a nun buoy, 100 yards across the channel, which had to be left to port—obviously a set-up for a "red-right-returning" entrance from Vineyard Sound toward Buzzards Bay. Inside the nun was a nasty, foul ground of rocks and ledges. The first few boats astern of the flagship made the turn without mishap, but then the concentration became so heavy that the nun buoy was obscured and could no longer be used as a reference point. We happened to be in the vanguard of the fleet in our own boat, since we were in the class scheduled to start first. We rounded the can and made the 45-degree turn to starboard without any special concern, though unable to see the nun in the press of boats ahead. The current was raising a great rooster tail on the down-tide side of the big, scarred, black can as we swept by it and put the helm over.

Suddenly two boats just off our port bow hit bottom with a great thunk and a sickening lurch. I spun the wheel hard to starboard for a 90-degree emergency turn, and as I did I saw that we had been carried sideways and were right next to the nun, which was leaning way over as the current sucked it under. We were barely able to stay on the correct side of it, but were soon out of the crosscurrent and headed toward Vineyard Sound under a directly fair current. The boats that had hit bottom near us managed to bounce off and make it into safe water, but astern, as the bulk of the fleet crowded together, further obscuring the buoys from each other, several boats missed the nun and were swept below it.

The first was a big, clipper-bowed ketch. She was hurled sideways onto a shallow ledge and hit it with a tremendous, clanking crash. She heeled over with her rail under as she surged onto the rocks, but such was the force of the current that she was carried over the first reef and then bumped and banged across the entire foul middle ground before being released into clear water. Astern of her, a 48-foot yawl was not so lucky and hung precariously on a ledge at a 75-degree angle of heel. We found out later she was stranded there for hours and was joined by several other boats. Aside from the shock of seeing them hurled onto their beam ends, the noise as they crunched across the rocks was appalling. All in all, over a dozen boats from this top-notch collection hit the bottom during the parade that had started with such carefree high spirits. Only quick action by the crews and by some rescue boats, and the rapid cooperation of nearby boatyards, prevented the total loss of any boat in this unnerving experience. It was a shocked and sobered fleet that hit the starting line for the port-to-port run to Nantucket.

Perils such as these only seem to make the pleasures of cruising, especially in delightful surroundings, that much more rewarding. Skippers who negotiate Woods Hole safely on even the mildest of summer days spew out into clear water at the opposite end with a sense of accomplishment and of a challenge met. One can only wonder what it must have been like for Gosnold and his company to ply these tricky waters without charts in the clumsy vessels of the Elizabethan era.

Perhaps it was the clumsiness of their ships and the concern for uncharted dangers and contrary winds that made these early visitors so prone to putting their settlements on islands rather than the mainland. To a seaman, an island meant better nautical security because of easier approach and departure, and, as mentioned, there was always the thought that an island was easy to defend. Actually, Gosnold was more interested in quick profit than in establishing a settlement, and his voyage was a financial success because he took a cargo of sassafras back to England. At the time it was a highly prized medicinal commodity for the treatment of "the French pox," today better known as syphilis.

• *MARTHA'S VINEYARD* •

All the pressures that the Elizabeth Islands have escaped through private ownership have descended on their bigger neighbors farther offshore, Martha's Vineyard and Nantucket (see Chapter 5). After slumbering peacefully through three centuries of rural isolation, with farming, fishing, and a little whaling satisfying the economic needs of the small population, Martha's Vineyard has had the twentieth century thrust on it with tremendous impact. There were intimations of things to come in the late nineteenth century, when summer people began to build cottages on East and West Chop, two points at the island's east end, and a religious campground grew up at Oak Bluffs. A maze of small gingerbread cottages, jammed together and known as Cottage City, was the site of the revivalist community. Not far from it the graceful old houses of Edgartown, the first settlement on the island, began to attract visitors eager to acquire them as summer homes.

It was not until after World War II, however, that the Vineyard began to feel the crunch of tourism. Just six miles from Cape Cod by ferry, and with air service from New York and Boston increasing yearly, it is no longer isolated enough to have this great flow of visitors naturally controlled. The big question has become one of preserving the charm that brought visitors there in the first place—open moors, miles of beaches, and quaint towns—without stifling natural economic expansion.

Amid all this, the charms of the Vineyard are still very much in evidence. The afternoon southwester still riffles across the salt grass and the multicolored cliffs of Gay Head stand guard at its southwest tip. The striped bass still feed in the surf of Squibnocket, Edgartown's stately houses are neat and trim (and terribly expensive), and boats by the thousands make a marine spectacular of Edgartown, Vineyard Haven, and the picturesque fishing village of Menemsha. It is a charm that is definitely derived from island atmosphere and it is probably strong enough to withstand the pressures on it.

· THE MAINE COAST ·

Cape Cod, technically an island itself created by the canal across its base, divides the island world of New England into distinctive halves. North of the Cape in Massachusetts Bay there are no major islands. The Bay has the sandy, dune-clad shores, scrub pine, and bayberry that set the atmosphere for the southern islands, but Maine is something else again. Maine's southwest coast is one of bold, rocky shorelines, broken by the long flat stretch of Old Orchard Beach, so firm and straight that it has been used for auto racing. Early transatlantic fliers sometimes used it for takeoff, because few airports then had runways long enough to handle their overloaded planes.

Just beyond it is drab, utilitarian Portland, Maine's major city because of its deep-water location on Casco Bay, and from here to the Canadian border Maine's seafront is like the hem of a torn skirt, a ragged succession of points, rivers, coves, and bays, with not a straight stretch on it. Like pieces of cloth ripped from the hem, hundreds of islands straggle from these points, some large and imposing, like Mount Desert (pronounced like the course at the end of a meal), others mere pinnacles of rock. The two major bays, Casco and Penobscot, are chock-a-block with islands, and others like Muscongus, Blue Hill, Frenchman, and Machias have their own share. Few of these islands lie offshore, like Block, Martha's Vineyard, or Nantucket. Only Monhegan, a dozen miles from Boothbay Harbor, is really isolated, a situation that is especially emphasized by the amount of fog that plays around it. Monhegan, with its loud, active fog signal, is lonely, rugged, and possessed of a sense of complete independence, but it is unique for Maine. And, typical of colonial settlements, its inaccessibility and good defensive position caused it to be one of the first places settled in Maine.

All the other islands have a close relationship with the mainland. Most of them are tucked into bays or seem to be mere extensions of the points they lie near. Often it is hard to tell whether a hunk of land is actually an island or just the end of a long point. Only viewed from certain perspectives do the narrow channels appear to open up and show the Maine islands as separate from the mainland or from one another. Causeways and bridges are enough to link many of the islands to the shore, although some of the islands are far enough out to necessitate a ferry ride, and some groups are clustered so close that they almost seem like one island. Mount Desert has a convoy of satellite islands around it, and only narrow Fox Islands Thorofare keeps Vinalhaven and North Haven Islands from being one. Rather than that distinctive, individualistic feeling of being on a Nantucket, the Maine islands foster a sense of entering a special world of community. The clear, cool air, which makes the afternoon southwester tangier and more bracing than it usually is below Cape Cod, the bold, surf-lashed rocks topped by stands of pine and fir much taller and statelier than their scrubby cousins to the south, and the backdrop of elevated land like the graceful Camden Hills or such real mountains as Cadillac, Pemetic, and Norumbega on Mount Desert, all lend something special to Maine's unique atmosphere.

It is an ideal area for cruising, once an accommodation has been made to living with the ever-present threat of fog. Many of the smaller islands, and the hundreds of coves tucked into them, can be reached only by private boat, and there are enough of them to absorb a large cruising population. Except in a few developed centers like Boothbay, Camden, and Northeast Harbor, there is nothing like the jam-up of yachts in any one harbor in Maine that there is in dozens of ports in southern New England. Most Maine cruising devotees feel the world has come to an end if they see more than one or two boats when they anchor for the night. I have cruised for a whole day in Blue Hill Bay at the height of the season and seen no more than a dozen other boats, and not because it was foggy. Yet such is the reputation of the Maine coast islands for providing escape from the rest of the world that many a "Mainiac" yachtsman would feel this a terribly crowded scene.

For those without boats the Maine islands are not totally inaccessible. Ferries take mainlanders to most of the bigger islands, and Mount Desert is an island merely by virtue of a tidal cut, almost bare at low tide, crossed by a short causeway. Its Acadia National Park attracts millions of visitors, many of them campers. The park is highly organized and beautifully maintained, and, despite the number of visitors, the sense of wilderness is never lost. On a clear day the view from the top of Cadillac is a stupendous one— the interplay of sea and islands, stretching to the horizon, east, south, and west—as this is the highest point on the east coast of the United States. Nowhere from here to Mexico is there anything approaching Cadillac's 1,530 feet, not exactly Alpine or Himalayan, but quite impressive when compared with the endless succession of barrier beaches, low bluffs, and sand dunes that border the ocean the rest of the way.

From Viking times on, fishermen and trappers ranged the Maine coast, but it was not until the late sixteenth and early seventeenth centuries that explorers kept records. We know about Gosnold and his voyage, but it was Samuel de Champlain, who left his name for history farther inland, who did some of the earliest exploring in Maine of which accounts remain. From 1604 through 1606 he cruised the coast from the Canadian border all along Maine, and down around Cape Cod as far as Martha's Vineyard, making excellent charts. With about 30 men, he used a pinnace, a small two-masted vessel of 17 or 18 tons, perhaps 35 feet long, propelled by sail and oars. It was Champlain who gave two names that remain today: Isle au Haut and Mount Desert (*Monts Desert*). The latter, for which the French pronunciation has remained, got its name from the fact that there are no trees on its several mountain peaks, the highest of which is Cadillac.

If the French had been more interested in colonizing than in fishing and trapping, Maine might today be a part of French Canada, but instead it was the English who were more intent on establishing themselves on the land. The first attempt was at the mouth of the Kennebec in 1607, the same year that Jamestown, Virginia, was settled, but the Maine winter was too much for the colonists. Those who were left gave up in 1608, sailing home in the 30-ton pinnace *Virginia*, which they had built themselves. Maine got its name as a province in 1637 to set it apart from the offshore islands to the south, but the territory eastward from the Kennebec, known as Sagadahoc, was a disputed area until the end of the French and Indian War in 1763. From then until it became a state in 1820, Maine was part of Massachusetts.

Captain John Smith was another famous explorer who came to Maine. He arrived at Monhegan in 1614 and, in expeditions along the coast as far south as Cape Cod, gave the area the name New England. Despite the absence of gold and copper, which he had hoped to find, and a notable lack of success in chasing whales, Smith felt that the area was a great one for development, based on its fish, furs, and timber. Just as Jamestown, which he helped to colonize, had been on an island, albeit a low, swampy one on an inland river, Monhegan, in its lonely splendor offshore, was settled as the base for his New England expeditions.

The islands have made all the difference when Jane and I have cruised in Maine. Our first trip, which was from South Freeport, near Portland, to Somes Sound on Mount Desert, saw almost an entire week of fog lying along the coast during an inland heat wave. In many coastal areas we would have been held in port for much of our eight-day cruise, but here we could head inland through the maze of channels and rivers that make so many of Maine's long points end as islands. It was not sailing, as we were under power most of the time, but we were in bright sunshine and weaving our way through a country of pine forests high above rocky shores, most of it in tidal waters. We went up the Kennebec River, leaving a low bank of fog at its mouth that hid offshore Seguin Island and its throaty diaphone hooting into the void, as far as the old shipbuilding town of Bath. Here we branched off eastward through the Sasanoa River that makes islands out of the ten miles of land between it and the sea. The Sasanoa is tidal, and a narrows in it, called Upper Hell Gate, has even stronger currents than Woods Hole, complete with overfalls and whirlpools. This inland waterway goes through Hockomock and Knubble Bays, with an equally fearsome Lower Hell Gate to negotiate between these two, and finally leads to the Sheepscot River, the next big indentation in the coast to the east. The whole day, with a feel of being far inland in the north woods, was spent among coastal islands, and several others like it saved the cruise.

Another week-long cruise was based entirely on Mount Desert Island and never once touched the mainland. Night by night we made different harbors on the big island, such as Pretty Marsh, Bass Harbor, Southwest, and Northeast, with side expeditions to smaller islands nearby, like the Cranberry Islands off Northeast, and magnificent Burnt Coat Harbor on Swans Island. All the charms of the Maine coast are tied up in one package in this well-protected spot on the southwest side of Swans, which lies five miles off Mount Desert and is surrounded by a fringe of smaller islands of its own.

Burnt Coat has a graceful, pine-covered point, with a typically stubby, little white lighthouse perched on the rocks at the end for its main entrance. A "backdoor" entrance is on its south side, and it enjoys plenty of good holding ground, and a pleasing shoreline with summer cottages and the homes of year-round islanders spread widely across open fields and in the patches of forest between the fields. Local lobster boats share the harbor with visiting yachts, and a few fishing shacks along the shore add a quaint touch. The name, too, is an interesting relic of Maine history, coming originally from the French words for burned coast. There had been a forest fire on shore when Champlain's expedition came through, hence the French *côte brulée*. In due time the *côte* became "coat" but the *brulée* was properly translated.

Many of the varied experiences that are so special to the Maine islands were wrapped up in this one cruise. We had the expected fog for a day or two, while feeling our way into Southwest Harbor up Western Way by the sound of waves lapping on the rocky shoreline and the twitter of shorebirds above it, as a large whale suddenly surged out of the murk and broached in a fast "blow" a few yards astern. The fog was blown away the next day by a fresh northwester that gave us a gorgeous view up Somes Sound, called the only fjord on the Atlantic coast, cutting deeply northward into Mount Desert. Towering over it in brilliant sunshine were the St. Saveur and Acadia mountains on the west and Norumbega, Pemetic, and Cadillac to the east.

On another day, we beat out to Swans into a salty, tangy southwester bringing the feel of offshore waters in one of its smoky gusts, and mornings in several harbors started with the sound of lobster-boat motors chugging to life in the soft dawn, the twangy voices of their skippers exchanging gossip and information across the still waters. The Maine islands are a continuous, distinctive assault on the senses unmatched because of this unique combination.

Nantucket Harbor; Brant Point in the center.

5 · Nantucket

*E*ven before they are sighted, certain islands make themselves known by some special trademark. Polynesian voyagers could tell where atolls lay beyond the horizon by cloud formations over them. In the approach to Bermuda, a subtle reminder of oleander drifts far to leeward over the open sea. A Maine lobsterman can smell his way home through the fog, and the cool, damp sou'wester that patterns the green waters of Nantucket Sound with whitecaps will suddenly bring a warmer gust, freighted with the scent of bayberry and heath, and of sun on the grasses and ferns of the moors that could only be Nantucket.

Nantucket for me will always mean memories that are awakened by the senses. When I hear an afternoon breeze humming through screens, the moan of a diaphone in fog, or a seagull's cry, or see sunlight slanting through a smoky sou'wester, Nantucket comes back to me wherever I am as it was where my fascination with islands all started. The first trip I can remember to Nantucket was when I was three years old, followed by summers there throughout childhood and adolescence. The impressions of those early years have become imbedded in a nostalgia that increases as time goes by. Consciously or not, I am sure that I use Nantucket as a comparison with all the places I have been where land and water meet.

Each time I return to Nantucket by boat, I reexperience the initial excitement of that first visit as we headed out from New Bedford, Massachusetts on the island steamer *Sankaty*. After we left Oak Bluffs on Martha's Vineyard and cleared by Cross Rip Lightship (where it was a great show to watch *Sankaty*'s crew throw newspapers to the lightship sailors), my father took me to the bow to catch the first sight of Nantucket, the instant when the slim black pencil of the water tower popped over the horizon. It was a moment of high excitement, with the long yellow cliffs of the north shore gradually rising into view as we drew closer. Ever since then I have gone to the bow of the steamer as that time approaches. That first glimpse of the tower, to me as enduring a landmark as the Parthenon, is always a joyful moment and a symbol of the special sense of a beginning, of a new life and a new adventure, that can only be aroused by going to an island.

The approach would then continue with entry through the jetties, and the steamer would blow her whistle three times as we came even with the bathing beach at the landward end of the jetties, another sound that evokes instant nostalgia for me. As she blew, a red tablecloth would be waved in greeting from the porch of my uncle's house located at the back of the bathing beach at the foot of The Cliff. Next was Brant Point, with its squat little lighthouse, where there would be another blast of the whistle as we rounded into the harbor that was crowded with yachts at anchor, and a full view of the town spreading along the shore, its gray and white houses rising from the waterfront to the ridge topped by the gold-domed tower of the Unitarian Church.

Nantucket is where I learned to sail and swim, and eventually to drive, careening over the rutted roads of the moors. There was my first airplane ride, costing five dollars for fifteen minutes of sightseeing over the town in a Ford trimotor in 1928; sailing picnics to Pocomo Head; early dating and dances; movies at the Dreamland Theater; fishing off the jetties; beach parties; and the Fourth of July fireworks. When I return now the associations come crowding back. But for those without this head start in nostalgia, Nantucket is still unique in its combination of physical charm and a history that is fascinating, for there are literally hundreds of pieces of history that remain intact.

Nantucket town is perhaps the purest example there is of eighteenth- and nineteenth-century America. There are over 400 houses that date from 150 to 250 or more years ago, providing a living continuity of tradition, not a restoration like the colonial ones at Williamsburg, Virginia or Sturbridge, Massachusetts. This atmosphere has been maintained by building codes that restrict new construction to the simple, shingled cottages of the Cape Cod saltbox style. Illuminated signs are not permitted, and there are no fast-food outlets. Even the supermarket fits the image.

The history of Nantucket, with its blend of Indian culture, Quaker dominance for many years, whaling and a brief period of opulence, and the modern era of tourism, shows on every side and is carried on by whaling and historical museums, a library called the Atheneum, and in the very special atmosphere of Main Street. Cobbled with ballast stones from ships, with red brick bank buildings and trading houses still standing from the era of whaling prosperity, and lined with elms, the only tall trees on the island, it is unique as an example of America's past, so strong in character that it easily withstands the tremendous influx of visitors.

Nantucket's climate is also its very own. Nearer to the Gulf Stream than any land north of Hatteras, it has a milder, softer air than the mainland, and in the salt tang of the breeze, the sudden materialization of fog, and the power of northeasters when they sweep in from offshore, sending spray far inland across the moors, there is always awareness that you are 30 miles at sea.

The islanders too are unique. Since the seventeenth century they have maintained an unmatched individuality for independence of character. Non-natives are considered "off-islanders," although they may have lived there for half a century. The first settlers arrived in the middle of the seventeenth century to avoid religious persecution, and since then they have not taken kindly to outside interference. When a summer resident, Walter Beinecke, whose personal fortune came from a trading-stamps company, proposed an elaborate plan to revive and remodel the rundown waterfront of Nantucket Harbor, there was tremendous controversy in town meetings and in the pages of Nantucket's highly individualistic newspaper, *The Inquirer and Mirror*, which still prints on presses that give it the dimensions of a tablecloth. Beinecke finally prevailed, but the general opinion had been that only Nantucketers knew what was good for Nantucket, and it was not the business of an off-islander to make such drastic changes in the face of the town.

In 1977, when a change in apportionment of election districts deprived Nantucket of direct representation in the Massachusetts legislature, there was serious talk of secession, and the island received bids from Rhode Island, Vermont, and Connecticut, as well as, improbably, Michigan and Hawaii, to join with them. Nothing came of it, but the talk was a fine example of the lively independence of attitude that exists.

As unique as the town is in architectural purity, equally unique is the land outside the town, on the moors that make up most of the fifteen-by-five-mile spread. The open, rolling fields are called moors on Nantucket, even though that name is supposed to apply to bleaker, boggier landscapes. Botanists claim that the Nantucket moors contain the widest variety of ferns and grasses of any similarly sized piece of land, with heath, heather, and bayberry predominating, and no trees higher than scrub pine. Crisscrossed by sandy, rutted roads, the moors give a wonderful sense of space and freedom to walkers and bicycle riders.

The history of white settlement on Nantucket dates back to 1659. Before that, the explorer Bartholomew Gosnold sighted it in 1602. He gave many of the islands in the area the names they use today, but Nantucket retained the name it was given by its original inhabitants, the Indians, which can be roughly translated as "faraway land." The Indians had been there for perhaps 6,000 years before the white man came. The island itself is a geological newcomer, a product of the most recent ice age that started 18,000 years ago, when great glaciers pushed south from the Arctic to what is now southern New England and sat there for some 10,000 years. When they melted and receded, helping to fill the Atlantic that had been several hundred miles farther out, heaps of rubble that had been shoved ahead and piled up by the leading edge of the glaciers remained as the offshore islands, rising above the great spread of sandy shoals. A ridge east and west across the center of Nantucket marks the limit of glacial advance, and the southern half of the island is made up of the sand and gravel washed down when the glaciers melted.

By the early seventeenth century, Nantucket was divided between two tribes of Wampanoags, both from the Algonquin nation. One group had come from Cape Cod, some 25 miles distant, and lived on the eastern end, while the other had come from Martha's Vineyard and lived on the western side. Their legend of how the islands were formed had it that a giant Indian named Maushop, who lived on Cape Cod, was bothered by sand in his moccasins as he slept and, kicking in irritation, sent the moccasins flying into the offshore waters, where they landed and became Martha's Vineyard and Nantucket.

The first white man known to have contact with Nantucket was Thomas Mayhew, of Martha's Vineyard, who purchased rights to Nantucket from the Earl of Sterling, who held the royal patents. Mayhew used it as sheep pasturage, building a pier at what is now Madaket, at the western end, to facilitate landing. In 1659 a group from Salisbury, Massachusetts, unhappy with the rigid Puritanism there, decided to settle elsewhere. One of them was Tristram Coffin, who had been to Nantucket and liked it, and another was Thomas Macy, who was threatened with jail for having given shelter to some Quakers during a storm. A group of ten families, with Coffin as their agent, went to deal with Mayhew, to seek settlement in Nantucket. The agreed price was 30 pounds sterling and two beaver hats, so Nantucket had a wealthier start than did Manhattan.

Macy was particularly anxious to leave Salisbury because of his difficulties with church officials, and he headed for Nantucket right away, with his wife, five children, and three young friends, Edward Starbuck, Isaac Coleman, and James Coffin. After weathering a storm in their small boat they landed at Madaket and built a hut, where they barely survived the first winter, and would not have were it not for Indians who gave them food. The next year they were joined by nine more families, and one Peter Folger, who could act as an interpreter with the Indians. The names of these early settlers are still prominent on Nantucket today. One of the Macys gained somewhat wider fame. Rowland Hussey Macy, a descendant of Thomas, tried whaling and, not liking it, moved to New York to open a dry goods store in 1858.

The settlers and Indians got along well, with minimal friction, although there was little the Indians could do to preserve their lands in the face of constant additions to the settlement, and a tragic accident in 1763 all but wiped them out. Two sailors from a brig carrying immigrants from Ireland came ashore to seek information while their ship was anchored off the beach. At the first house they were taken in and given food, and the mistress, Molly Quin, in an act of kindness, had her Indian servant wash their ragged, filthy clothes. Soon Mrs. Quin and the servant became ill. Mrs. Quin recovered, but the servant, who had gone to the Indian settlement, died. The disease was smallpox, and before long 258 of the 358 Indians on the island had become infected, and 222 of them died. This was, in effect, the end of the Indian population on Nantucket, but their memory is carried on by many names such as Wauwinet, Sankaty, Siasconset, Quidnet, Miacomet, Madaket, Coskata, and Sesachacha.

The Indians had taught the settlers whaling. In their long canoes the Wampanoags pursued the creatures as they swam by the south shore. They used the technique of a harpoon attached to a long line that coiled out of a bucket. The whale would tow the boat until he tired, at which point the exhausted beast could be easily killed. These techniques later became standard in white man's commercial whaling. From lookout stations at Tom Nevers Head, 'Sconset (which is never called by its full name, Siasconset), and Sankaty, the new settlers would sight the whales and give chase, but gradually they had to go farther and farther from the island to find them. Eventually the sperm whale of distant seas became their chief prey, so Nantucket whalers roamed the globe in three-year voyages. By 1842 the Nantucket port had become the third richest in Massachusetts, behind Salem and Boston.

In this economic heyday, Nantucket became a showplace of wealth. Imposing Georgian and Greek Revival homes were built in the town and the shops dealt in the latest fashions. The island was a matriarchy run by women during the long absences of their men, and tales of the whaling days are a colorful part of Nantucket's heritage.

The golden era of the early nineteenth century came to an abrupt end with the discovery of petroleum, which resulted in a decline in demand for whale oil. And, in 1846, a great fire wiped out one-third of the town. Also, the natural sand bar across the harbor became so shallow that it prevented deep-water ships from entering. A long depression followed in which many of the men had to leave the island to make money. In one way, it was a long-range blessing for modern Nantucket's position as a tourist attraction, because almost no houses were built during the following era of gingerbread decorations and mansard roofs, thus maintaining, even if by accident, the purity of Nantucket's heritage.

One of the best known members of Nantucket matriarchy was Kezia Coffin, née Folger, an ardent Tory who dealt with the British during the Revolution to obtain goods for her store. She thus gained an economic stranglehold on much of the island. Quakers were very powerful and quite numerous at the time on Nantucket, and Coffin, originally one, was read out of the Meeting for her high-handed ways. This bothered her not at all, as she continued a flamboyant life-style in the face of island austerity. It was said that her country house, built near the harbor at Quaise, was used as a headquarters for smuggling, and that it contained a secret tunnel leading to the harbor's edge, although these activities were never proved. When the war ended, neighbors that she had exploited united to boycott her store, and she ended her days in poverty after a siege in debtors' prison.

Of better reputation and also an original Nantucketer was Maria Mitchell, daughter of a Nantucket banker, who had a small observatory in the cupola atop her father's bank. In 1847 she discovered a comet that made her world famous as an astronomer, and in 1861 she was appointed professor of astronomy at the newly opened Vassar College. She was a forceful, distinguished member of that faculty for 21 years, and during her lifetime she was given more awards and honors than any other American woman of her generation.

From early on, the quaint shacks of 'Sconset began attracting visitors, and "summer people" grew to be Nantucket's major industry. The necessary ingredients were all there, in a mix that has proved attractive to owners of summer homes, hotel vacationers, and day trippers alike. Since the late nineteenth century, Nantucket has gradually built up a summer colony of intensely loyal, emotionally involved people who feel just as strongly about the island as do the natives, and third and fourth generations are now carrying on the tradition. The houses on The Cliff, which begins a half mile west of the jetties on the north shore, and those on Brant Point's sandy shoreline are as attractive and as beautifully maintained as any summer homes anywhere. Many of the old houses in town are now owned by summer residents, and colonies with individual characteristics have developed at Monomoy across the harbor from the town, Wauwinet at the head of the harbor, and along the bluff between Sankaty and 'Sconset at the highest spot on the island (about 100 feet).

'Sconset has grown into a big community, and the little fishing shacks that originally attracted Nantucket's first vacationers are a picturesque feature at the heart of it. Parts of several of these buildings are actually older than the restored Jethro Coffin House, officially publicized as Nantucket's oldest house, dating from 1686.

The summer colony swells the resident population from about five or six thousand in the winter, including an increasing community of retired people who first came as summer residents, to perhaps 50,000 in the summer, with hundreds more coming in each day on one-day excursion-boat trips from Hyannis, Massachusetts. For the established summer colony the Nantucket Yacht Club, right next to the steamboat dock, is the center of social activities and much more than just a sailing club.

One concession to summer trade that was a feature over the turn of the century was a narrow-gauge railroad to Surfside and 'Sconset, for auto-mobiles were not allowed on the island until 1918. When they came, the railroad, a Toonerville trolley affair that would stop on the moors if a passenger happened to want to pick wildflowers, soon expired. Automobiles now create a serious traffic problem in the narrow town streets, and bicycles are a favorite means of transportation.

Almost every bit of Nantucket's shoreline is beach, with the warm, pro-tected waters of Nantucket Sound on the north side, and the colder, rougher Atlantic on the south and east coasts. Until recently, one could drive, walk, or bicycle across the moors and find a stretch of beach with no one in sight in either direction. Now the beaches are well populated with swimmers, and fishermen ride dune buggies along otherwise inaccessible stretches to reach the bluefish rips off Madaket, at the western end, and Great Point on the northeast.

The controversy over waterfront development has subsided, and it is now an established part of Nantucket's image. In place of the fish piers, coal yards, oil tanks, and machine shops of a grubby commercial area, there is a large marina, surrounded by stores, art galleries, restaurants, and marine service shops. Everything has been done carefully, in keeping with the traditional, shingled building style of Nantucket, and the area has been extensively planted in flowers and evergreens. It is a magnet for the visitors flooding off the excursion boats, and for yachts cruising in from all over the Eastern seaboard. The marina is so popular with visiting yachtsmen that slip reservations must be made weeks in advance for the height of the season.

The marina is the biggest change in the face of Nantucket since the end of whaling, but the old houses of the town retain an atmosphere that withstands the heaviest visitation of sightseers. The showpieces of all ar-chitectural treasures are the "three bricks," Georgian houses on upper Main Street, built at the height of the nineteenth-century prosperity by whaling magnate Joseph Starbuck for his three sons, with the two high-columned Greek Revival houses of their in-laws across the street. These were the ultimate in Nantucket's days of economic glory, even though the side streets like India, Pleasant, Fair, Orange, and Centre are lined with beautiful examples of Nantucket houses. These are typically built at the sidewalk line, the front steps paralleling the sidewalk and a yard at the side. They are often three stories tall with a basement that is half above ground.

As I have returned through the years, watching the developments and changes, Nantucket has lost none of its original charm as far as I am concerned. It is still my first island, the classic standard, and its charm is still forcefully individual. The moors, though threatened, still have a sweep of grandeur and loneliness, and the view from The Cliff is a lovely panorama of sand, dunes, seascape, and the curving beaches of Coatue and Great Point, with the hustle of the harbor and the gray and white huddle of houses and spires of the town as counterpoint. Out at Sankaty, the lighthouse stands high on its bluff looking out over the open sea ("Nothing until Portugal out there," we used to say on visits to Sankaty), the surf booms in at Surfside, and the fog often slides in unannounced after a day of hazy southwest breeze, sending its gray fingers over the moors and across the hills of Monomoy and Shimmo to wrap the harbor in quiet, shrouding the riding lights of the yachts at anchor. Nantucket remains as it was in the beginning for me.

Lake Ontario from Main Duck Island.

6 · The Great Lakes

*J*ust two months after she had been skimming across the limpid waters of the Great Bahama Bank one spring, our 24-foot sloop *Mar Claro* was in a dramatically different setting. Through the magic carpet of trailing behind the family car, she had been transported to the Great Lakes, and Jane and I sat in her cockpit in the snug, postage-stamp harbor of Main Duck Island and watched the Aurora Borealis blaze across the northern sky to the zenith. The brisk northwest breeze had a nip of autumn in it, though this was just the first of August, and windbreakers felt good. A modest Lake Ontario surf splashed and rustled on the low, shale-covered point that separated us from the open lake just off our bow.

Somehow it was hard to believe that we were in the middle of a lake, far inland from salt water, although the breeze held a reminder of meadow grass and frog ponds as it hummed through the rigging. The feeling of space, of open waters, and of separation all seemed to belong to the oceans, according to our seacoast-oriented senses, but the great flickerng spasms of green and white sweeping across the northern half of the sky told us that this was indeed a different world. It is still one, however, in which islands hold that intriguing fascination for those who dream of escape.

Each of the Great Lakes has its special insular attractions. Located near Main Duck, the Thousand Islands fill the St. Lawrence where it joins the eastern end of Lake Ontario. Lake Erie's are off Sandusky, centered in Put-in-Bay. Lake Huron has more islands than anyone can count in Georgian Bay and the North Channel, plus Mackinac. The Manitous and Beaver Island lie athwart the head of Lake Michigan, and Isle Royale is the major mass in Lake Superior, which includes the Apostle Islands, nearer shore, which form a large group.

• *MAIN DUCK* •

For us, Main Duck was as intriguing as an island can be. We had headed there, 24 miles from the little mainland resort harbor of Chaumont, across the steep and slow-breaking chop of fresh water, on an afternoon of brilliant sun and brisk breeze. It was a glorious sail, and now, on a weeknight, we had the tiny harbor to ourselves. Even better, we had the run of the island via a letter of introduction to the caretaker. Main Duck, located in the Canadian half of Lake Ontario, had for years been the favorite retreat of John Foster Dulles and his family and was still owned by his estate. Since it was a privately owned island, visitors were not allowed ashore without special permission, and the caretaker was delighted to see us. He and his wife, the only permanent residents, had to spend most of their time asking people to leave or preventing them from landing. The harbor, of course, was open to all for anchoring, but not landing. This policing really was contrary to the caretakers' friendly natures, especially in such a lonely setting, and they welcomed us, and our daughters, who were teenagers at the time, as a fine chance to show off the island they loved.

There was plenty to see. The three-mile-long splinter of land athwart the main steamship channel between the open lake and the St. Lawrence was unspoiled and untouched except for rustic Dulles family cottages. They sat high on a bluff in a setting of magnificent trees, and included the caretakers' cottage near the harbor, and a Canadian lighthouse on the

Toxotis *in the Meltemi.*

The Meltemi at Mikonos.

The harbor at Ios.

Vlacherna Monastery at Corfu.

Grecale *at Bonifacio, Corsica.*

The cliffs of Bonifacio.

Dubrovnik's main street.

←*The Aga Khan's high-powered yacht.*

Waterfall on the Dalmatian coast.

Lingering northern light over Fjallbaca, Sweden.

Mover *approaching Smögen in the Swedish skerries.*

The jam-packed harbor at Smögen.

Lohals, Denmark, a typical lystbodhavn.

Morning fog burning off in Somes Sound, Maine.

Busy Edgartown, Martha's Vineyard.

Sunset over Goat Island, Newport.

Burnt Coat Harbor, Swans Island, Maine.

western end. A single Jeep track provided the only road on the island. The land varied from forests with open meadows to some marshy areas with small streams, and in general teemed with wildlife, including a big deer herd.

This was an exciting, faraway land for our girls, who were used to tropical snorkeling, or clamming and building sand castles in our home islands in the Shrewsbury. The caretaker drove them all over in the Jeep, showed them the lighthouse, taught them to fly cast, and, on a special trip just at dusk, took them to a hiding place near the swamp, where they could watch the deer drift quietly in to a salt lick. After that they spent the night on shore, and this was exciting enough to make up for missing the Aurora Borealis. They were asleep in a cabin in the woods by the time that show began.

Much of Main Duck's shorefront is lined with rocky cliffs, deeply sculptured by wave erosion into odd, corrugated patterns. In many places the bottom of the cliff is eaten away more than the top, in a laminate of weird projections and semi-caves, and the trees at the top, not all evergreens as might be expected in this northern area, seem to soar out into space as they stand at the very edge of this receding escarpment.

Main Duck sits like a natural fortress in the middle of the blue lake, all by itself on an empty horizon as one heads offshore for it, and, knowing what it must have meant to Dulles and his family to retreat to its comfortable lodge on the cliff, one can take it as an almost perfect symbol of escape.

· LAKE ERIE ISLANDS ·

The Lake Erie Islands are far different. At the western end of the lake, they are links of a land bridge across a relatively shallow section of it to Canada from Catawba Island, which is actually a peninsula that forms the north side of Sandusky Bay. At one time this land bridge made a separate lake out of what is now the shallow western basin of Lake Erie. Gradually, parts of it submerged, and the names of the islands that remain are a picturesque litany: South Bass, Middle Bass, North Bass, Squirrel, Starve, Ballast, Kelley's, Pelee, Green, and Gibraltar. This is grape country, and the Catawba grapes make a good wine and a pleasant, effervescent grape juice that is popular as a "champagne" with teetotalers and teenagers. Wineries, rather than the usual bars and taverns, are the social meeting places in the Lake Erie Islands.

The whole chain is overlooked by a 352-foot fluted shaft on South Bass, the Perry Monument, a memorial to Captain Oliver Hazard Perry, who led an American fleet to victory over the British in the Battle of Lake Erie on September 10, 1813. Naval control of Lake Erie determined the fate of the whole upper midwest along the Canadian border during the War of 1812, and Perry, at the age of 28, was put in command of American naval forces in the spring of 1813. In what amounted to wilderness territory, a fleet had been assembled at Erie, Pennsylvania, through purchase and arming of commercial schooners and the construction, out of materials from local forests, of two 500-ton brigs, each with eighteen 32-pound carronades, short-range guns, and two 12-pound long guns. The British, with similar vessels also built locally on the Canadian side of the lake, had been in control of communications on Lake Erie, and Perry's job was to challenge this control.

While his fleet, badly undermanned despite his repeated requests for more crew and virtually unprotected in the rudimentary shipyard on Erie's Presque Isle Bay, was being outfitted in July, a fleet of British ships under Commander Robert Barclay patrolled the harbor's entrance. If Barclay had attacked the unfinished ships, he could have wiped out the force that eventually defeated him, but there was only five feet of water over the sandbar at the harbor's entrance, and Barclay was content to keep watch offshore.

Perry's problem was to get his ships over the bar safely, and this he did in early August while the British ships were absent, resupplying at their home base. The two brigs had to be lightened by removing all their guns and were then lifted even higher through the use of "camels," floating pontoons that raised them out of the water. While they were negotiating the bar, fortunately in calm weather, they were completely open to attack and defenseless, but the British had not returned, and Perry's fleet was safely underway before they reappeared.

Once operating in the open lake, the American fleet was able to disrupt the British line of supply along its bases on the north shore of the lake, and a big British fort at Malden, 30 miles across from the Lake Erie islands in Canada, was running out of food. Including army and navy personnel and a great force of Indians who were cooperating with the British, there were some 14,000 mouths to feed, and Barclay, forced to act, decided he had to do battle.

On the morning of September 10, Perry's fleet was anchored in Put-in-Bay. His two brigs were *Lawrence,* named for the U.S. Navy officer who had uttered "Don't give up the ship" as his dying words in a losing battle the year before, and *Niagara*. At sunrise, a masthead lookout on *Lawrence* sighted the British fleet in the northwest, reaching in on a favorable south-west breeze, and Perry ordered a sortie. The American fleet was slightly bigger, and, fortunately, a shift of wind to southeast gave them the wind-ward gauge, so necessary in sail combat, as the forces drew near to one another. In a day-long struggle, in which the wind lightened and hampered operations, *Lawrence*, closing first, did great damage but was eventually put out of action. Perry then transferred himself to *Niagara* and the battle was finally won. It effectively broke British control in the area and ended hos-tilities.

The monument to this feat, a major triumph for the young American Navy, dominates a scene that teems with marine activity today, although nothing like the military doings of 1813. Put-in-Bay personifies the herd instinct common in island escapes. It is difficult to find isolation or loneliness here, but, in genial banding together in the wineries on these busy islands, served by stubby little ferries and, unbelievably, Ford trimotor planes, there is that sought-after sense of separation from the "real world," of laissez-faire, and come-what-may tomorrow.

We saw these islands at their busiest and most carefree during the In-terlake Yachting Association Regatta, a fixture at Put-in-Bay since 1893. It brings hundreds of sailboats, and an attendant fleet of power cruisers, from the area between Detroit and Buffalo. Where Perry and Barclay once coursed down the lake in search of each other, offshore racing yachts home in on Put-in-Bay via feeder races from all points of the compass, and one-design boats, the smaller day racers, are trailed in from all over the Midwest for a week-long festival of serious racing and serious partying. The partying is given a peculiar impetus by the fact that most of the racing is in the morning, when summer breezes on Lake Erie are at their most reliable, as Perry and Barclay discovered during their battle. Also, the afternoons in summer are often given to vicious thunder squalls. Competition is over by early afternoon, which is usually the time racing starts in most sailing areas, and the wineries ring to an early assault by ready-to-relax sailors.

There is a homey atmosphere about the Regatta. While the younger element cavorts in the wineries, there are bingo parties for the wives of officials and sailors; a Commodore's dinner at the firehouse, served by the housewives of the island; parades; and a stage show; all in a sort of Fourth of July atmosphere—mid-America at play.

The close formation of the islands provides protected water that is good for racing, cruising, and fishing in small boats, and the race courses have interest and variety as they wind between the low, green islands; little bits of farmland dropped into the open water, some fairly heavily wooded, others more open. It also gives them a community of interest that has been fostered for years by the unique agency of the Ford trimotors. These relics of pioneer aviation days in the late 1920s and early 1930s have been kept alive as inter-island transport, serving as delivery trucks, school buses and mailmen, as well as passenger carriers.

We were there on the same trip that took in Main Duck, and one of the major thrills of it for our daughters was to take a trimotor flight from South Bass to North Bass and back, purely as a sightseeing junket one afternoon after the racing was over. We were the only passengers, along with a can of paint and one auto tire as freight, as the old plane lumbered into the air and made its stately way across the water at 80 m.p.h. The pilot warned the girls and then did an up-and-down wiggle with the plane to make them squeal and giggle, and they could not help thinking back to the old Ford a couple of months later, when they had their first flight in a 707. In winter, when the lake is frozen, the planes are the only form of passage unless the ice is smooth and unbroken so that cars or trucks can cross, and the trimotors seem to symbolize the unique way of life of the area.

· *MACKINAC* ·

One year while racing to Mackinac Island from Chicago in what is at 333 miles the longest regularly scheduled freshwater sailing race, we were all but becalmed as we drifted toward the finish line along the island's cedar-topped limestone cliffs. High above us on the wooded slopes, the long, white mass of the Grand Hotel, said to have the biggest porch in the world, looked down in regal Victorian splendor, and near us on the shore, a young girl was riding a horse. From a lazy canter along the water's edge, she reined it up to watch us for a while.

"Are you racing?" Her clear young voice carried across the water to us.

"We're trying to," someone on board called back.

For a minute more, she remained poised and still, watching us, and then she called again. "Well, you're not doing so good. Better get a horse!" And with a derisive laugh, she nudged her mount into action and tore off down the beach at a good clip.

Somehow, this seemed like an appropriate welcome to Mackinac, as it is one of the few places remaining in this world where you have to "get a horse." No cars are allowed on its land mass of three by two miles—a conscious effort of preservation. Once a fishing village and trading post, it is now a resort that is dependent on its atmosphere. Despite the rush of tourists swarming in by ferry from St. Ignace and Mackinaw City, and the special invasion frenzy that prevails when hundreds of boats sweep in from Detroit and Chicago in the annual races, Mackinac appears isolated.

There is also confusion about its name. When you race from Chicago, you say you are racing to MackinAW, whereas Detroit people talk about MackinAC. "You starts from a city and you takes your choice." Its origin was as a French fort in 1670, in the days of the *voyageurs* and adventurous trappers. Before that, Chippewas, Hurons, and Ottawas variously held it. The British took it from the French in the French and Indian War in 1761 and held it until after the American Revolution. They reclaimed it in 1812 in a surprise attack on the American garrison, which did not yet know that the War of 1812 had been declared, but it was finally returned to the United States in 1815. Old Fort Mackinac is now a park, and to stand at it and look at the wooded hills along the Straits of Mackinac stirs a nostalgia for the days of the fur trade. However, to achieve this sensation, one must ignore the large bridge that spans the Straits connecting Michigan's Upper and Lower Peninsulas, and the constant flow of steamer traffic.

On traveling up Lake Michigan from Chicago, toward Mackinac, the emptiness of the early part of the lake is left behind. For the first 300 miles the lake is open, but after that it is filled with islands, including the Manitous, Foxes, and Beaver Archipelago. These lie 35 miles west of the Straits of Mackinac and consist of Beaver, Hog, Gull, High, Squaw, Trout, Garden, and Whiskey Islands. Beaver is thirteen by six miles and has three lakes and several streams, the largest of which is called the River Jordan. The only real settlement is at St. James at a harbor on the north end of Beaver Island.

These are resort islands in a semiwilderness setting, giving little evidence of their lurid history between 1847 and 1928. Before 1847 the only white settlers had been French *coureurs de bois* of the early seventeenth century, who used it as a hunting base. After that, it was left to Chippewa and Ottawa Indians until a scouting party of Mormons arrived during the summer of 1847. They had a base in Wisconsin, but their leader, James Jesse Strang, was looking for a site where he and his followers could live without interference. Over objections by mainland fishermen and trappers who wanted the islands left undisturbed, the Mormons established a colony, built the town of St. James, and, on July 8, 1850, Strang had himself crowned king with full pomp and circumstance. He ruled as absolute monarch, forbidding tea, tobacco, and liquor, advocating and practicing polygamy, and demanding tithes from his subjects, with which he paid Michigan property taxes.

The bitter mainlanders, who objected to his kingdom off their shores, forced a U.S. Federal investigation of conditions on Beaver, and Strang and several followers were arrested on charges of counterfeiting, stealing public timber, and tampering with the mails. He was tried in Detroit and proved so eloquent in his own defense, blaming religious prejudice for the charges against him, that he and twelve followers were acquitted. By now his "subjects" were so numerous that he was elected to the Michigan House of Representatives, and the Beaver Islanders gained political control of Emmet County, moved the county seat to St. James, and gave all positions of authority to members of the colony. This led to further confrontations with mainlanders, and an expedition to Charlevoix to summon three jurors to the island led to a shootout known as the Battle of Pine Ridge, in which one mainlander was killed and many islanders were wounded.

Bolstered by political success, Strang became ever more tyrannical, even in small ways, and aroused special resentment when he decreed dress rules for women, banning long skirts and ordering them to wear bloomers or knee-length dresses. As women defied the edict and dissension grew, Strang had their husbands publicly whipped and carried out personal vendettas against them. Opposition increased to the point of open rebellion and Strang was shot to death by angry dissidents on June 16, 1856. His killers were assisted in escaping by naval authorities. They were taken off the island to the sheriff's office at Mackinaw City by the *Michigan*, a U.S. revenue cutter, and immediately turned loose. Mainlanders then formed an expedition that cleared the island of Mormons, numbering over 2,500, and seized all their property, turning them out as homeless and penniless refugees.

Irish immigrants followed the Mormons to Beaver and reestablished St. James. Their descendants, many with fine brogues, remain there today. Despite what happened to Strang, Benjamin Purnell, founder of a religious colony called the House of David, calling himself King Ben, tried to set up another "monarchy" on Beaver in the 1920s, but there was so much opposition that his plans had to be abandoned. He did, however, gain control of High Island and banished members of his cult who had fallen into disfavor to virtual slave labor on it. When he died in 1928, 500 exiles on what had come to be called "Siberia" were freed. Elderly sports fans will remember the bearded, barnstorming House of David baseball teams of that era.

• *THE NORTH CHANNEL* •

Beyond Mackinac to the northeast lies a tremendous spread of islands in the North Channel and Georgian Bay. These sizable bodies of water are separated from Lake Huron by one big island, Manitoulin, and a host of lesser ones. The shores of both are lined with small islands. The atmosphere is like that of the Maine coast, or perhaps Puget Sound, and the cruising opportunities are equally as good and as fascinating. It is a country of rocks and pines, a land of clean, bracing air freighted with the scent of evergreens. Navigation is tricky through the intricate labyrinth of channels and reefs, but worth the effort in rewards of solitude and scenery. At the height of the summer season, solitude may be a comparative term, but enough harbors, coves, and cuts are there to hold thousands of boats.

At the far northwestern end of the North Channel, almost to the Soo Canals that connect Huron and Superior, in a little town called Thessalon, I once attended the annual rendezvous of the Great Lakes Cruising Club, and solitude was certainly not the key, although conviviality and hospitality were. Sail and power yachts converged from all of the Great Lakes, many of them cruising to it in company, for a weekend of festivities, receptions, parades, banquets, and cookouts. Visitors in hundreds of boats outnumbered the few hundred townspeople of Thessalon, but the whole show was staged with an efficiency and aplomb that would rival any big city's attention to a political convention, and with much more friendliness. It was a Canadian version of the kind of hospitality shown the Interlake Regatta at Put-in-Bay.

After the rendezvous, the boats dispersed into the North Channel and Georgian Bay Islands to be completely swallowed up by a week or two more of cruising. Jane and I moved on to a place near Thessalon called Desbarats (pronounced Deborah) for a visit with my college roommate and family at their summer "camp," and this water-oriented little settlement was a fascinating example of a special kind of resort. Most of the summer cottagers are from Lake Forest, Illinois (Desbarats is sometimes called "Lake Forest on the Rocks"), and the third generation is carrying on a family tradition that started in the nineteenth century when railroad executives from Chicago, Lake Forest residents, decided to form a resort that would provide business for railroads running through the Soo area. It is the kind of community in which most of the people, although they nominally come from some big-city suburb in the winter, have their emotional involvement and personal identity tied up in their summer home, which was the focus of their growing up during boarding school and college days. My roommate's wife, from Lake Forest, was named Deborah in honor of Desbarats and has, for more than half a century, spent every summer of her life there without fail. Naturally, family connections and friendships are deep-rooted, and the pull of the place is so strong that the fourth and fifth generations are now beginning to turn up, if only for short vacation visits.

Physically, everything at Desbarats revolves around the water. There is a central landing-cum-boatyard and a general store just off the main highway from Sault Ste. Marie to Sudbury, where everyone leaves the cars needed for trips to the Soo airport to meet visitors and for major shopping trips, but for little else in the life of Desbarats. All of the houses are on isolated points or islands in the intricate archipelago that strings offshore toward the main waterway of the North Channel, and are only accessible by boat.

Launches, Boston Whalers, and all sorts of utility boats are the "station wagons" of Desbarats, ferrying people from their "camps"—a term something like the Newport euphemism for "cottages," in that the camps are usually very comfortable, rustic houses with all the amenities. You travel by boat to play tennis, to shop, and for cocktail and dinner parties. There is sailboat racing sponsored by a local "yacht club," which has no clubhouse, and some of the houses sport rather large cruising sailboats or cabin cruisers for ranging farther afield, although these are in the minority. Most people like to stay put once they are in Desbarats, and an occasional spin through the islands is enough of a nautical adventure.

And adventure it is to wind through the ever-changing perspectives, as channels open up for a moment into the middle distance when an open stretch of water is passed, only to be lost as the view closes in to the nearby bank of the next island, with its "camp" and its crown of trees. Quiet coves smile in the sun, and a more open stretch will have a parade of dancing whitecaps as the wind suddenly finds a long enough straightaway to make itself felt.

There are surprises in the shifting vistas in the maze. Here a local landmark, a house designed by Frank Lloyd Wright, tops a cliff, jutting dramatically into space, its windows an intriguing pattern that must provide gorgeous views from the inside. There, suddenly on a point, all by itself, is a building containing just a squash court, built by a fanatic who could not leave his city sport behind for the summer.

For a few short months when the sun is high and benign, the grass is green, and insects hum and buzz in the trees, Desbarats is a self-contained world, complete in its perfect insularity, whose time ends until next year when the north wind whistles down from Hudson Bay, and the moment has come to return to Lake Forest.

Saddle Cay anchorage in the Exumas.

7 · Offshore in the Atlantic

Bermuda and the Bahamas are often linked, erroneously, with the Caribbean, usually in a glamorizing attempt by advertising copywriters, but they are very much in the Atlantic. Actually, they should not even be linked with each other. They are separated by 800 miles of ocean and are different in climate and in the lay of the land. Bermuda is one small isolated archipelago, farther from any other land mass of any sort on the globe except St. Helena in the South Atlantic. (The British knew what they were doing when they sent Napoleon there.) Located at 32 degrees North Latitude, Bermuda is not a tropical island, although it has the palm trees, water colors, and coral reefs associated with one. The Bahamas spread over thousands of square miles of ocean and are made up of hundreds of islands, large and small. The Tropic of Cancer, where the tropics technically start (at 23 degrees and 30 minutes North), bisects the Bahamas. Bermuda is still a colony, one of the few Great Britain has left, while the Bahamas are an independent nation in the British Commonwealth. Linked with the Bahamas physically, but separated politically, is the Turks and Caicos group far to the southeast, another one of Britain's few remaining colonies.

• *BERMUDA* •

The nearest land to Bermuda is Cape Hatteras on North Carolina's Outer Banks, 600 miles westward; New York is about 660 miles away. Bermuda, a collection of coral reefs on top of an underwater mountain, is all by itself and there is always a sense of being at sea there in the look of the clouds, the way the wind blows, and the ever-present sound, sight, and smell of the ocean. The air is filled with it.

Bermuda was my first landfall away from continental North America, and I will never forget the sight of its brilliantly colored waters as the *Queen of Bermuda* made her way along the north shore in early morning sunlight. We were just rounding Catherine Point, the northeastern end of the island at St. George's, when I came on deck, and the pastel greens and blues of the inshore waters, varicolored over the reefs and shallows, burst with dazzling impact on eyes accustomed to the grays, dark greens, and browns of northern seas. Although Bermuda is not tropical, the clarity of the water around it and the play of colors in the water matches anything the tropics can produce. That was in 1937 and from the Great Bahama Bank to the Barrier Reef of Australia, I have seen many a gorgeous display of tropical water hues, but none has ever aroused a more excited reaction than that first glimpse of Bermudian shallows.

That was a primitive attraction of nature unadorned and unspoiled, but Bermuda's basic one is actually in its civilized structure of houses, roads, plantings, and gardens gracefully arranged against a backdrop of ocean vistas, rocky shoreline, and the sweep of surf creaming against the long white curve of a beach. Its lonely 21 square miles of connected islands are now so densely developed that there is no place left on it to be alone with nature and away from an awareness of the works of man, unless tucked away on a tiny cliff-enclosed beach with a view across the empty sea. But the civilizing has been well done. Every house has a white, rain-catching roof; but pinks, limes, lemons, blues, and a whole rainbow of hues make up the wall colors that flash into view between cedar trees, oleanders, and royal poincianas, usually with a riot of blossoms around them in gardens and hedges.

Those who can remember Bermuda before automobiles were allowed in after World War II miss the added quaintness of carriages, bicycles, and a small train that puffed its way from Hamilton to St. George's, but Bermuda driving is at a leisurely pace because of the narrow, winding roads, and all the cars are subcompacts. Visitors are not allowed to rent cars because of the traffic congestion this would add, and motorbikes have replaced bicycles as the major means of transportation. Their exhaust fumes have replaced the homey odor of horse manure that used to pervade Bermuda's coral roads.

Bermuda's late surrender to the automobile was just one more example of an individuality that has marked life there through almost four hundred years of history. Its name comes from its discoverer, the Spaniard Juan de Bermudez, who first saw it in 1515, and for the next century, the tight little archipelago was mainly known as a very real navigational hazard for Spanish ships heading home from the Caribbean. To take advantage of the Gulf Stream and prevailing wind patterns, they followed a route north along the North American coast to the general latitude of Bermuda, which is close to the latitude of the Straits of Gibraltar, before turning eastward for Spain. Some would stop in Bermuda hoping to find water, although there is no natural supply in lakes or rivers. The Spanish also left pigs ashore to fend for themselves so that they would be available as a source of fresh meat on future homeward passages. That not all the ships made it safely past is dramatically demonstrated by the number of wrecks on the reefs discovered off Bermuda's north shore, especially by modern-day divers. In addition to navigational dangers, Bermuda was also thought to be a place of evil spirits and haunts, and there was no thought of anyone living there until some European travelers were forced into it.

In 1592, a French ship left Santo Domingo for home with one English passenger, Henry May, on board. He was a seaman whose East Indiaman had put into port in distress, and he had been sent home to make a report on her condition to her owners. It was the custom on homeward-bound ships for the crew to be given "wine of height" to celebrate reaching the latitude at which they would change course for Europe, and this was done when it was mistakenly estimated that the vessel had passed safely east of Bermuda. With the effects of the "height wine" at a height, the crew was blind drunk when the ship grounded on a reef northwest of Bermuda. May was one of two dozen survivors who made it to shore.

The castaways lived on turtles, fish, birds, and berries but passed up the wild hogs, which they considered too lean to eat, and found rainwater in some depressions in rocks. They built an 18-ton bark out of native cedar and salvage from the wreck, and set sail for Cape Breton on May 11, 1593, getting there in nine days—a fast passage in any kind of sailing vessel. Eventually they returned to Europe on fishing boats, and May published an account of his experience, the first Englishman to set foot on, and to write about, Bermuda.

The hogs had the islands to themselves for a few more years before another shipwreck brought the next "settlers." This was the vessel *Sea Venture,* one of a fleet of nine proceeding in company to the new colony in Virginia. *Sea Venture* was the flagship of Admiral Sir George Somers and on board was Sir Thomas Gates, who was to be the new deputy-governor of Virginia. In a severe storm that lasted for four days, she was separated from the other ships and almost sank; but hard, continuous work at the pumps kept her afloat until Bermuda was sighted, the ship was grounded, and all 150 aboard taken safely ashore. This was July 28, 1609, and Bermuda's history really dates from that day.

The *Sea Venture* survivors spent nine months in Bermuda and found the hogs far from inedible, feasting on pork as well as turtles, fish, birds, and berries, while managing to make a strong wine from palmetto palm hearts. This was while they were building two vessels from the local cedar, the 80-ton *Deliverance,* and *Patience,* a 30-ton pinnace, which Somers personally built with the help of 20 workmen. Lacking caulking cotton, Somers used a gooey mixture of lime and turtle oil as a putty to seal the seams.

The following May 10, these two ships set sail for Virginia with almost the entire company aboard, but two men, Christopher Carter and Robert Waters, stayed behind. They were in disfavor with Governor Gates and fully expected to be hanged when they arrived in Virginia, so they hid in the bushes when *Deliverance* and *Patience* were leaving. Admiral Somers abetted them, secretly vowed to come back for them, and made good his promise. Actually, he found the Virginia colony in such a sad state from lack of food that he headed back to Bermuda to bring new supplies from there, and he found Carter and Waters so pleased with their lush existence that he decided that Bermuda should also be settled. Unfortunately, he died there in November. His heart and entrails were buried in an area at the east end of the island that is now named for him, St. George's. Carter and Waters decided to continue their island existence rather than take the long, nasty voyage back to England on Somers' ship (carrying the rest of his body), and they were joined by a third man, a servant of Somers' named Chard.

This triumvirate thought that a plantation would soon be established in Bermuda and that they would be in a good position as original settlers, but three did not get along as well as two had, and they fell to feuding in their lonely paradise. A find of precious ambergris on the beach was the cause. For a while they battled with oars, bashing each other's heads, and then Waters and Chard became serious enough to prepare to fight with swords. Carter prevented bloodshed by hiding their weapons in a masterful display of "arbitration."

After two years, however, they decided to return to civilization and were in the process of building a boat to take them to the fishing grounds of Newfoundland, the surest way of getting a transfer home, when a ship, *The Plough*, arrived with a party of more than 50 colonists under a master carpenter named Richard Moore, and Bermuda's tripartite rule came to an end. Carter, Chard, and Waters joined with the new settlers, who were under commission from the same Company that was running the American colonies under a March 12, 1612, grant from King James I. It was an august Company of 150 of England's leading citizens, and eight of them gave their names to the parishes that are still designated by them today in Bermuda. The town of Hamilton is named for a governor of that name in the eighteenth century; Smith's after Sir Thomas Smith; Devonshire, first called Cavendish for the Earl of Cavendish, was changed to Devonshire when he became a Duke; Pembroke after the Earl of Pembroke; Paget after Lord Paget; Southampton after Shakespeare's patron, the Earl; Warwick after the Earl of Warwick; Sandys, after Sir Edward Sands; and St. George's after Somers.

Bermuda's first economic attraction was the ambergris that the three first settlers had fought over, but no more was found. At first tobacco seemed like the best economic bet, but Bermuda's soil produced a bitter, almost unsmokable leaf that was considered as "only fit for Dutchmen to smoke," and from then on its history is a roller coaster of ups and downs based on changes in economic fashions as well as historic events like the American Revolution and Civil War. Bermudians have traditionally been loath to engage in any form of agriculture, so they have always been dependent on off-island supplies for food. It was not until some Portuguese immigration during the nineteenth century that much of the soil began to be tilled. In any event, there is not very much of it that can be tilled, and the economy of this isolated yet dependent spot has successively, and not always successfully, been based on a strange variety of items and trades. Starting with that first find of ambergris, it has attempted seed pearls, tobacco, cedar, salt, shipbuilding, shipping trades, shipwrecking, privateering, whaling, palmetto hats, blockade running, arrowroot, potatoes, onions, Easter lily bulbs, and, finally and most lucratively of all, tourism. And, as in other colonial areas, the importation of slaves was to lead, eventually, and at long range, to deep-seated problems.

Shipwrecking, a phenomenon in isolated maritime communities throughout history, gave Bermuda an unsavory name among seamen in the lean years after the privateering of American Revolutionary days eased off. False lights on reefs or cliffs would lead ships onto the reefs, and the wreckers would then take over ship and cargo. There is one story told in W. B. Hayward's 1910 book, *Bermuda Past and Present,* about the rector of St. Ann's Church. He was preaching his sermon one stormy Sunday when he noticed that a latecomer was whispering to several parishioners, who were seen to be reaching for their hats. Interrupting his sermon, the rector asked what this was all about and was told that there was a ship in the southwest breakers.

The parson's reply was: "The congregation will remain seated until I take off my surplice, and then, boys, we'll all start fair."

Before the golden flood of tourism began slowly in the late nineteenth century, spurred by a winter visit by one of Queen Victoria's daughters, the two most prosperous periods were the privateering era in the late eighteenth century and four frantic years as a base for blockade runners during the American Civil War. Some of the oldest Bermuda fortunes were founded in these eras, and some of the most handsome examples of Bermuda architecture, still standing today, were built with privateering money. It was also during the American Revolution that Bermuda almost joined the American colonies, or at least might have been forced to. A Franco-American treaty in February 1778 provided for annexation of Bermuda. Lafayette was in favor of it, but somehow it was never executed. Then, during the War of 1812, the U.S. Congress decided by one vote against a plan for capturing Bermuda.

And so Bermuda has retained its unique position, physically, socially, and politically, in its isolated mid-Atlantic splendor. Dependent as it is on American tourism for its livelihood, which has given it one of the highest standards of living anywhere in the world, it has nonetheless remained very British in its traditions, social structure, and loyalties, and has developed, on the basis of British traditions, a distinctive life-style. Its parliamentary system, which is claimed to be the oldest continuously self-governing one anywhere, started in 1620, under the sponsorship of the Company that then operated Bermuda, and came under the Crown, where it remains today, in 1687. In that year the first assembly under the Crown was called, with four men elected from each of the nine parishes, a system that continued unchanged into the twentieth century.

As in the American colonies, Bermuda has had to live with the consequences of slavery, which was abolished in the 1830s. Blacks make up over 60 percent of the population of over 60,000 and enjoy the highest standard of living of any black community in the world. There is no unemployment and virtually no poverty, but the consequences of years of rigid segregation of the races have had a severe effect. Despite the general prosperity, and the conservatism of a large middle class of blacks who live very comfortably, there has been continuing black resentment over white control of Bermuda's economy. Ownership of the banks, shops, hotels, restaurants, and other establishments that bring tourist dollars has always been in white hands, and blacks have filled subsidiary roles as clerks and in service positions for the most part. With the world racial unrest of the 1960s bringing new emphasis to such situations, Bermuda has gone through two severe riots that shook the community deeply and temporarily hurt tourism.

The climax of a centuries-old situation came in December 1977. Two men, who had confessed to the ambush and assassination of the Governor of Bermuda and an aide in the garden of Government House in 1973, and to the murder of the police chief of Hamilton in 1972, were to be hanged. There were vehement protests against the hanging until the very last minute, and, when it was announced that the executions had taken place, rioting broke out and continued for two nights, mostly concentrated in the black areas of Hamilton, but spreading sporadically to isolated spots throughout Bermuda. I happened to be visiting a Bermudian family that week, and it was a tense, unhappy time; not so much one of physical fear, but fear for the future of Bermuda and the quality and fabric of life there. Since then, concerned Bermudians of both races have worked hard to overcome the effects and eradicate the causes of the unrest. The vast majority of islanders of both races want the peace and cooperation that mean continued prosperity, and a sincere effort has been made to correct the imbalances that led to the situation. This same majority goes out of its way to be hospitable to visitors. Perhaps fostered by realistic recognition of how the bread is buttered, there is nevertheless a delightful atmosphere of friendliness and genuine warmth in dealing with Bermudians, and pride in their very special island-bound situation shines through. Bermudian hospitality is genuine.

And nothing can change the magnificence of Bermuda's natural setting. An approach by sea through the brilliant colors inside the reef, with the white roofs of the houses dotted through the trees on shore, or a first ride from the airport over the roads winding around the glorious blue of Harrington Sound between hedges of oleander, dusty pink and white, sets the atmosphere for a continuous assault on the senses. This is made up of the soft touch of Bermuda air on the skin, the pungency of the riot of flowers, and the constantly changing perspectives of hills, trees, hidden harbors, beaches, and the open sea, ever present as a cobalt background to almost every Bermudian vista.

Because it is not tropical, Bermuda has its seasons—not as sharply defined as on the mainland at the same latitude, but still a distinct variation in winter and summer weather. Temperatures around 50 degrees Fahrenheit are rare in even the coldest spells of winter, and summer heat hardly ever rises above 90 degrees Fahrenheit, especially in the almost ever-present breeze. Being far at sea keeps the climate equable and moderate, and the Gulf Stream's course of about 300 miles to the north breaks up cold blasts from the continent. Still, fireplaces are well used in winter, and no self-respecting Bermudian would be caught dead swimming in the ocean between November and May—that activity is for "crazy" tourists. Winter weather is ideal for golf, which is one of the major tourist attractions on several beautifully laid out and situated courses, and tennis is naturally very popular. Indeed, it was from Bermuda that the United States originally learned the game. In 1874 Mary Ewing Outerbridge, an American visitor, saw a form of lawn tennis being played by British officers of the Bermuda garrison. Fascinated by the game, she took a set of equipment home with her, and with her brother's help established a court on the grounds of the Staten Island Cricket and Baseball Club.

It is the sea, though, that is the main attraction, and it is responsible for much of Bermuda's local color. Handsome cruise ships crowd Hamilton's tidy harbor from April to November, and the most glamorous nautical sight is the arrival in June of every even-numbered year of the ocean race for sailboats from Newport, Rhode Island. Started in 1906, it has become one of the top sailing events in the world, with the reward of the delights of Bermuda at the end of a rugged offshore passage as one of its main attractions. It brings the cream of the ocean-racing crop from the United States, Europe, South America, and even Australia and New Zealand. The fleet, 150 or so strong, makes a brilliant spectacle when it assembles in a dress-ship array of signal flags flashing bright colors in Bermuda's breeze and sun. The Royal Bermuda Yacht Club's pink building at the edge of Hamilton Harbour is the focus of activity, with sailors swapping yarns at its open-air bar on the lawn; but boats are moored all around the perimeter of the long, narrow harbor at guest houses, hotels, and the Royal Hamilton Amateur Dinghy Club, near Foot of the Lane. So popular has racing to Bermuda become, that an odd-year event for cruising boats was started in 1977 and has also brought large fleets to Hamilton, so that there is now a yachting spectacular every June.

· *THE BAHAMAS* ·

Despite often being linked in the popular mind, the Bahamas are a marked contrast to Bermuda in almost every possible way. They do have striking colors in their surrounding waters, from deepest purple to the palest pastels, and it is definitely an island world. Nowhere in the Bahamas is it possible to forget that these are islands, with the sea around them, acting as a dominant influence on everything that goes on. In Bermuda, all this is contained in a compact world of twenty-one square miles set far out to sea and away from any land influences. The Bahamas, however, are only 45 miles from Florida at their westernmost point, Bimini, and have 5,400 square miles of land spread over 100,000 square miles of ocean in a northwest-to-southeast arc of about 700 miles. There are almost 700 islands and a couple of thousand more rocky cays. Since 1973 the Bahamas have been an independent nation in the British Commonwealth.

The vivid limestone-and-coral islands rise from a submarine plateau, and are generally low and flat. They are riverless, but dotted with mangrove swamps and brackish ponds, and depend on rainfall and desalinization for fresh water. Their many reefs and shoals make navigation hazardous, and many outer islands are uninhabited and undeveloped.

For the visitor, they have the double fascination of complete change from the mainland combined with easy access. One can move very easily into a whole new island world, excitingly exotic in scenery and life-style. It is not unalloyed paradise; there are some grubby realities to face amid the sparkling waters and fresh trade-wind breezes. As in any new, relatively insolvent independent country with no natural resources and a long history of tension between ruling whites and working blacks, there has been a backlash of reaction under the native regime that took over in 1973. Bureaucratic meddling and bungling can produce real frustration, and poverty is a depressing reality and an unnerving contrast to the opulent trappings of tourism. Sometimes these combine in unpleasant personal confrontations, but through the overall atmosphere there breathes a sincere effort to do well by the tourist trade. In official circles of the new regime there is full recognition that without tourism the Bahamas would have no basis for an economy of any kind. And, in natural features there is much to offer. The climate, the waters, the beaches, the excellent sailing, and sportfishing add up to a great plus.

Before tourism, the economy and the history of the islands went through cycles similar to Bermuda's. It is not exactly a secret that Columbus discovered the New World (if you forget the Vikings and generations of north European fishermen and trappers) on October 12, 1492. It is generally accepted that San Salvador, lonely eastern outpost of the central Bahamas, was the site of the historic landing, although there is a reasonable school of thought that gives this honor to the Turks and Caicos group. The late Samuel Eliot Morison, historian, author, naval officer, and the foremost expert on Columbus, has made the case for San Salvador, and that remains the official story.

During the period of Spanish development of the West Indies that followed the voyages of Columbus, the Bahamas lay unsettled and almost forgotten, occasionally used by pirates, and the Spaniards transported most of the Indians to work the mines of Hispaniola. It was not until 1649 that William Sayle, who had been governor of Bermuda, led a group of 70 people to the long, fishhook-shaped island the Indians called Seagatoo to set up a community where there could be "liberty of conscience." He renamed Seagatoo as Eleuthera, and the company of settlers was called the Eleutherian Adventurers, after the Greek word for freedom. All did not go well, however, and the group split to form a second community on St. George's Cay, off the northern tip of Eleuthera at what has become known as Spanish Wells. Both went through hard times, but names from these early settlers, such as Bethel, Knowles, Kemp, Pinder, Sands, and Sawyer, among others, are still predominant through much of the Bahamas.

Later, American Loyalists fleeing the Revolution joined these communities "to be closer to the King." Over the years these families have stayed together, and all-white settlements like Spanish Wells and Man o' War Cay in the Abacos have retained a way of life that goes straight back to colonial days. Religion is a strong, everyday factor in their lives—you cannot buy liquor by the bottle on Spanish Wells—and churches are very much in evidence, with prayer meetings several days a week, not just on Sundays.

The inbreeding that has resulted from generations of the same few families intermarrying has produced a physical type of distinctive look-alikes, remarkable especially in what is now an almost all-black nation. The people are fair-complexioned, blue-eyed, and freckled, with sandy hair, thin-lipped mouths somewhat sunken in bony faces, prominent jaws, and lean, leathery necks. The resemblance is so strong that you will start a conversation with a man thinking you have already spoken with him only to find it is a different person.

In the 1970s Spanish Wells became a boom town based on lobstering. It had neat new houses, new cars in every driveway (on an island less than two miles long), towering television antennas capable of bringing in Florida stations almost 200 miles away, and youngsters zooming through the quiet streets on motorbikes, a shock in the otherwise decorous surroundings. The talk is nasal and peculiarly accented with quaint phraseology.

My favorite encounter with a Spanish Wells resident came when I needed some repair work on our boat's engine a few years ago and had made advance arrangements at the local machine shop for it to be done. When I stopped in to check when the mechanic would be available, I found him hard at work just finishing another job. I explained who I was and asked when I could expect him to work on our boat.

"Right after now," was the prompt reply, as he picked up his tools and marched out the door toward our boat.

Under proprietorship, the Bahamas did not prosper, and Nassau, soon after it was settled, became an important pirate base, because of its strategic location, for waylaying Spanish ships heading home via the Gulf Stream with New World treasure. The Spanish did not suffer these attacks meekly and made many raids on Nassau, sacking it completely in 1703. This resulted in the Crown's attempts to sort out the chaos with their own administration, and Captain Woodes Rogers became governor. He managed to eliminate the pirates and organize a stable government, which led to the motto of *expulsis piratis commercia restituta*. In the boom days after World War II, when merchants known as "the Bay Street Boys" were running Bahamian business with high-handed concern solely for their own profitable interests, which eventually led to their political downfall, there was an undercurrent of amused irony in some quarters over whether *piratis* had been *expulsised*, although commerce had certainly been restored. In 1776 Nassau was captured and held for a year by the young United States Navy, and was under Spanish rule briefly before being restored to British rule.

Through all this, plantations in the Bahamas were never as successful as in the lush islands farther south in the Caribbean, although they were the basis for the little economy there was in the eighteenth and early nineteenth centuries. There was not enough good soil or acreage for the vast crops of sugar and cotton the bigger West Indian islands could produce, and the final blow to plantation economy was the freeing of the slaves in 1838. Today plantation ruins on some of the Out Islands are ghostly reminders of a vanished past. The Out Islands refer to everything in the Bahamas except Nassau and New Providence, the hub. The new government has tried to rename them the Family Islands in an attempt to erase any stigma implied by "out," but the old title remains in use, as it is completely apt geographically, with no insult intended.

Through the nineteenth century the Bahamas dozed except for one frantic flash of prosperity, as was the case in Bermuda during the blockade-running days of the American Civil War. Shipwrecking, also as in Bermuda, was one of the staples of the economy, and was such an accepted practice that it was actually done by license until the British Government eliminated it in 1848 by establishing a system of proper aids to navigation. It took tourism, starting slowly with improved steamship service from New York in the late nineteenth century—and blossoming mightily during American prohibition when the islands were a base for rum-running to Florida, a mere 50 miles away—to bring at least partial prosperity back to the Bahamas. Now visitors are numbered in seven figures per year. Gambling in Freeport and on Paradise Island (formerly Hog Island) at Nassau has brought with it large Miami Beach–style hotels. More than a dozen cruise ships a week keep the dredged and deepened port of Nassau constantly busy as one of the two or three most active cruise ports in the world. And smaller resorts, some barefoot casual, some truly sumptuous but low-key, can be found in attractive settings on most of the Out Islands. Bimini, on the rim of the Gulf Stream 50 miles from Florida, is a major center for big-game fishing.

It is in and on the water that the Bahamas are at their best. The sea has acted as the prime historical influence, and today's yachtsmen have a ready-made "escape to the South Seas" right at their doorstep. Crossing the Gulf Stream to get there cannot be taken lightly. I have done it 17 times, both racing and cruising in sailboats, and have had only two "easy" trips. However, hundreds of boats do it each month. Some stop right at Bimini and Cat Cay on the eastern rim of the Gulf Stream for the excellent big-game fishing, but many more go on to cruise through the almost limitless choice of harbors. Each big island—Grand Bahama, Abaco, Andros, and Eleuthera—is a cruising ground in itself, and the Exumas are among the world's finest cruising waters. The Exumas are a 100-mile north-to-south string of slender cays and islets never more than a few hundred yards apart and veined with creeks and channels, offering hundreds of places to drop the hook.

We have had our own boats in the Bahamas for four winters and have also cruised there in charter yachts many times, and we always head for the Exumas whenever possible. It is 32 miles across a portion of the Great Bahama Bank, known as the Yellow Bank, from Nassau to the northernmost Exumas, usually a good day's sail, but miles and miles away in atmosphere. As the high rises on Paradise Island fade below the horizon astern you are eerily alone on the Bank for a while, with no land in sight except for the bottom, 10 to 12 feet away and clearly visible through the pellucid water. On the Yellow Bank, named because the bottom gives a greenish-yellow cast to the water, there are isolated coral heads showing as yellowish-brown, purple, dark green, or black patches that may be seen under the surface if the light is good. It takes some experience to pick out coral patches from small cloud shadows, and most skippers prudently steer around them, even though a six-foot draft can supposedly clear all of them.

After perhaps an hour or so of being alone with the heads—this would be on a five- to six-knot sailboat—a tiny dot pokes over the horizon beyond the bow, the top of the highest hill on Highborne Cay, soon joined by two more little humps. Then Ship Channel Cay separates from the water in isolated clumps. Most boats head for Allan's or Highborne as their first Exuman anchorage, and, as the details of the low, scrubby cays begin to take shape, the water over the Bank pales from greenish blue to a powdery azure, with coral patches near the islands showing up in warning hues of yellowish brown. And no matter how many times one approaches the Exumas, there is still a sense of wonder, almost of astonishment, at the clarity and shadings of the water, shifting with the depth from blinding white over the shallows to the inkiest, richest blue where a finger of deep water threads its way in from the expanse of Exuma Sound on the other side of the narrow islands.

The relative accessibility of the Bahamas and their abundant attractions for cruising yachtsmen have brought many more boats in recent years, and it is not as easy as it used to be to get away from it all in a snug, private anchorage. There are so many of them, though, that the Exumas are still far from crowded, and their charms are neverending. The islands themselves are nothing special in scenery or landscaping although flowers can be found in protected corners, and there are gorgeous, untouched beaches on many of them, some pure white, some pinkish, all symmetrical and clean. Sailing here is a constant delight, and there is an extra effervesence, almost a sense of flying, in surging through these limpid waters while watching the bottom flash by just beneath the keel, with an occasional starfish, sea urchin, or patch of grass to provide a focus on the long, clean stretches of corrugated sand. The Exumas are an intoxication to the sailor, a place where the clichés of dreams of escape manage to come true.

They are the best of the Bahamas, although there are many other areas that are almost as satisfying. The Berry Islands just north of Nassau are almost the Exumas in miniature. The Abacos have much of the same escapist charm, with more civilization and fewer nautical challenges. And the far Out Islands—the San Salvadors, Acklins, Mayaguanas, Long Islands, Rum Cays, and Jumentos, to name a few—still have an unspoiled away-from-it-all aura, as few yachts get that far from Nassau.

While the Bahamas trade on this sense of the remote, they are not so isolated from North America when it comes to weather influence, especially in the winter. The normal weather sees day after day of fresh easterlies, the tail end of the warm trades that blow so steadily in the Caribbean, and an equable year-round climate, but weather systems from the big continent to the west can move on through and bring marked changes. An average winter season—mid-December until late March—will see a dozen or more cold fronts sweep out across Florida and the Gulf Stream and blast their way southward. Usually the Gulf Stream moderates their temperatures, if not their gusty north and northwest winds, although there was the one infamous occasion in January 1977, when it actually snowed in the Abacos and Grand Bahama, something unmatched in recorded history there. The normal cycle for a norther starts with a weakening of the easterlies and a definite warning is a shift into the south or southwest for a day, usually with strong winds from that quarter, followed by a cold front with squalls, rain, and dropping temperatures. Behind the front comes the norther (or northwester) and moderate ones just mean a day of clear, cool weather, while the stronger ones have winds in the 40-knot range and temperatures down around 50 degrees Fahrenheit. The front usually blows itself out in a day or so and the breeze then swings gradually into the east, with a warming trend, or a flat calm results as the center of the high pressure system takes over, before the normal breezes come back. In January 1979, there were eight cold fronts, some as close as three days apart, one or two viciously cold, but the rest just calling for a few hours in port until the weather moderated. In spring and summer the weather steadies down to prevailing easterlies and temperatures from 72 to 85 degrees Fahrenheit.

Despite the burden of the cold fronts, the Bahamas repay the rest of the North Atlantic world in a tremendously important way. If they were not situated where they are as a vast underwater plateau with canyons and a few peaks poking above the surface, the Gulf Stream would not be formed as it is, by being forced into the narrow Straits of Florida and impelled northward in a concentrated flow by a nozzle effect. If this warm flood of water that dead-ends in the Gulf of Mexico after being pushed across the equatorial Atlantic by the northeast trades merely dissipated back out into the open Atlantic, instead of being concentrated and forced into the vast northward-flowing ocean river of the Gulf Stream by the Bahamas barrier, the Atlantic basin to the north would be tremendously different. The northeast coast of the United States and northern Europe would have a Labrador-like climate, and New York, Paris, Rome, and London would have temperatures like Archangel or Nome. Thanks to the Bahamas, we have a livable climate in the centers of western civilization.

· TURKS AND CAICOS ·

Speaking of remote, this group really is. Physically it is a part of the Bahamas, an extension of the same topography of the peaks of a sunken plateau barely protruding above water. They are in the Atlantic Ocean, at the southeast tail of the Bahama chain, and oddly enough, the Anglican church considers them part of the Bahamas although they have not been that politically since the mid-nineteenth century. For a while they were a dependency of Jamaica, but now they are a separate British crown colony. One must go through customs and immigration when arriving there from the Bahamas.

The remoteness is not so much geographic as psychological. True, the Turks and Caicos (Kā́-kōs) are in an out-of-the-way corner geographically, a crossroad to nowhere in world commerce, about 100 miles north of Hispaniola and 50 miles from Mayaguana, the last of the Bahamas, but the Caribbean is farther away. For years there was no real reason for anyone to travel to them except for those Bermudians who worked the extensive salt flats quite profitably until relatively recent times, and the world knew nothing of them. Gradually a small group of settlements grew for fishing, lobstering, and the salt works, but even the postwar tourist boom passed the islands by until very recently.

Now, with direct air service to Nassau and Miami, several companies are promoting land sales and informal resorts with marina facilities, so the world is gradually catching up with an area it truly forgot for centuries. Increased yacht traffic to and from the Caribbean has also brought more boats this way in recent years.

Physically they are very similar to the Bahamas. The islands are low and scrubby, the beaches are beautiful, and the islands perch on the rim of a big, shallow bank. The native settlements are almost primitive, and the speech and manners are very similar to Bahamian ways. If you like bone-fishing this is the place to do it, as the Caicos Bank is ideal for this very special sport. It is a great, flat, protected expanse of white sand, never more than 10 or 12 feet deep, and often shoaling to a few inches. The islands form a semicircle of more than 50 miles across the northern edge of the bank, and their layout can often be seen from far offshore, when they are well below the horizon, by the pattern of cumulus clouds that forms over them in the heat of sunny afternoons.

Ocean tides flow onto the bank in narrow cuts between the islands that send fingers of dark blue onto the white, only to disperse gradually and blend with the pale bank waters. These bring small forms of marine life in from the ocean and provide food for the strong, wary bonefish that drift across the flats like pale shadows. Guides from Providenciales, the big island on the west side of the bank where most of the resort clubs are, know where these currents meet in extra concentrations of bait. It is a long trip through one of the cuts and along the edge of the bank to the special holes where the bonefish live, and the weather must be right. We spent a windy week there when not a boat could move, forcing the bonefishermen to sit at the bar of the Third Turtle Inn and bemoan the conditions, trading taller and taller tales during the long days of waiting.

So pale and easily spooked are bonefish that the water must be calm, with excellent light. When a breeze roils the water and the bottom sand is stirred, there is no way to spot their elusive shadows. In addition to bonefish, the Caicos bank has one of the greatest collections of conch, the big shellfish that is a staple of Bahamian and West Indian diets, anywhere in the world. This fishery has only lately received any commercial attention.

Preparation of the prevalent conch is one of the great challenges of island cookery, and there are quite a few methods. The meat of the conch, which is difficult to remove from the whorled shell unless you know how to slip a knife into the right place, is white and rubbery, too tough to eat unless well handled but delicious when done with the right touch. To open a conch, you whack off the second point from the top with a hammer or stone and insert a sharp knife in the hole this makes to cut the muscle that holds the animal to the shell. A sort of sickle of flesh sticks out of the main opening of the shell, and pulling this will remove the conch's body. The sickle-shaped flesh is then thrown away and the body is cleaned by splitting it and throwing away everything that is not white.

Some people tenderize conch meat by pounding and beating it. Others boil it in a pressure cooker in a half-and-half mix of sea water and fresh water, with onions, bay leaf, and potatoes. Another method is to dice it fine, boil it for at least 20 minutes and then simmer it in butter with onions and potatoes until it is browned. Minced conch, called *lambi* in Spanish-speaking countries, is ground to a mince and cooked with spices and rice. Other ways of serving it include conch fritters, with chunks of tenderized conch fried in batter, or in conch salad, where the meat has been boiled and tenderized in lime juice and the seasoning is supposed to be as peppery as individual tastes can stand. In addition to the various ways conch can be cooked and eaten, conch shells can make a melodious horn if they have the right shape and are pierced correctly, but it takes a good "trumpeter" to get a sound out of one.

To get to the Caicos we thrashed our way across Caicos Passage from Mayaguana on a windy April night. A stiff northeaster obscured the stars with low-flying scud, and short, steep seas charged the port bow of our sloop, the white of their foaming crests providing the only break in the blackness. There were anxious hours when the lighthouse at the west end of Providenciales was not visible. The point on which it is located is ringed with reefs, and it would have been hard to pick them out of the darkness amid the welter of wind-driven whitecaps breaking around us. The first gray easing of the blackness at dawn showed the point where it should have been off the starboard bow, and we later found that the lighthouse had not been working for two years, standard operating procedure in this part of the world. At least there were no licensed wreckers to lure us falsely into the reefs.

Providenciales—"Provo" to all in conversation there—is the most developed of the Caicos, with land sales for vacation homes increasing steadily. Many houses have been built, although they are still scattered over the hills and bluffs that command magnificent views of the reef to the west and the pale greenish white spread of the bank in the other direction. The passage through the reef and the intricate maze of coral heads inside it is one of the trickiest I have ever seen, and a pilot, absolutely necessary for new-comers, is provided by the marina at Third Turtle. Third Turtle is located on a landlocked pond that has been opened up by a man-made cut, and it perfectly embodies the spirit of an Out Island resort. The guests are well and comfortably cared for in an informal atmosphere, everyone mixing in the bar and at meals, and locals stopping in for a drink and to watch whatever impromptu entertainment happens to pop up during the evening. The rest of the world seems very far away.

Palaminos Island off Puerto Rico.

8 · Into the Caribbean

Through a dark, moonless night we motorsailed southeastward, leaving the Caicos and Bahamas astern. Heavy-looking stars shone fuzzily between clouds hanging low in nighttime humidity, and instead of the expected trade wind, a fitful breeze barely ruffled the long swells of the Atlantic. We were alone in the void, and only the flicker of lightning from Haitian thunderstorms on the starboard horizon gave a hint of the existence of land.

The April dawn came early in a gradual seeping of gray through the wall of night soon after 0430. In half an hour there was enough light to see a darker area of gray on the starboard bow. Yes, there was land there, and it was Hispaniola. The heavy outline, growing more distinct by the minute, was Cabo Isabela. As the eastern horizon began to show streaks of red and gold, a higher shape bulked directly over the bow. A double peak loomed through the mists, the taller one topped by a statue of Christ, arms outstretched, showing as a tiny, pale shaft. This was Isabela de Torres, rising 2,600 feet behind Puerto Plata, our destination in the Dominican Republic, which shares Hispaniola with Haiti.

At first, Isabela de Torres was bluish gray, indistinct in the mists around its slopes, but as the light strengthened, the gray disappeared and the blue began to deepen. The sun, hidden for us by horizon clouds, sent random shafts of light to isolated spots on the mountain, turning them to gold. Gradually the glow spread over the whole face of the double peak, burning the mists away. By the time we arrived off the harbor entrance, in full sunlight, the statue of Christ gleamed in the horizontal rays, and the mountain was a lush green. Ranging behind it into the interior were higher mountains, fading from purple to pale blue in the distance under towers of cumulus. It was a landfall to remember, the essence of the magic that islands can generate.

After many trips by plane, Jane and I were bringing our own boat to the West Indies for the first time, and what could be more dramatic, more rewarding, than the misty unveiling of the corrugated profile of Hispaniola, Columbus's favorite island? In these storied waters, you sail with the legends of the early voyagers, in the wake of Columbus, Drake, Morgan, Nelson, Rodney, de Grasse, and the galleons of Spain. The cultures they represented, and many more, from the Netherlands, Denmark, France, Africa, and India, have blended over the centuries into a very special mix.

In a 30-mile passage between islands that stand on the horizon in a repeated pattern of cloud-capped peaks and shifting color values of blue, purple, green, and brown, there can be a dramatic change in customs, language, and modes of living. From *arroz con pollo* and mournful songs about *mi corazón* in Santo Domingo to the neat Danish streets of the towns of St. Croix, from cricket in Barbados to smart boutiques and haute cuisine in Martinique, from the tourist traps of St. Thomas to the trim Dutch cottages of Saba, from the whalers of Bequia, cane cutters of St. Vincent, Indian shopkeepers of Trinidad, Breton fishermen of the Saintes, and banana farmers of Grenada to tourists in the high-rise hotels of San Juan's Condado Beach, the Caribbean has a multitude of facets under the common denominator of sun and trade winds. The African heritage has mixed with many other influences so that a Haitian and a Grenadan, for example, would struggle to find a common ground of communication.

The beat of African music comes out in the liquid rhythms of a steel band from Antigua, the oddly accented lilt of a Trinidadian calypso singer, the rasping insistence of a "scratch band" in Virgin Gorda, or the swirling dance called the meringue in the Dominican Republic. In the Spanish-speaking countries, the smooth cadences of Iberia have been mixed with an African tempo.

The term *calypso* has been applied to almost all music of the Caribbean, but it is really the distinctive style of singing in which topical lyrics, sometimes improvised at the moment, are sung in a jazzy, accented rhythm. It originated in Trinidad and soon spread to most of the islands, including the Bahamas and Bermuda, and it is a feature of carnival time leading up to Mardi Gras, when contests are held to pick a calypso champion. The singers use names like Houdini, Sir Launcelot, Lord Invader, The Mighty Sparrow, and Lord Caruso, and their subjects range from a local marital scandal to world affairs.

The steel band, also started in Trinidad, is an outgrowth of calypso. Lacking instruments for a proper band, natives cut off the tops of 55-gallon oil drums and beat the metal into a pattern of panels that sound a scale when struck with a padded stick, something like a xylophone. The depth of the slice determines the pitch of each drum. A steel band of a dozen or more skilled drummers produces a remarkably rich and full effect. Most songs are played with a tremendous driving beat that is almost hypnotic, and the sound of a good steel band rippling through the tropical night across a harbor or along a beach is seductive. The band members always seem indefatigable; however, a long session of music can develop a measure of monotony.

Language in the Antilles is a mixture of cultures as well. It is "¿Qué pasa?" and "¿Como está?" in Puerto Rico and the Dominican Republic, "Comment allez-vous?" in Haiti, Martinique, or St. Martin, "Hey, mon" in St. Thomas, plus a variety of special dialects and patois that are distinctive to St. Lucia, Guadeloupe, or St. Vincent. The Creole patois of Haiti is notable for wry aphorisms: "Only the shoe knows whether the sock has a hole." Or, "The little dog barks loudest in his own yard." You can converse in English with a native in most of the English-speaking islands and reach a level of understanding, but let the same native break off and start talking to a fellow islander and you will be completely lost in a whirlwind of elisions, misplaced accents, and local idioms as the conversation goes into high gear. Where Spanish, Dutch, or French are spoken, there is much less likelihood of getting along in English, although tourism has forcibly spread English through most of the islands.

The tourists come by jet and great white cruise ships, lured by the prom-

of romance and exotic surroundings. Some, oblivious to the great beauty around them, can mar it, although it can never be completely spoiled. There is too much of it. For every St. Thomas there is a Tortola, for every San Juan a Culebra, for every Jamaica a Bequia, and those who seek them can still find isolation and native charm.

Politically the Caribbean is a volatile cockpit of change, and has been through the centuries. From the fifteenth-century discoveries until World War II, it was a story of colonialism, exploitation, and destruction of the native Indians, slavery and its aftermath, and the ever-shifting balance of power between European countries competing for control. From their head start the Spaniards were soon challenged by the English raids of Sir Francis Drake. By the eighteenth century the Caribbean was the major area of colonial competition. Admiral George Rodney, concerned with the French in Martinique, was not impressed by the plight of Lord Cornwallis far to the north in that cold land where there was no sugar cane. He refused to come to the aid of the British in Virginia, contributing to the well-known result, in which the French Admiral de Grasse had a hand as an ally of the Americans. When de Grasse returned to Martinique, Rodney, who had been waiting there, defeated de Grasse in a fierce battle in the channel between Martinique and Dominica, capturing seven ships and the admiral himself.

Rodney was informed about French activities in Martinique through a unique advance signalling arrangement. A force of British marines took over Diamond Rock, a steep mound rising from the sea, just off the southern tip of Martinique. Landing there, where there is not a beach or cove of any sort, had been considered impossible, and scaling its perpendicular sides even more so, but this was done from small boats under cover of darkness, with cannon lifted to the rock's crest by block and tackle, and the French were caught by surprise. The British called this unusual outpost *H.M.S. Diamond Rock*, flew the Royal ensign from the heights, and checked the French moves from it, secure from harassment and under the protection of their own guns. The French in Fort de France were furious but incapable of retaliation.

Rodney established a lookout post atop a hill on tiny Pigeon Island, off St. Lucia. It was British occupied and directly south of Martinique. Rodney went there each day to receive heliograph (sun-mirror) signals from Diamond Rock. He thus was ready to intercept de Grasse when the French sortied from Fort de France.

Each island is rich in background, and since 1945 the attitude has been one of self-determination, declining colonialism, and the emergence of many of the islands as independent nations. It is a story that never ends, as each island in turn undergoes a revolution, coup, or some quieter form of change. The political situation of the nations in the Caribbean has never remained the same for any length of time, and there is no reason to believe that there will be any difference in the near future. Whether in throwing off the protective arm of colonialism or effecting a local change in control, some of the islands are sure to be in a state of ferment. Grenada in 1982 was a graphic example. Over 25,000,000 people, mostly descendants of African slaves, live here and are participants in this drama of emerging nations.

The islands share this political disorder as well as the danger of hurricanes, sun and breeze, calypso beat, and year-round climate cooled by nature's great air conditioner, the easterly trade winds that sweep in unimpeded from Africa. Most of them also share a volcanic origin that thrust up the soaring peaks of the big islands, although the foundations of some of the smaller islands are coral, or outcroppings of sand. Geographically the northern and eastern Caribbean can be divided into three groupings: The Greater Antilles, consisting of Cuba, Hispaniola, Puerto Rico, and Jamaica; the Virgin Islands; and the Lesser Antilles, stretching from Anegada Passage east of the Virgins to South America. The Lesser Antilles were split by the British into political groups known as the Leewards—Anegada Passage to the channel south of Guadeloupe—and the Windwards—Guadeloupe south to Grenada. This was based on an assumption that the trade winds were southeast, which they are in the summer, but they are northeast in the winter, which would reverse the terminology of the two groups from a nautical viewpoint. The British stuck to one terminology and administered the two sets of islands separately no matter how the wind blew.

· THE GREATER ANTILLES ·

The four islands of this group are big and mountainous. They are major land masses that are in sharp contrast to the low, sandy Bahamas and Turks and Caicos just north of them, and to anything on the east coast of the United States. After months of seeing the low, pencil-like sliver of Bahamian landfalls, the impact of Hispaniola on us as we sailed toward Isabela de Torres out of dawn mists was tremendous.

Cuba is the largest of the Greater Antilles. It is a beautiful land rich in agriculture, scenery, and history. However, it is not exactly news that political problems have isolated it from most visitors since 1959. The weather is benign and the shores are ringed with cays, reefs, and islets in fascinating profusion, looked down upon by the majestic mountains of the interior. It was in the Sierra Maestra Mountains that Fidel Castro gathered the small force around him that eventually carried off the revolution of 1959. In this same area the United States Navy still maintains its base at Guantánamo Bay, one of the finest harbors in the Caribbean.

Based there for a month in World War II, I was fascinated to take my ship the short distance west to Santiago through the narrow entrance to its magnificent bay, where one of the decisive actions of the Spanish-American War was fought, ending Spain's 400-year history of Caribbean colonialism. In the old city, with its central plaza where the populace comes to promenade in the cool of the evening, the cathedral dominating the plaza dates from 1512, just 20 years after the first voyage of Columbus.

Hispaniola is not as big as Cuba. It is 350 miles long and encompasses 28,000 square miles, but it is a solid land mass that contains the highest mountains of the West Indies, topped by Loma Tina at 10,000 feet.

My first flight past Loma Tina was in a United States Navy C-47 from Guantánamo to San Juan in 1943. Our route was directly across the center of the island, flying at about 9,000 feet, and when we reached the middle all sight of the sea was lost and we were looking up at peaks on both sides of the plane. The landscape below was an awesome wilderness, forbidding in the rugged, jumbled pattern of its peaks and valleys. Returning via a coastal route, the climax came in circling The Citadel, the mountaintop fortress built by Henri Cristophe near Cap Haitien, an unbelievable stone labyrinth of walls, towers, and battlements at the very top of a soaring crag.

Cristophe is perhaps the best-known figure in the bloodily turbulent history of Hispaniola. Out of a slave revolt in 1804 in which all the whites on the island were massacred, he eventually emerged as the leader, established himself as King Henry I, and built The Citadel and a palace called San Souci with the use of prisoners as a labor force. He reigned for nine years of terror and bloodshed. Since then the island has known little political stability, as it has been continuously swept by revolutions and civil war. In 1844 the present political split was established. Haiti, the poorest nation in the Western Hemisphere, is French in language but black and African in background, and occupies the western third. The Dominican Republic,

Spanish in language and heritage but an Afro-European mix ethnically, is on the eastern part of the land mass. Each nation has undergone continuing political turmoil, largely under dictatorships such as "Papa Doc" Duvalier's in Haiti and Trujillo's in the Dominican Republic, although the 1970s did bring a measure of order and calm and the chance for visitors to enjoy reasonable peace and safety.

I first stayed in the Dominican Republic in 1956, when Trujillo was still in power, and the capital city of Santo Domingo, named by Columbus for his father's patron saint, was then known as Ciudad Trujillo. In an attempt to bring visitors to the island, Trujillo had just staged an unsuccessful world's fair and it was eerie to see the garish buildings standing untended on a seaside hill, overlooked by an imposing hotel, El Embajador, that was almost empty. At night chauffeur-driven Cadillacs deposited the elite of Trujillo's clique at the hotel's nightclub casino, where Porfirio Rubirosa's brother was a croupier. A worldly group would gather at the tables around Trujillo's daughter, Flor de Oro, who had been married to Rubirosa before he moved on to the conquest of American millionairesses. Flor de Oro and friends exuded an ersatz sophistication and pose of ennui that failed to cover a basic, wary uneasiness.

Outside, in the streets of the city, an armed soldier was stationed at every street corner for 24 hours a day, and in every house and building there had to be a photograph of Trujillo in a prominent place with the inscription, *En esa casa, El Jefe es el benefactor*—"In this house, the Chief is the benefactor."

Puerto Plata, when we came there more than 20 years later in our own boat, seemed a century behind the hollow modernity of the Ciudad Trujillo of 1956. In its narrow streets running up from the harbor, the gutters were open sewers, and the houses stood together in a dusty huddle, balconies leaning over the sidewalks. Men in carts and wagons lashed scrawny, tired horses to keep them moving through the heat, and siesta time would find the whole city in a doze of inactivity. In the inevitable plaza, with cathedral, city hall, and hotel surrounding it, young men lounge on the benches, laughing and erupting into horseplay, lottery ticket vendors set up their tall boards fluttering with paper at strategic corners, and Latin music wails from a radio in a tavern. In the evening, the age-old ritual of Latin American towns takes place, with girls parading in one direction and boys in another, giggling and making eyes, although there is much less of a formalized pattern to it than in the days when duennas dominated a young girl's life. Visitors are always convoyed by insistent preteen youngsters offering to be guides, selling bedraggled flowers, or openly begging.

There are no modern buildings in the old city, but on the outskirts, the market, which would normally be a collection of ramshackle stalls and booths, has been established in a futuristic, concrete, open-sided dome. Under it there is nothing futuristic about the heaps of avocados, limes, bananas, sapodilla, cristofine, mangos, ginger, and a host of unidentifiables, with the usual haggling over prices and spicy mingling of odors sweet and sour. There is one concrete-and-glass hotel near the sea that seemed completely empty when we drove by it, and we did our eating ashore in town. The city's hotel is an old building with balconies above the street and a high-ceilinged dining room with tongue-in-groove panelling where big fans overhead stir the humidity in lazy eddies.

For lunch one day we had the daily three-dollar special, *criolla*, starting with fish soup and then a platter of rice, meat, and gravy, bean sauce and fried plantains. At other meals we had *arroz con pollo* (chicken and rice), *pastellas* (taco-like meat pies), *lambi* (minced conch), and *patchugas* (chicken wrapped in cheese and batter). Anyone not brave enough to try these could always get a hamburger. The local beer, *Cerveza El Presidente,* as in most Latin American countries, is very good, and so are the two local rums, Bermudez and Brugal.

On a Monday, two cruise ships arrived simultaneously, a weekly occurrence, their huge white hulls and superstructures towering over the small harbor, and the sleepy little city erupted into a madhouse of tour buses, street vendors, begging children, and jammed curio shops. The big attraction at Puerto Plata is a funicular to the top of Isabela de Torres, which takes much of the in-port time for cruise passengers, and the rest of the visit is a frenetic whirl through the market and gift shops as everybody in Puerto Plata tries to sell something to somebody simultaneously. Meanwhile, the crews of the cruise ships are doing their part in keeping Puerto Plata's houses of prostitution prosperous. On other days, the women can be seen lolling on the porches of their houses, smiling idly at passersby, but on Mondays the porches are empty. Everyone is busy.

We made the funicular trip on a Sunday, practically the only Americans in evidence in a crowd of hundreds of Dominicanos who had come by bus from all over the island. The view from the swaying cable car was spectacular until we were suddenly engulfed in the almost perpetual mountaintop clouds. We wandered through acres of tropical gardens in a fine, blowing mist. A meringue band was performing for contributions on the sidewalk at the exit from the funicular, and many of the locals had a quick whirl of a few steps as they went by.

On the peak of the mountain is a statue of Christ, a tiny dab of white when first sighted from sea, but immense and dominant when you are standing under it on the peak. The sense of brooding concern that is dramatized by the outstretched arms was heightened in the swirl of clouds that engulfed it, reducing it to a dark outline, and occasionally opening up to let a glimmer of sun shine whitely on it for a moment.

From Puerto Plata we moved on to lonely, remote Samana, 100 miles to the east on a big bay of the same name that cuts a ten-by-thirty-mile gash into the eastern end of Hispaniola. Before the era of paved roads and air service it was so isolated that a colony of slaves, escaping from southern United States plantations, was shipwrecked at Samana early in the nineteenth century and lived there for 50 years without being discovered. Their descendants, with Anglo-Saxon names like Green and Jones, still live in Samana, and many of them still speak English.

Samana was eventually razed to the last chicken coop, and new concrete houses, shops, a hotel, and a casino were built, as well as a large pier for cruise ships. This was all done in advance of any effort to attract tourists, and when we were there the facilities stood empty except for one weekly visit by one cruise ship. In the surrounding countryside the fields are incredibly lush, abundant with sugar cane and bananas, but we were told that no one wanted to work in the fields. They were all waiting for the tourists to come.

Samana sits in anticipation of a future, while 20 miles up the bay the town of Sanchez gives, in its crowded, dusty streets, an idea of what Samana must have been before the rebuilding. It is closely packed with wooden houses, brightly painted and teeming with life on porches and balconies, and the bustle and stir of its market. Wagons of cut cane lurch down the streets to a railroad siding and cocoa beans stand in shiny mounds waiting to be sorted and processed.

We saw all this as guests of a local entrepreneur named Nadim Bezi. I had been given a letter of introduction to him by a yachtsman in Caicos who explained that Bezi owned much of the land in Samana and was instrumental in the development of tourism there. An imposing man with flashing dark eyes, pencil moustache, and gold-toothed smile, Bezi spoke no English, and our conversation when I went to his concrete-block house near the harbor to introduce myself left a question in my mind as to just what he had offered to do. As I understood it, we would be taken on a tour the next day, although I was not certain about the hour. But, sure enough, there he was at our berth at the town dock at nine o'clock in the morning, ready to take us on a sightseeing tour.

Our vehicle was a pickup truck, and I sat in the back with the interpreter, a young black named Green, a descendant of the stranded slaves. I asked him what his first name was, and he answered that his grandfather always called him "Turkey." He was eager, friendly, and knowledgeable, with a good command of English, so I had a good guide. It was a great perch for seeing the sights (until it rained), but Jane, in the seat of honor in the cab between Bezi and the driver, was largely confined to communication by gesture and an occasional "Sí," as we drove through the rich, green, hilly countryside. Bezi stopped now and then to confer with workers in farm areas he owned, and I gathered his story as we sat for a few moments on a lovely curve of beach at Rincon Bay, outside the entrance to the Bay of Samana, drinking the milk and eating the meat of fresh coconuts Turkey had gathered from the palms along the beach.

Bezi is a Syrian name and his parents had come to the Dominican Republic in 1914 as visitors, only to be stranded there by World War I. By the time it was over they had decided to stay, and Bezi's father had already acquired a great deal of land around Samana, the basis of his current holdings. Despite his heritage, Bezi thinks of himself as completely Dominican and Latinized, and he is an important member of the community.

After the visit to Sanchez, via a stop at the lovely, curving Bahia de Flechias (Bay of Arrows) where Columbus had his first hostile encounter with the usually peaceable Arawak Indians and had built a small fort, we stopped at the great long finger of concrete built out in the bay west of Samana. This was not the day for Samana's sole cruise ship, and the only vessel there was an incredibly rusty ex–United States Coast Guard buoy tender named *Hickory*. In talking to her crew, we found that she was owned by a United States company operating under private contract with the Dominican government searching for treasure in the dozens of wrecks the reefs of the Bay of Samana have claimed. Its thirty-by-ten-mile gash that forks the eastern end of Hispaniola is full of unmarked reefs, except for one clear channel into Samana and Sanchez along the north shore. In the days before modern charts many ships ventured into the bay as a likely refuge and were soon trapped by this confusing maze.

Hickory had a great canister with a fanlike propeller in it rigged on her stern. The crew explained that this was used to uncover wrecks by blowing silt and sand away, so that divers could concentrate their search. Naturally, they gave no details on success or lack of it. Treasure hunters are incredibly suspicious and close-mouthed. These same crew members, husky young men from Chesapeake Bay, had also worked out on the Silver Bank, 80 miles north of Puerto Plata in the open Atlantic, one of the most difficult and treacherous reefs anywhere in the world, in the search for the Spanish ship *Concepción,* reputed to have one of the greatest treasures of gold and silver ever lost in a shipwreck. After months of incredible hardship, a Florida-based salvage firm eventually located *Concepción* in the spring of 1979. Treasure hunting is a risky, frustrating business that continues to lure the adventurous.

Jamaica, south of Cuba and southwest of Hispaniola, is mountainous over more of its terrain than the other Greater Antilles, with few plains or lowlands, and its past encapsulates the whole Caribbean story. Piracy and privateering were dominant in the early days, and through the years it has seen prosperous plantations (in the era of slavery), colonial exploitation, colorful native music and folkways, and primitive savagery in native life. Later came tourism and bauxite mining, and finally political independence. The result of all this is a Third World nation with more than its share of economic, political, and social problems, and racial tension that has led to violence and tended to put a crimp in the important tourist business. At times, the plush resorts of the north coast between Montego Bay and Port Antonio have been virtual armed camps, and Kingston, the capital on the south coast, has had a history of violence since the days of Henry Morgan's piracy. An earthquake in 1692 hurled the old city of Port Royal, situated on a peninsula forming the harbor at Kingston, into the sea, and divers still explore its ruins. Life has rarely been peaceful there and Kingston is now a big, sprawling city with a history of political rioting and bloodshed and an enormous amount of poverty, although not as abject as the level in Haiti's Port au Prince.

The abruptness with which Jamaica's peaks rise from the sea to as high as Blue Mountain Peak's 7,388 feet at its eastern end produces a great amount of rainfall as trade-wind clouds hit them and quickly unload their moisture. The result is rich green vegetation and some of the wildest and densest growth in the Caribbean. The mountain scenery is impressively dramatic and the beaches of Jamaica are long curves of gold against an idyllic background of palms and soaring peaks, but, due to all the island's political troubles, a visitor must be concerned with more than a beautiful view of the mountains.

Puerto Rico is the most crowded and developed island in the Greater

Antilles with less to offer in scenery than its larger neighbors, although its center is mountainous and wild. Although not the tallest, the dominant mountain is 3,400-foot El Yunque, The Anvil, at the eastern end, named for the shape of the clouds that form over it. It is also called The Rainmaker because of the way it forces the clouds it collects to spill their moisture. The lower islands to windward of Puerto Rico, the Virgins and Culebra, are not high enough to break up the flow of trade winds blowing in from the open sea, and it is not until El Yunque creates an obstruction that this moist air forms into great cloud castles on its higher slopes. It is almost always surrounded by a tumbling array of cumulus that towers high above it, the rolling, billowing tops creamy white in the sunshine over black shrouds of rain, while long shafts of light angle through cloud breaks in ever-changing patterns.

Under this almost continuous parade of showers, the slopes of El Yunque are covered in a rain forest that is a riot of tropical vegetation, dense and impenetrable, but easily seen because a good road winds all the way to the top. In the forest, with cool sprays of rain drifting down through the trees and the greenish light dimming and glowing in the swift passage of clouds over the sea, it is almost possible to forget the problems of overcrowding and unemployment, superhighways, fast-food outlets, shopping centers, and high rises in the great urban sprawl of San Juan. There, even the ancient, peeling buildings and narrow, odoriferous streets of Old San Juan, the sixteenth-century Spanish colonial city on the heights over the harbor entrance, have been seduced by North American influences.

Just east of Puerto Rico and belonging to it politically, a few small islands in Vieques Sound are an out-of-the-way enclave. The United States Navy controlled them for military training and they were the scene of bombing, gunnery practice, and amphibious landing drills. There were no facilities for visitors, and the local residents of the two biggest islands, Culebra and Vieques, lived in an atmosphere of continuous explosions and the whine and roar of dive bombers. They were not in danger but the atmosphere was unsettling, and they resented their own lands being off limits. They were mostly farmers and fishermen whose families had been there for generations, long before the involvement of the United States. They were not happy living under these conditions, but they did not want to give up their homes and land, and they gradually formed an increasing resistance to the treatment they were receiving. Culebra was the first focus of the agitation. It is smaller than Vieques and the bombing was noisier and closer to the one little town of Dewey, also known as Playa Sardina, than any of the activity on Vieques was to its inhabited areas.

The Culebrans persisted, and the United States Navy finally ceased all operations there in 1975. It still has a major base at Roosevelt Roads, on the eastern end of Puerto Rico, and Vieques is still used for exercises amid protest and controversy, but Culebra has taken a new lease on life. Now its lovely north-shore beaches, off limits for years, are open, and no longer do the sounds of explosions punctuate every phase of daily activity. Tourism and its developments will no doubt spread to these lost islands from the eastern end of the main island, where the 20 years following 1960 saw a sleepy area of fishing villages and farms turned into a booming resort complex of high rises and 300-boat marinas. But when we were in Culebra in 1979 there was still the atmosphere of an isolated backwater in the Spanish Caribbean. The streets are narrow and steep, and the houses are close together. Music with a Latin beat blares out from kitchen radios along with the smells of garlic and frying, and children, their big liquid eyes turned momentarily up to an off-island visitor, scamper along the dusty, littered gutters. A shallow, debris-strewn creek cuts through the town from a harbor on Vieques Sound to Ensenada Honda, a big, well-protected bay that almost bisects Culebra at Dewey's back door. Nothing bigger than a rowboat could travel the creek, but it is spanned by an enormous drawbridge for some reason.

Ensenada Honda, about four miles long with a dozen pleasant coves along its largely uninhabited shores, is such a good natural harbor that Theodore Roosevelt thought of it as a major naval base before the selection of Roosevelt Roads (named for him, as Dewey is named for Admiral George, Teddy Roosevelt's good friend and hero of the Spanish-American War). We spent a solitary night anchored in one of its coves, exploring a scrub-covered hillside on the west shore, where we found extensive ruins of a plantation, sugar mill, and massive cistern. Now only cattle and horses, wary and skittish, roam the lonely hillside.

From it we could see St. Thomas, only 20 miles to the east but light-years away in atmosphere from almost-forgotten Culebra.

Dockyard at English Harbor, Antigua, before restoration.

9 · Down the Antilles

· THE VIRGIN ISLANDS ·

St. Thomas, capital of the American Virgins, may be the ultimate example of how tourism can alter the natural charm and beauty of a place. It has many hotel guests and it is the most popular cruise-ship harbor in the West Indies, if not the world, bringing passengers swarming ashore to its duty-free shops. Main Street in Charlotte-Amalie, really just a narrow alley, is two long rows of establishments catering to the duty-free shoppers, who crowd into every corner of them in the few hours they have ashore, and disappear in a sudden rush of cabs, leaving the stores strangely empty by late afternoon. Watches, cameras, jewelry, perfume, clothing, and liquor are siphoned off the counters in a mad rush.

Over all of this the sun shines brightly, trade-wind clouds sweep in from the east and scud across the island's peaks, occasionally dropping a quick dash of rain, white sails dot the indigo sea, the sunsets are gorgeous, and palm trees frame vistas of hills and beaches. Even so, there are difficulties. Amid this tropical splendor most of the ills that plague less glamorous cities to the north can be found: traffic jams, crime, overcrowding, high prices, litter, and racial tensions. Some of this has spread to St. Croix, 35 miles to the south, where there is still a bit more room for living than on jam-packed St. Thomas. In St. Croix civilizing influences have become so prevalent that it is sometimes called "Connecticut in the Caribbean," or "Darien South."

It is not all bad on St. Thomas and St. Croix. The climate is still marvelous, the beaches are lovely, and the views of islands and tropical sea in juxtaposition are of proper picture-postcard quality. Many of the inhabitants are cheerful, pleasant, and graciously helpful, and there is a full share of entertainment and night life for those who want it. It is just that too much has been jammed into too little space, so the pressures inevitably build up.

St. John, the third big island of the American Virgins, is something else again. Much of it is a national park, and it is therefore nowhere near as heavily developed as the other two "Saints." Cruz Bay is the major settlement, a pleasant little village compared to Charlotte-Amalie or St. Croix's Danish-named towns of Frederickstead and Christianstead. Caneel Bay, an early Rockefeller resort, is quiet and elegantly informal, with beautiful beaches. Much of the rest of St. John is semiwilderness. Lovely bays indent all its shores, and at Trunk Bay, the Parks Department has set up a marked underwater trail for skin divers, with signs identifying plant life, coral formations, and the most common fish. All the Virgins are great for snorkeling and scuba. Camping is so popular on St. John that reservations must be made months ahead.

St. John is the farthest east of the American Virgins. A mile away across a stretch of water called The Narrows is Tortola in the British Virgins. The International Boundary runs down the center of The Narrows and out between St. Thomas and Jost Van Dyke, and these islands in the northeastern half of the Virgins are a colony of Britain. Customs and immigration procedures apply when going between the two parts of the Virgins.

The proportions and extent of the Virgins can cause confusion. Because they are so well known in the resort world there is a tendency to imagine them as covering a large area, but from one end to the other, the American and British Virgins are only a bit more than 40 miles, and, excluding St. Croix, the width is less than 15 miles. In both of them driving is British style, on the left of the road, and the American Virgins are the only territory under United States control where this driving practice applies. The story is that when the United States tried to switch to right-side driving after purchasing the islands from Denmark in 1917, the people were willing, but the donkeys would not change their habits.

The elevations of the Virgin Islands are generally lower than those of the Greater Antilles to the west and most of the Lesser Antilles to the south. Sage Mountain on Tortola is the highest at 1,740 feet and most of the hills are under 1,000 feet. Rain clouds do not collect on these as often as they do on higher peaks, sweeping instead to their demise on El Yunque; thus the island vegetation is often brown and sere for much of the year. And at night, when the daytime clouds have dispersed and the stars fill the sky from horizon to horizon, there is a special excitement in being able to see the North Star, 18 degrees above the horizon, with the Big Dipper wheeling over it, and, opposed to it in the south, the heavy, blazing stars of the Southern Cross.

For centuries, the British Virgins have been the quietest, most undeveloped area of the eastern Caribbean. Too hilly and dry for successful agriculture, they have never had the big plantations that were so profitable in colonial times, although a few managed to keep going. And there has been very little resort development over the years. Few cruise ships come in, as there are no deep-water ports and little for cruise-ship passengers to do or see on shore; no high-rise hotels, casinos, or nightclubs, and life has been at a donkey's pace. Road Town, Tortola's capital, has been a scruffily somnolent little port huddled along a single street at the base of a hill. Gradually over the years, a few out-island, club-type resorts have opened, and tourism was boosted when another Rockefeller resort, Little Dix Bay, opened on Virgin Gorda. This was a major addition for the British Virgins but a small resort by Miami, San Juan, or St. Thomas standards.

Now, however, the British Virgins have an "industry" and can rightfully be called the world capital of it. This is sailboat chartering, mostly in bareboats, which means there is no professional crew aboard. The charterers must be able to handle the sailing—and the galley work—by themselves. There are also professionally crewed yachts, usually bigger and more comfortable, in which the crew does all the work and the guests relax, or pitch in if they feel like it. St. Thomas started as the major chartering center, and it is where most of the professionally crewed boats in the Virgins— over a hundred by the 1980s—base. There is bareboating out of St. Thomas as well. In 1965 the fleet numbered ten boats, and today about 150 boats. The big concentration of bareboats is in Tortola, where there are at least 250 boats, and the number is growing annually. Two-thirds of the seats on airplanes arriving in the British Virgins are occupied by bareboat charter parties, and Road Town, no longer dozing in the sun, presents a forest of aluminum masts in several big marinas and a major service yard. Waterfront development has left the old main street stranded a few blocks inland, and modern shopping centers and hotels dot the shoreline. There is a constant traffic of sailboats in and out of the harbor, and at least one sail, and usually a whole fleet, can be glimpsed in looking out over the harbor. Outside, in Sir Francis Drake Channel, sails dot the blue in every direction at all daytime hours. It is not yet like Long Island Sound on a summer Sunday, but the traffic is steady. Drake Channel is an ideal body of water for supporting all this, and the whole fabric of the British Virgin Islands life is built around the theme of island escape, using a sailboat to do it.

From a high vantage point outside Road Town on the Tortola shore, the view across Drake Channel takes in 500-foot high Peter Island, four miles across the way, with a 180-degree panorama of islands spreading out on each side of it in a pattern of peaks and hills. In the blue distance to the west, St. John is all curves and mounds, with a glimpse of St. Thomas beyond it, and Norman Island, claimed locally as Stevenson's inspiration for *Treasure Island* as pirates did bury loot there, partly shows behind Peter. To the east of Peter, a string of small but hilly islands—Dead Chest, Salt, Cooper, and Ginger almost blend together, leading to a jumble of rocky cays called Round Rock, The Blinders, and Fallen Jerusalem—which is aptly named, as it looks like a ruined city—and then the bulk of Virgin Gorda blocking the eastern horizon. Against its rounded mass, Beef Island, an extension of Tortola, shows more distinctly in the middle distance.

This view, which encompasses little more than 15 miles between its western and eastern extremes, takes in at least 15 anchorages for cruising boats, with double that number just around the bend or behind the islands that can be seen. Probably nowhere on earth has nature put together better ingredients for sailboat cruising. The climate is as predictable as climate can be, with its steady flow of trade wind. There are rain squalls, and even longer periods of rain when an "easterly wave," a form of minor storm center, curls along the normally even advance of the trades, but the sun is in evidence for one of the highest yearly averages anywhere. Sometimes the trades gust up to 40 knots or more, but the usual strength is just under 20 knots, much lighter in the fall. Hurricanes can be a factor in the Virgin Islands weather, as in all the southern islands.

Assured of a breeze, a cruising sailor is also assured there will be no long slugs through crashing seas to reach an objective. There is no stretch of the Virgins where one goes more than three miles to find another harbor, and this makes for an easy, varied itinerary, with stops for lunch, or just a swim, before choosing a new nighttime anchorage. Overcrowding is a problem in some popular harbors at the height of the season, but there are so many harbors tucked away all through the area that this is only a comparative problem—comparative, that is, for those who remember the days before the 1970s when the bareboat boom started.

One of the pleasures of charter cruising here is to eat ashore at a resort. These range from the studiedly informal luxury of Little Dix and such newer places as Biras Creek on Virgin Gorda or Peter Island Yacht Club, through the easier-going atmosphere of Virgin Gorda's Bitter End, Cooper Island, Marina Cay, or the zany and informal Last Resort, to such native-run spots as Abe's on Jost Van Dyke, where you eat lobster family style at plain board tables. Marina Cay, with A-frame cottages scattered along the steep bluffs of its two or three acres, is perhaps most typical of the little out-island clubs. Its main building remains from the early 1930s when a young American couple, Robb and Rodie White, built it as a honeymoon retreat. They had the usual difficulties getting a building permit from officials who thought they were crazy, and dealing with suspicious natives who could not understand white people moving in for no obvious reason except "escape." The Whites built the place themselves, with a minimum of local help, scavenging materials from the ruins of old plantation houses on Tortola and Beef Island. From one dilapidated mansion on a hill overlooking Trellis Bay, which lies between Beef Island and Marina Cay, they got marble blocks and columns and roof slates, and found the outline of a wall that surrounded a hundred-foot ballroom. Tracing its history in talks with locals, the Whites learned that it had been the home of a widow named Catherine George who raised cattle on Beef Island (hence the name) and who was annoyed by pirate raids on her herd. Once, the story went, when buccaneers were careening their vessels on Marina Cay, she invited them to her home for a party. Thirty-six came, and none left after partaking of the Widow George's poisoned tea. That was long ago. The house evidently was sacked in a nineteenth-century slave rebellion and thereafter was worn down by wind and weather.

The Whites' idyll ended with World War II, and the house stood deserted on its hilltop for almost 20 years before becoming the bar and dining room of Marina Cay resort. Robb White wrote a book called *Our Virgin Island,* which was made into a movie in the early 1950s with Sidney Poitier in one of his first roles, featured as a friendly native whose help made the project a success. The movie company people, expecting the usual cliché of a tropical paradise with golden, palm-fringed beach and lush vegetation, took one look at Marina Cay's barren, scrub-covered rocks and built their set nearby on a cay that fitted the image better. For one scene the script specified a small sailboat with red sails. Because colored sails were almost nonexistent in the Virgins, the film's technicians daubed the boats' sails with house paint to get the color they wanted.

· THE LESSER ANTILLES ·

Beyond the Virgins, the Antilles swing southward for almost 500 miles to South America. Here Anegada Passage, the longest open-water stretch in the whole arc of islands from Cuba to Grenada, sets off the Lesser Antilles. This current-racked area, where Atlantic and Caribbean tides mix in a tricky roil, has been a hazard for ships since the days of Columbus, and the unmarked reefs that dot it are rich in wrecks.

The islands between Anegada Passage and Antigua saw some of the earliest settlements in colonial times. St. Christopher (universally called St. Kitts), was the first British colony, in 1623, and it was from here that many of the other islands were settled. In the days of a plantation economy, the grouping of St. Martin, St. Bart's, St. Kitts, Nevis, Statia, and Saba was the most important part of the West Indies but was long virtually ignored by travelers. Except for St. Martin, it was a lightly visited backwater that kept much of the look and atmosphere of colonial times. Now the big jets do fly in, but there are more sophisticated destinations, such as Antigua, Martinique, and Barbados. Islands like Saba and St. Bart's have an individuality not found in the calypso-accented ones that are closer to the accepted concept of what a Caribbean island is like.

St. Bart's, with a mostly white, French population and a little harbor town with the look of a European fishing village, was for so long a forgotten spot that it was a haven for smugglers. It now has a steady flow of tourists and some quietly luxurious vacation homes for the super-rich who want a hideaway.

Saba is unique in the Caribbean, or anywhere else. Through the lack of a harbor and difficult communications, it has hardly changed in 200 years. An extinct volcano of only five square miles, its cone soars into the clouds for close to 3,000 feet. Landings can only be made at two stone jetties in the open sea and there is STOL (Short Take-off and Landing) plane service from St. Martin to a tiny airport. Always under Dutch rule, Saba has retained its character through almost complete isolation. Two towns, holding most of the population of about 1,000, are called Bottom, because it is at the bottom of the old volcanic crater, and Windward Side, because of its location. Their narrow streets and picture-book, red-roofed, European-style cottages seem unchanged since early settlement. The people are mostly of Dutch stock, but speak English.

There is little local industry except for fine lace made by Saba women. Most of the men live and work off the island, as seamen or in the oil refineries of Curaçao, and send money home to their families until they return to retire. Few Sabans seem to leave forever, showing an intense loyalty to their homeland.

In a part of the world where colonial rivalries have been a factor for some 500 years, St. Martin is also unique. This 37-square-mile island has been peacefully shared by Dutch and French since 1648, when a division of the island was made by the simple procedure of having a Dutchman and a Frenchman walk around it in opposite directions from a starting point that would be one end of the dividing line. The spot where they met on the opposite side established the other end of the boundary. For some reason the Frenchman was a little faster, or had an easier shoreline, and the French have three more square miles than the Dutch. Although there are no formalities in going from one side to the other, it is amusing to see national characteristics clearly followed on each of the halves. Sint Maarten, as the Dutch call their side, booming touristically is trim and neat, with modern buildings in the capital of Philipsburg. The French half, called Saint Martin, is very Gallic, noisier, and messier, with the usual clutter encountered in the Caribbean.

Anguilla, the smallest and least significant of all the inhabited islands, made headlines in the late 1960s when its residents staged a reverse revolution. Instead of breaking the colonial yoke of a European power, they rebelled against the poor-relation treatment they were receiving in the newly independent country of St. Kitts-Nevis-Anguilla and asked for renewed status as a British colony. After comic-opera events that would have delighted Gilbert and Sullivan, including "invasion" by a force of London bobbies in full winter uniform, Anguilla finally managed a reverse revolution and happily became a colony again.

On the subject of throwing off colonial power, it was at Statia (formally St. Eustatia), least known of the Dutch islands, that the United States government first received recognition from a foreign power. In November 1776 the fort there replied in kind to a national gun salute by the United States brig-of-war *Andrea Doria,* Captain Isaiah Robinson of the Continental Navy commanding.

There is another story from colonial days of quite a different sort at Barbuda. This sandy satellite of Antigua remains as remote and untouched as any Caribbean island, with only a few natives and one club resort devoted to fishing, diving, deer hunting, and quiet luxury. It is low and scrubby and ringed by reefs and gorgeous beaches, and its place in history comes from the fact that it was the site of a slave-breeding farm in plantation days. The strongest male and female specimens from plantations throughout the West Indies were selected and sent there to produce a rugged strain of worker.

Antigua combines a sense of history with the development of cosmopolitan resorts. Not as striking in scenery as some of its neighbors to the south, it is low and dry in all but the southern end, but it makes up for lack of mountains with many good beaches and harbors. English Harbour, on the south coast, was an important base of the Royal Navy in colonial times. Its deep, completely landlocked inner harbor, surrounded by the highest hills on the island, made it a perfect naval base in the days of sailing ships, secure and easy to defend. Horatio Nelson operated from there and the restored red brick buildings along the quay show what it looked like in his era, although the scores of modern, fiberglass yachts, aluminum masts shining in the sun, are far different from the frigates of Nelson's fleet.

English Harbour is now base for a big fleet of charter yachts and a popular cruising port, and the yachting activity reaches a climax each spring in Antigua Race Week. This was started in the late 1960s as an end-of-season picnic for the charter fleet. It has developed gradually into a formal regatta that attracts boats from all over the Caribbean, North America, and Europe for port-to-port racing by day and all-out partying by night. The sailing is hard and serious, with multicolored spinnakers flashing in the sun, and the post-race partying is equally as vigorous, if not so serious. While the crews gather at beachfront bars at a different Antiguan harbor each night to toss down rum punches, the beat of a steel band sets the palm trees vibrating and the dancers gyrating. It was during an Antigua

Race Week that topless female crews first made an appearance in the Caribbean and in general fewer clothes are worn per square inch than in any other yachting event.

Antigua has been a leader in resort development. The exclusive enclave called the Mill Reef Club, which was started in the 1950s, was a foretaste of the type of resort now found on islands in all parts of the world. A central club, with restaurant and bar, surrounded by luxurious private homes spread over bluffs and hills above a fine beach, it also has a golf course and waterfront facilities. Before the jet age, Mill Reef even had a special Friday afternoon flight from New York. Antigua was early with a good airport as the United States–built Coolidge Field was part of President Roosevelt's lend-lease deal with England, and this had much to do with the development of its resorts.

Mill Reef was intended for the independently wealthy, but it set a style and tone that many have tried to emulate since, either in the club format, or in public resorts that are called clubs. They are found all through the islands. Some manage to capture the proper blend of privacy, luxury, and the atmosphere of being an "in" place, while others go through frequent changes of management and never make it. One that seems to have found the right combination and is a favorite of ours in all the places we have stayed from Bermuda to the Barrier Reef, from Martinique to Moorea, or St. Martin to Sardinia, is Curtain Bluff on Antigua's south coast. It sits on a small peninsula athwart the trade wind's natural air conditioning, facing a windward beach and ocean waves, and there is a quiet harbor and beach on the leeward side. There is Sunfish sailing, reef diving, fishing, and a major emphasis on tennis. Guests play in early morning and late afternoon to avoid the direct sun, and for the rest of the time the management encourages youngsters from nearby villages to use the courts.

The central building, with office, gift shop, bar, and dining room, is on the ridge of the peninsula, and room units line the windward beach. Everything is well maintained, and special attention is paid to the food. The atmosphere is clubby as guests gather in the bar before dinner, strangers turning quickly into friends. Many are repeaters who have met before, and there is a genuinely festive air as the sun slants down over the leeward harbor and the entertainment of the evening—local singers or musicians—tunes up. There are many Curtain Bluffs, and I use it simply as an example of that kind of relaxed establishment people think of when an island vacation seems a good idea.

South of Antigua steep, jagged peaks denote volcanic islands, three of which have erupted in the twentieth century: two Soufrieres, one on St. Lucia and one on St. Vincent, and Mt. Pelee on Martinique. Pelee's eruption in 1902 was one of the great natural catastrophes, wiping out the 40,000 inhabitants of the town of St. Pierre, except for a condemned murderer who was in the innermost dungeon of the jail. St. Vincent's Soufriere was violently active in the spring of 1979, spewing lava down its slopes and covering much of the island in a gray film of ash.

The progression of islands south from Antigua for 330 miles is: Guadeloupe, Iles des Saintes, Dominica, Martinique, St. Lucia, St. Vincent, the Grenadines, and Grenada. Guadeloupe (including the Saintes) and Martinique are overseas departments of France, as much a part of it as Hawaii is of the United States. The others are newly independent and are British in background, with a French mix on St. Lucia. Columbus is responsible for the surviving Spanish names.

The islands vary in sophistication from the bustling cities and smart shops of the French islands to the primitive interior of Dominica, where the last reservation of the once fierce Carib Indians holds a few pitiful survivors. In the Saintes, the blue-eyed, fair-haired fishermen are descendants of Breton settlers, and on Montserrat, a small island out of the main chain that can be seen on the western horizon from Antigua, the original settlers were Irish, and the local patois is a strange mixture of Irish and African accents. Every island has a distinctive dialect of some sort, with local idioms. Another island off by itself is Barbados, 90 miles east of Grenada, and, with over a quarter of a million people, the most densely populated of all Caribbean lands. Although independent now, it has retained many British customs, including cricket and afternoon tea, and the pace there is extremely civilized. Rum drinkers also know it as the source of Mount Gay, a special favorite with sailors. Despite its heavy population, Barbados' low hills are bright green with sugar cane rippling in the trades.

In the mountainous islands there is that constant interplay of clouds and peaks, in the same condition that makes such a dramatic spectacle of Puerto Rico's El Yunque. The trade wind lashes the windward side of every island with spray-flinging surf, and there are almost no usable harbors on the east coasts. When the moisture-laden wind hits the inland peaks, great cloud caps form and rain squalls then drift down the leeward slopes to the becalmed western shore. Each high island has a big area of calm under its mountains, an unbelieveable change from the boisterous conditions on the windward side, and in the passages between the islands.

This these islands share, each with a variation in local conditions brought about by the special shape of the mountains and valleys. The south end of Dominica, site of the largest lime plantation in the world, has a local phenomenon called white squalls that burst down the leeward slopes out of a clear sky, frothing across the water in a welter of foam that gives them their name. They can knock a sailing vessel down without warning, and the wind has a peculiar extra force on a sailboat in that it is cold and heavy as it rushes almost vertically down from the rainy heights. This same condition also exists in the lee of the Pitons, the distinctive twin cones that are virtually a trademark of St. Lucia.

The islands may share the look of their peaks (we once flew with a charter pilot who confused Dominica and Martinique), the sun, the squalls, and the towering cloud caps, but the character of each is distinct. It is possible to be one night in Fort de France in a restaurant as good as the highest rated ones of France, amid smartly dressed locals in the latest Paris fashions, and the next day to take a car into the wild mountains of Dominica, where civilization seems never to have existed. In doing this, we drove upward on the bumpy, ever-winding serpent of asphalt into the untamed rain forest, as the air became sharpy cooler. Below us, occasional glimpses of the shining sea, caught through gaps in the trees, gradually grew less frequent until we were completely surrounded in an overwhelming riot of green pressing in from all sides. Vines coiled around trees, great purple, white, and scarlet flowers shone in the dim, greenish light, and birds flitted by as bright spots of color, their cries strange and raucous.

Eventually we came into a cleared area at an old plantation house now serving as an inn, a sprawling, white affair with wide porches roofed in red. We were served drinks on a terrace with a view limited to the tangled riot of vegetation at the edge of the clearing. The Caribbean had disappeared long since, and we could have been a thousand miles inland in Africa for all the nautical atmosphere. As we sipped our rum punches, the sun darkened and gray curtains of clouds sped by overhead, swooping down through the trees from nearby mountaintops in damp veils, followed by a quick, cold splash of rain, a continuous occurrence, we were told. Dominica is the highest of the Windwards and collects the most rain on its steep, jagged complex of peaks. Rather than aiding cultivation, the excess of moisture makes nature too hard to tame, and it has remained the least developed and poorest of the Lesser Antilles. The lime plantation and banana cultivation are the major economic factors in a deficit economy that was a burden to Britain while it controlled Dominica. This presented difficult problems to a new government that faced riots and dissension on taking over with the granting of independence in 1979, and the devastation of Hurricane David was another severe setback.

It was in Dominica that we first saw that peculiar phenomenon of the tropics, the green flash at sunset, which some say is an optical illusion and others attribute to atmospheric conditions. This was at another old house, dating from the eighteenth century and poised high on a hillside above the coast near Roseau, the capital of the island. We were in a group on the verandah watching the sun send slanting shafts through well-spaced trees as it plunged toward the sea horizon. If there are clouds at the rim, there is no chance for a flash, but this night the line of sky meeting sea was clear and well defined, when the sun, fiery red by now, touched it and began to sink from view.

The lower limb of the sun spread out in a peculiar distortion as it melded with the horizon, and then only the upper half remained in sight, an even semicircle of red slowly diminishing. Our hostess had alerted us, as we held our drinks, that this seemed a good night for the flash, and all sat in hypnotic fascination, trying not to blink at the crucial moment.

Then, just as the upper rim of the sun slipped to the horizon, there was the briefest glow of molten green slithering out on each side of it for a moment, and an apple-green light flashed in the clear sky above.

"There," cried our hostess. "Did you all see it?" And as she spoke it was gone. Just a faint pink glow remained.

Dominica is accented on the third syllable, which is pronounced "neek," and there are peculiarities in the names of many West Indian locations. St. Lucia is St. "Loosha," Bequia is "Beck-wee," and Grenada is "Gren-aid-uh," accent on the "aid." It is also my favorite of all the islands of the West Indies. At the bottom of the Lesser Antilles, 90 miles from Trinidad and Venezuela, it is the richest in scenery, loveliest in the symmetry of its peaks and valleys, has the most picturesque city, the best beach and the most interesting vegetation, and the people are as genuinely pleasant and friendly as in any of the islands. For a time, it was the smallest (120 sq. miles) independent nation in the Western Hemisphere.

The people are proud of their island and proud to be Grenadans, and over the years they have been more self-sufficient than some of their neighbors. Despite the character of the people, Grenada has not been free of the political troubles that have beset so many of the islands, however, and destructive riots have marred its history. It made the transition from Associated State to independence by succumbing to dictatorship during rioting in 1974. A bloodless coup in the spring of 1979 ended the capricious dictatorship of Sir Eric Gairy while he was off the island, and there was hope that a period of corruption, favoritism, repression, and loss of civil liberties, devastating to the economy, had ended, but the new government swung just as radically to the left, and the events of October 1983 brought it worldwide attention.

Grenada's economy has been dependent for centuries on its exotic crops—nutmeg, ginger, cinnamon, vanilla, and cacao—as well as the more usual sugar and bananas. Bananas were a late addition, turned to in 1955 as a quick-growing crop after Hurricane Janet took an unusual veer. It was the first hurricane to hit Grenada in the century and it all but wiped out the delicately nurtured spice trees, which take years to bring to maturity. Now banana freighters, large, modern, and white, are steady visitors to the compact little harbor in St. George's, Grenada's capital. When a ship is loading, trucks careen down to the harbor over the incredibly narrow, deep, and winding roads, banana stalks bulging out in what would seem to be far more than capacity, and it is a rare thrill to be on the road with them. The trucks sweep around corners, scattering chickens and pedestrians, and any vehicle not on the very outer edge of the pot-holed asphalt is fair game to be bumped into a ditch.

St. George's is the best protected and most picturesque deep-water port in the Lesser Antilles. A rocky promontory topped by an old fort encloses the harbor, which is rectangular and surrounded by steep hills. A stone quay lines the waterfront on three sides, with native freight boats moored fore-and-aft in a colorful jumble. Along the quay there is a cobbled street backed by shops, restaurants, markets, and warehouses. There is a continuous rattle and rumble with the passage of trucks, wagons, mules, autos, and ancient buses with names like "Happy Days," "Confident in God," "Pleasure Palace," and similar whimsies. Behind this one row of buildings, the rest of the town rises in tiers on the almost perpendicular hills, a multihued huddle of pastels, faded brick, and European architectural styles that delight the eye in bright sunlight. Splashes of color from flamboyant trees, oleanders, poincianas, and poinsettias, frame the buildings, and the midisland peaks form a dramatic backdrop. The poinsettia, incidentally, gets its name from the first United States ambassador to Mexico, J. R. Poinsett, who noted the plant there in the 1820s. The poinciana tree honors a seventeenth-century French governor of the Antilles, M. de Poinci. Rain squalls spilled by these peaks make Grenada's vegetation as rich as any of the islands, but not as overpowering as Dominica's. There is a beautiful lake, Grand Etang, high in the mountains, and Annandale Falls, a narrow cascade tumbling through luxuriant growth, and in all but the densest mountain growth there is cultivation.

A Grenadan taxi driver is always glad to stop and pick samples of the island's spices from trees growing along the roadside, explaining how mace is found as a red liner covering the inner seed when the fruit of a nutmeg tree ripens and splits open. Nutmeg trees grow to 70 or 80 feet. Cacao trees are shorter with bright green leaves and red pods that contain the beans. The taximen are polite and enthusiastic, with a courtly air rarely associated with their trade, and their lot, driving Grenada's atrocious roads, is not an easy one.

For several days once we had the use of a friend's house on a beach at the south end of Grenada, offering a fine chance to get to know the people. We had Norma Desmond (a housekeeper-cook, not the aging movie star of Sunset Boulevard) looking after us, a laundress named Lydia Scragg, and a gardener called Gresham St. Bernard, not unusual names for Grenada. Jane found it fascinating to go to the native market in St. George's, a teeming, reeking collection of stalls in a square up the hill from the harbor, to do the household shopping. In addition to familiars like tomatoes, cucumbers, limes, and bananas, she was also dealing in such strange, to her, items as cristofine, a form of squash, and tanya, a potato-like root.

Her arrival as the only white customer in the all-native market set off a flurry of activity as the women in the stalls called out how fine their wares were, poking samples in front of her and crying "Come see my tomatoes, mistress. De best in de i'lan, I tell you. Come see! Come see!"

They wore straw hats or bandannas and simple print dresses, and flashing gold teeth were very much in evidence. Once Jane settled on one of them, they became all business, taking an intense, helpful interest in her selections. From loud shouting when competing for trade, their voices softened to a musical lilt.

Norma, who took shy delight in making her own very special brand of rum punches for us as a small ceremony before dinner, did wonderful things with the local produce, and also had some fisherman friends who showed up at the door one day with *langustas,* the clawless lobster of the tropics, which she broiled to perfection. While running our house, she also managed a household of her own, and several of her children played quietly outside the kitchen door while she was at work.

Beyond St. George's, there are market towns called Gouyave and Grenville, one on each coast. Sauteurs, a small town at the north end, looking out across the Grenadines to St. Vincent, got its name when Carib Indians, in a battle with French invaders in 1651, leaped off cliffs into the sea rather than surrender. These are small native towns with rusting tin roofs on most of the houses, and chickens, pigs, and dogs mixing with roadside pedestrians. The south coast is quite different, indented by a series of beautiful bays, with off-lying reefs and cays. Here, in developments like Westerhall and L'Anse aux Epines (pronounced "Lansapeen") non-Grenadans from North America and Europe established vacation or year-round houses in well-manicured surroundings that could almost be a Westchester, New York, suburb. In the years before 1983's invasion, many of these people left the island in fear of the new government's intentions.

The Grenadines, a 40-mile string of low islands that lie between Grenada and St. Vincent and are shared by them politically, are known for some of the best sailboat cruising anywhere in the world. At the southern end, north of Sauteurs, Atlantic and Caribbean currents meet in a turbulent confrontation that for centuries has made a sheer pinnacle of gray rock called Kick 'em Jenny a famous landmark for sailors. Halfway between Grenada and Carriacou, it rises from a bright blue welter of whitecaps and tide rips that is almost always rough going. The name is a corruption of the French *quai c'on gêne*—"worrisome island"—as it was particuarly hard for the bluff-bowed, square-rigged ships of colonial times to fight their way past it.

Carriacou, where oysters grow on trees in Tyrell Bay, is the largest Grenadine, and belongs to Grenada. From here north is St. Vincent territory, and vessels must clear and enter customs in making the three-mile passage between Carriacou and Union, an island easily identified by a distinctive *U* between its two peaks.

The Grenadines are relatively low and do not receive much rainfall. Water supply is therefore a problem and has held back development of many of the islands, although Mustique has been turned into a hideaway for the special few, including Princess Margaret of England, who has a house there. Bequia, five miles south of St. Vincent, has developed from a haven for commercial sailors and whalers, last in the hemisphere, into a quietly sophisticated resort island. The Tobago Cays in the center of the Grenadines are everybody's idea of perfect tropical islets, with brilliant waters, perfect beaches, and some of the best snorkeling and scuba diving in the world. Except that they are inundated by visitors from the charter yachts and bareboat fleets that operate in the area, the Tobago Cays will remain unspoiled, as they are now a national park of St. Vincent.

The Grenadines and Grenada are the end of the line for the Antilles. The great arc that swings east and south for 1,500 miles from Cuba ends here. At the lower end of Grenada on the west shore, Grand Anse Beach, a broad two-mile curve of powdery sand, is the southernmost, and perhaps finest, of all the ones through the islands that are such magnets for worshipers of sun and surf. Below it, Grenada's mountains slope to a plain atop a long, flat point. Here, at the very end, a lighthouse, candy striped in bright counterpoint to the gray cliffs below it, stands above surf breaking in columns of spray and foam that shoot far up the perpendicular facade. This is Point Saline, and it looks out on empty blue sea. Here, at last, there is no mountain standing purple on the southern horizon, as it is 90 miles to the Venezuelan coast of South America.

Cruising the Utila Cays in the Bay Islands of Honduras.

10 · The "Other" Caribbean

The little single-engine plane threaded its way around great castles of cumulus and the mountain peaks of the Isthmus of Panama, heading north from Panama City. The pilot, who had just finished a jet flight from Miami and was moonlighting, yawned and chewed at his thumb as we banked and turned to avoid squall clouds and the higher peaks of the Continental Divide. I looked ahead with some anxiety, trying to figure out where we were to land. The Caribbean was a dull, cloud-specked platter far ahead, with faint smudges of dark on the surface that could be either clouds or islands. The coastline came into view with nothing resembling an airport that I could see.

Then the pilot stopped yawning long enough to point to a small speck of brown against the shoreline as he tipped the wheel and started a descent. I raised questioning eyebrows, pointing at the speck, and he nodded. Yes, that was where we were headed. Although it looked no bigger than a jumping pit at a track meet to me, we continued our downward path and soon bounced safely to a stop about 20 yards from the edge of the water. I pretended that all this was routine, and we stepped out of the plane into a waiting outboard. The boat was no Boston Whaler, though. It did have a new Evinrude for power, but the hull was an Indian dugout canoe, or *cayuco,* and it was our next transportation on a visit to the San Blas Islands, a 100-mile chain along the Caribbean coast of Panama. Somehow it seemed appropriate to step from a plane to this Stone Age vessel, because in coming here we were entering pre-Columbian society.

Nominally under the protection of Panama, the Cuna Indians of San Blas have in effect kept their independence over the centuries, as well as their racial purity, one of the few tribes in the western world to do so. Cuna women seldom leave the islands, and visitors are not allowed to spend the night there, except in a few special resorts. The result of his isolation is a glimpse of what life was like when Spanish explorers first invaded the area. In their island existence the Cunas had no nearby Indian enemies to war on them, and they had nothing the Spanish wanted to take away. A coconut economy has kept them going through the years. If Panama will not pay the price for their coconut crop they sell instead to Colombia, just to prove their independence.

The San Blas archipelago typifies the contrast of these islands to those visited in the last chapter, where jet planes and tourism have brought the twentieth century to what had been a quiet backwater. The western Caribbean has hardly felt the impact of tourism. Now more tourists are drifting in, and in time the San Blas may be as tourist-heavy as the Virgins. The same can be said of most of the rest of the Caribbean beyond that now highly developed arc of the Greater and Lesser Antilles. Except for the ABC Dutch islands—Aruba, Bonaire, Curaçao—which are now thoroughly visited, and local tourism to the Venezuelan islands close to the Spanish Main, the "other" Caribbean lies relatively unspoiled and waiting.

· THE SAN BLAS ISLANDS ·

As we slowly motored away from the air strip in our *cayuco,* with the great mountains of the Continental Divide looming behind us in the mist, the calm sea ahead was dotted all across the horizon with specks of land. So flat and low as to appear as rafts, most of them had a fringe of palm on

Commercial Wharf, Nantucket, before the new marina was built.

Nantucket ferry passing Brant Point light.

*The Nantucket
waterfront.*

A Bahamian sunset at Nassau.

*Rose Island anchorage
near Nassau.*

*Bermuda Race yachts
dress ship at Hamilton.*

Samson Cay in the Exumas.

Crowded English Harbor, Antigua.

Caribbean cloud formations: Puerto Rico.

Caribbean cloud formations: Nevis.↓

Caribbean cloud formations: Statia.↓

A quiet harbor on Roatan, Bay Islands of Honduras.→

Looking down on Belize's blue hole.

A jungle river on Raiatea.

Looking at Bora Bora from Tahaa.

Along the beach at Bali Hai, Moorea.

Walking the Great Barrier Reef, 40 miles off Australia.

top and not much else, but here and there one would seem about ready to founder under a density of thatched huts. Fortunately, the tide range here is less than one foot.

It is a common publicity ploy in many areas to say that an archipelago has 365 islands—one for every day of the year, as in Bermuda. Or, a big island may provide 365 rivers, as in Dominica. But, the San Blas goes beyond that and claims to have 368 islands in the chain. They sit safely behind a long, fringing reef that could be seen on the far horizon as we moved offshore, a wavering line of white where the trades were dumping blue Caribbean rollers onto the coral. We were headed for a little island called Pidertupo, which was, at that time, one of the two resorts that had been allowed in the San Blas. The other was at Porvenir at the western end of the archipelago, where cruise ships occasionally make a one-day stop. We were about 20 miles farther to the east.

Of all the little, isolated, out-island resorts we have seen in all parts of the world, Pidertupo still ranks as the simplest, most out-of-the-way, and certainly one of the most intriguing. It was first permanently inhabited by a "fugitive" from Pittsburgh. Tom Moody, his wife, and a small daughter, after a stint at Marina Cay in the Virgins where the crowds began to seem too much for them, came here on their own. It seemed an idyllic spot on our visit, but unfortunately the resort was burned down in an attack by masked raiders in 1982.

From the water, Pidertupo's little cay looked like most of the other islands scattered around at small intervals across the placid lagoon. Only a couple of feet above water, with a border of golden beach, it was topped by a grove of curved, gently rustling palms. Under them a row of well-separated thatched huts was strung out along the beach. These, it turned out, were the bedroom units, and we found them well-equipped and comfortable despite their primitive look. As we came to a small pier, the Moodys were there to greet us, and we had soon been given a tour of the island, not difficult to cover as its size is only a couple of acres. In addition to the bedroom huts, there was a large central hall for community, family-style dining, with an honor-system bar, and a collection of service units and huts for the staff at the other end of the island. A few guests were lounging around in bathing suits or preparing a snorkeling expedition on the hotel's diving boat, and we decided to join them.

The boat was as unusual as the surroundings. It consisted of a work float that had broken away from Aruba, 500 miles to windward, and drifted down to the reef off Pidertupo, where the Moodys salvaged it. They equipped it with an outboard, a thatched canopy, and a couple of benches, and it served the purpose very well. The snorkeling was fine just off the island on a small fringing reef, and spearfishermen among the guests came up with a mammoth *langusta* that graced the table that night.

Lunch was simple but good, featuring cold seafood salad at the community table, after which we departed in Pidertupo's utility launch to visit an Indian village. It was less than a mile to the village island, toward the mainland. There the afternoon clouds had formed into great anvils over the mountains, creamy on top, black and purple underneath, with heavy showers shrouding the mountain slope. Here it was sunny and calm. The Indians farm on the mainland, commuting by canoe, as only coconuts find room to grow on the cays, and the inhabited ones are covered from end to end by native huts.

The village we were approaching was typically cramped with houses, which covered every inch of land on the cay. *Cayucos* clustered at the waterfront, some with small spritsails, a few with American outboard motors, and some worked by paddles alone. We were told that Cuna villages are run on a socialistic pattern with a chief as administrator. All adults have a voice in village proceedings and all farming products are pooled. Any Cuna over five feet tall would be considered large. They are stocky and broad-faced people, with blue-black straight hair, and bright, dark eyes. The women and girls dress elaborately in skirts, intricately embroidered blouses called *molas,* bright red head scarves, and gold rings in their wide, flat noses, while the men wear the simplest singlets and khaki pants, with no attempt at decoration.

Molas are sewn by the women, and each panel tells a story or presents an individual picture of animals, birds, fish, or plants. Each blouse has a panel front and back. Until recently these were all worked by hand, and it was easy for the occasional tourist to buy blouses very cheaply. That afternoon in 1971, Jane bought four or five for about ten dollars, each with two panels. One tiny child's blouse was sold for fifty cents. When we returned to the United States we found that a New York art gallery was selling single panels for $150, and now, we understand, *molas* are being produced by machine at a rapid rate for the increasing tourist market. When we were in the Caicos in 1979, machine-made *molas* were for sale in the boutique at the Third Turtle for thirty dollars.

The day of our visit coincided with a special ceremony. A young girl had reached puberty, and the women of the village were deeply involved in elaborate rites. The girl was confined to one of the huts, where women were bathing her and dressing her in ceremonial clothes. They were all in their best scarves and *molas,* and some had a dark line painted down the center of their noses. They proved very shy, especially when a camera appeared, and scurried away from us into the huts, where visitors were prohibited, although they could be lured out when the word was passed that there were customers for *molas.*

Actually, the ceremony also seemed to involve a great deal of drinking among the women. Some local firewater made from fermented plants was being served in one of the huts, and after a while we began to realize that much of the scurrying, giggling, and disappearing into doorways came from the fact that most of them were drunk.

With the huts close together and the alleyways between them rather narrow, there was a great deal of crowding and jostling in all this colorful swirl of scarves and *molas* and scampering children, along with the sound of giggles, shouts, and high-pitched squeals of female laughter. Meanwhile, a group of men oblivious to the feminine uproar were playing basketball in one of the few open spaces in the village near the town pier. They were quick and adept with the ball, although there were not any stuff shots. One man on another's shoulders might have just about made the average height in the United States' National Basketball Association.

We had been told to be out of the village long before sunset, making sure that the Cuna tabu against strangers staying in their villages after nightfall was not broken, and as we pulled away from the landing on our return to Pidertupo, we could still hear the cries and squeals of the women and see the bright flashes of red as they darted through the alleyways from hut to hut.

· *THE VENEZUELAN ISLANDS* ·

Most North Americans visualize the Spanish Main as a long, open stretch of coast along the northeast hump of South America, with great trade wind rollers pounding against an exposed shoreline. Not so. We found out the difference on a visit to Venezuela that included some offshore cruising and a survey trip by light plane. Islands are a very important part of the lay of the land here, and a good part of the Venezuelan coast is lined with close-in islands belonging to Venezuela.

To the west and farther offshore are Aruba, Bonaire, and Curaçao, which, with Statia, Saba, and the Dutch half of St. Martin, all far to the north, form the Netherlands Antilles. The Venezuelan coastal islands are about 130 miles west of Grenada and Trinidad, and directly downwind from these anchors of the Antilles chain. They are below the hurricane belt, but swept constantly by trades that are light in summer and blustery and strong in winter. During August the temperatures are around 70 degrees Fahrenheit.

The major island is the mountainous Isla de Margarita, over 30 miles long and lying 20 miles off the mainland harbor of Golfo de Cariaco. Margarita sits athwart the trades and forms a large lee that effectively breaks up the sweep of open ocean waves. Downwind of it a string of smaller islands, close to the coast, benefits from this lee with conditions reminiscent of the Virgin Islands. The string provides a wide variety and choice of anchorages. In a short cruise through them we saw nothing but local boats, some of them yachts, some of them commercial fishing skiffs, and we had our choice of many well-protected coves. As a backdrop, the magnificent mountains of the mainland towered off to the south, hues shifting across them as the sun changed angles and clouds swept by.

Many roughly informal vacation cottages are perched here and there on coastal points or above beaches on the islands, and we were told that most of their residents were technically "squatters." The houses were built over the years when no one paid any attention to the area, but now the government is beginning to check on who is using its lands. We were aboard the 65-foot Rhodes ketch *Sargasso,* a comfortable, luxurious cruising yacht belonging to Daniel Camejo, a Venezuelan architect, developer, and Olympic Star Class sailor for his country.

If Camejo has his way, these sleepily bypassed islands will be busier soon, as they lie on what he calls "The Sea of El Morro." El Morro is a high, rocky peninsula about a mile long that juts out from the mainland near the town of Barcelona. When we were there in 1975 Camejo had just started developing it and the nearby shore as one of the largest resort complexes anywhere. It will contain 30 hotels, condominiums, 560 individual vacation homes, 1,035 houseboat lots, several yacht clubs, golf courses, shopping centers, and commercial marinas. A similar but smaller development called Puerto Azul, near La Guaira, the port of Caracas, was the forerunner of El Morro. It has been hugely successful, and El Morro was expected to equal that success, although a recession in the Venezuelan economy in the 80s slowed progress. Certainly the accessibility of the offshore archipelago will greatly contribute to its success, and Margarita, at the far end of the chain, offers a contrast to the lonely islands in between as a full-fledged popular resort, with air service, ferryboats, resort hotels, and all the amusements necessary when a change of pace is needed.

Westward from El Morro there are more islands like Isla Piritu and Isla La Tortuga, which we flew around on an air survey trip. This was in a light plane from the general aviation field in Caracas. Caracas, a bustling oil-boom city of more than two million people, lies in a valley beyond the first range of coastal mountains. We had a good view of its serpentine sprawl along the valley floor and its incredible traffic jams as we climbed over the mountains and then slid down to the bright blue of the Caribbean on the other side. Our main objective was Islas Los Roques, 80 miles at sea north of La Guaira. Los Roques is a spread of cays and lagoons and a true atoll, a ring-shaped coral reef that is rare in this part of the world. It is a favorite cruising target for Venezuelan yacht owners. Its bright pastels—greens, yellows, and pale blues—emerged from the ink-blue background of the Caribbean. We banked and dipped low over some of its long, lonely white beaches. Here and there a yacht was anchored by itself, as isolated in tropical beauty as anywhere in the South Pacific and in surroundings quite different from anything to be found in the Antilles.

Our best memory of this area is of the night we spent at anchor off one of the many little islands near El Morro. At twilight the gentle summer trade had eased off and we were gliding quietly along, past a fleet of fishing canoes. There were perhaps 50 of them clustered together on the gentle heave of the sea, with the mauve-tinted mountains of the mainland behind them. In the evening hush we could hear the soft chatter of men and women's voices as we drifted by, a laugh now and then, or a snatch of song, and the occasional flurry of splashing as a fish was landed. Our course took us to the deserted cove we sought. It was open to the west with a view of the golden flare of the sunset. There are such places left.

· THE REEFS OFF BELIZE ·

The biggest barrier reef in the world is off the Queensland coast of Australia, and the second is just offshore of Belize in Central America. Belize is now a country, an independent state of the British Commonwealth. Before it achieved that status it was known as British Honduras, and Belize was the name of its capital city.

The city has all the sad and unpleasant features of impoverished areas everywhere, but offshore, untouched and pristine, is an array of gorgeous reefs, cays, islets, and lagoons. The barrier reef forms a smooth-water lagoon about 10 miles wide between it and the mainland. Beyond the long string of the reef itself more reefs and cays extend 30 or 40 miles into the Caribbean. The trades blow in ceaselessly with their cargo of puffy clouds. The air is often softly hazy from the spray of endless waves pounding on reefs.

My exposure to this strange, forgotten land was in an old Baltic trader built in 1895, which had been converted to a cruise ship with cabins for 12 passengers who book independently. That was in 1975, and she has since been removed from service. In a week we saw a couple of conch smacks and one powerboat with a diving group, but not another sail, and not even one airplane. We were by ourselves in a maze of reefs, cays, and brilliantly colored water. Again, we found ourselves alone on a vast, untouched seascape under an empty sky.

Except for a few shacks and a lighthouse or two, there was little evidence of man or his works. More startling was the sight of wreck after wreck piled on the outer reefs of this poorly marked area. We saw more wrecks than vessels during our week of ranging the Belize reefs.

We had a naturalist aboard as general nursemaid and guide. With him we explored cays that were bird hatcheries and the haunts of iguanas. Pushing our way through pungent, lime-encrusted vegetation on one little cay, we came to the roost of red-footed boobies, great, ungainly, trusting birds that perched on their nests and stared you down, eyeball to eyeball, from a couple of feet away. Their gawky, fuzzy-headed progeny sat unmoving under the closest scrutiny.

On another cay off by itself, stately frigate birds had their hatchery. The birds wheeled high in the sky as we approached the nest, ready to swoop down to the attack in forked-tail fury if we came too close. No staring at these proud birds from close range while they were in their nests. Nearby, another cay was home for iguanas up to several feet long. Perfectly camouflaged in the underbrush, they were very hard to spot as they stood motionlessly watching our approach. The shine of an eye would be the first sign of them, and only a direct move toward them sent them scurrying into deeper brush with amazing speed.

The outermost reef of the Belize complex is a big one called Lighthouse Reef, 30 miles at sea beyond the main barrier. Our old schooner was a cumbersome sailer with her maze of rope rigging, ratlines, and gaff-rigged sails, but she would move on a reach in a good breeze, and we had one to get us to this lonely outpost. There was the feel of an ancient sailing ship as we swept across the white-capped blue of trade-wind seas. Once there, we found the most fascinating phenomenon of the exotic attractions in the area. Winding through the pale-green reef waters with the skipper calling orders to the helm from the crow's nest high on the foremast, we followed a serpentine course to a fabulous anomaly of nature known as the Blue Hole. Taking right-angle and hairpin turns around ugly, threatening reefs, we snaked our nine feet of draft to the edge of this perfectly circular, inky-blue pit, 200 yards across and more than 400 feet deep, with nothing but the palest reef waters on all sides as far as the eye could see.

Captain Jacques Cousteau brought his ship *Calypso* here and found it a diving paradise, and the scuba enthusiasts on our vessel said it was the diving experience of a lifetime. The walls of this great natural canister, perhaps a prehistoric lake, are lined with stalagmite-filled caves, and marine life teems in the depths. Hammerhead sharks were reported in abundance, but not inclined to notice the intruders, and the light through the clear blue water was described as beautifully, translucently sparkling.

Not being part of the scuba set (I snorkel very tamely at my bravest), my thrills at the Blue Hole came from sailing the schooner's Sunfish in the brisk 18-knot trade that was blowing. It was an exciting sensation to sweep in on a planing reach from the lime green shallows surrounding the Blue Hole and suddenly, in half the length of the little boardboat, be on blue as dark as the open sea. Our schooner sat in the only cut through the reef into the Blue Hole, anchored to the rim. The rest of the reef was barely awash. As I skimmed along, I could see the dorsals of sharks weaving through the reef formation, with an occasional thrash of tail in the shallow water. I was very careful not to capsize. I have never felt nature's predominance more strongly than on the reefs off Belize.

· THE BAY ISLANDS OF HONDURAS ·

In 1861 Queen Victoria ceded a group of islands in the western Caribbean to the Central American nation of Honduras. This is not one of the epic events of history, and most people, if they ever knew about it at all, have long forgotten it. But the inhabitants of the Bay Islands have not. For more than 100 years they have been under the rule of the Spanish-speaking mainlanders—although they still speak English, albeit with a very special lilt of their own—and they live their own independent, insular lives to the best of their ability.

For most of this century the Bay Islands were a "lost" area, little-known to the outside world. Even mainland Hondurans wer so unconcerned about them that they paid scant attention to what went on there. The schools were conducted in English, the people fished and did a little farming, and many of the men shipped out as professional seamen. Other sources of income were boatbuilding and, more recently, shrimping.

Few visitors came this way. Transportation was difficult and there were no tourist hotels. If ever there was a land that time forgot, it was this little archipelago, sitting about 35 miles off the Honduran mainland where Central America juts eastward, forming the big bight known as the Gulf of Honduras with Mexico's Yucatán Peninsula as the northern arm. The Bay Islands stretch for about 75 miles in an east-west direction. Cigar-shaped Roatan is the major land mass. The easternmost part is the island of Guanacca; the Utila Cays are at the westward end. Halfway to the mainland on the south is a separate little archipelago known as the Cochinos—Hog—Islands.

Lately the world has been catching up with the Bay Islands. Air connections were established via ancient DC-3s, and a resort known as Anthony's Cay was established to cater especially to the diving trade. In 1978 Jack Van Ost, president of the pioneer bareboating charter company, Caribbean Sailing Yachts, decided to shift his Abacos operation to Roatan. He sent one of his charter yachts, the CSY 44 cutter *Basilisk,* to Roatan to do preliminary survey work, and we were invited to use her for a week to get a preview of what chartering would be like when the area opened up.

In getting there to board *Basilisk,* we found out just how remote the Bay Islands are. Travel agents answered with a "Where . . . ?" when inquiries were made, but finally we forged a route: an overnight stay in Miami and an early morning flight on TAN, the national airline of Honduras, to a town called La Ceiba on the Honduran mainland. This was a pleasant jet flight of two and a half hours and a stop in Belize. Very little time was lost on the clock because of two time-zone changes. La Ceiba had a good, big airstrip not far from the coast on a plain backed by high mountains, with a modern little terminal building. It also had close, humid heat, flies, and no one who spoke English. We checked in with an airline with the acronym SAHSA and were given boarding passes for a plane to Roatan, with no hint of delay or trouble. Old friends were traveling with us and we repaired to the lunch room, mainly because it was the only air-conditioned place in the building, for a *cerveza* during the wait for our connection. The beer was cold (again, most Latin-American beers are quite good) and we watched the flow of life around us as we sipped.

After one of those funny, exasperating, confusing, nervous-making experiences one always risks by traveling to exotic places, we overcame hours of delay, lost luggage, wrong boarding passes, impassive officials speaking no English, and found ourselves aboard a venerable DC-3. Taking off, we bounced into the air with a vibrating, rivet-popping rush, swooping low over the bright green of palm and banana trees along the coast to the blue of the sea, and, sooner than expected banked and began a descent. I could see that we were making an approach to a low, small, sandy island, and I knew Roatan was long and hilly, but someone shouted over the engine roar that this was Utila. No one had mentioned it as a stop, but there it was, and there we came, lower and lower over paling water. Suddenly there was dusty dirt under us and we bounced onto it with a crack that jarred the plane and knocked it back in the air for a moment. Finally we came to rest in front of a small building, a few passengers disembarked, and we were off again. A short hop across whitecapped seas took us to Roatan, where the airport was just as dusty, but much bigger than Utila's absolutely minimal strip.

There was no terminal, although construction was underway, and our luggage, covered with dust, sat in a forlorn cluster not far from the runway. I understand that conditions have improved since our adventure in 1978, but we really felt we had earned our wings in getting to these "lost" islands.

I do not know how he knew when our green passes would finally get us on board, but on hand to meet us on arrival was CSY's agent for Roatan, an engaging young man named Compa Galindo. He whisked us off to a private house, vacation home of an American in a development that was just starting on the south coast overlooking Brick Harbor, where CSY's base was to be built. The house was a long, rambling, one-story building of wood, with big, airy rooms, and an open veranda on the seaward side that soared out into space as the land fell away below it. Sitting there with a cool drink and watching the play of afternoon light across the mangroves below us, with the rolling blue of the Caribbean beyond and an indistinct loom on the far horizon that might have been clouds but was actually the mountains of the mainland, the trip finally seemed worth the effort. The white dot of a sail materialized up the coast to the east, gradually drawing nearer on the wings of the trade, until we could see the beige and maroon of CSY hull colors. *Basilisk,* finishing a week of survey work for a cruising guide, swept into the harbor, with the slanting light of the late afternoon sun gleaming on her topsides.

In our week aboard her we learned a great deal about the Bay Islands and their people. Compa was typical of the islanders, part Spanish in heritage, but English-speaking and very much an islander, quick, friendly, and efficient. Still in his twenties, he was into all sorts of enterprises and raising a family. His brother managed Anthony's Cay.

Our pilot aboard *Basilisk* showed us another type of Bay Islander. He was a professional seaman in his early thirties named Charlie Osgood, entirely of Anglo-Saxon descent from the days before Queen Victoria dealt the islands away; many of the family names are similarly Scottish and English. Charlie had worked on ships in many parts of the world and would continue to do so, although he too was raising a young family. He knew every inch of the waters in the Bay Islands. Charts of the area were old and vague, and the people making the survey cruise the week ahead of us found that his local knowledge was much better than the charts, as we did, too. We only used them for general reference as he piloted us unerringly in and out of the many harbors we visited.

His typical Bay Islands accent was an engaging mixture of Bermudian, Bahamian, and West Indian lilts, with a few touches peculiar to the Bay Islands alone. We understood him well, but whenever he conversed with other natives the tempo of the chatter picked up and it was much harder for us to follow. He could speak Spanish, but not well, and did not like to, and it was from him we learned of the real resentment Bay Islanders still have about being turned over to the SPON-ish, as they pronounce it. Anything that fails to work or goes wrong is derogated as "Sponish," with great scorn. It is more than idle resentment or ancient ethnic prejudice, because efforts are being made to make Spanish the language of instruction in the schools, and the Bay Islanders are not happy about it. Bay Island blacks, not heavily in evidence, are English-speaking too.

We had a young passenger named Joe Cooper aboard for several days. He came from Utila Cays, a tiny community of small wooden houses on stilts strung along a sandy bar at the western end of the archipelago, where shrimping is the major activity. In his fourteen years he had been as far away as Roatan only once, and we gave him a ride so he could visit relatives there. He was dark-skinned and small, with a flashing smile, bright, dark eyes, an engaging sense of humor, and an eagerness to learn everything he could about the boat. Joe more than earned his keep when we had a feast of lobsters Charlie bought for us while at Utila. With practiced skill, Joe showed us how to crack them and get the best and most meat out of them, working like a skilled, if frantic, surgeon.

Aside from the "Sponish," Charlie was obsessed with country-and-western music. Radio Roatan, which broadcasts a mix of canned evangelical programs, local news, and nondescript Latin music, as well as some popular songs, had two hours of country-and-western music every morning, emceed by a disc jockey pal of Charlie's. With an accent duplicating Charlie's, he bemoaned "old Charlie Osgood's" absence from town and dedicated numbers to him, while Charlie, hugging his portable to his stomach as he sat in the cockpit, chortled.

Having Charlie aboard meant that we met the local populace wherever we put in. He seemed to know everyone in the islands, and they all stopped by to visit. We never anchored, except in the Cochinos and Utila town, where there were no piers to handle us, as he always wangled a berth alongside a shrimp boat or at someone's private pier. In Utila Cays the entire population of the village crowded aboard the big shrimp boat we were alongside, chatting with Charlie and staring down with open curiosity at *Basilisk*. With no roads, only wooden walkways between the houses, and many of them off on separate cays of their own, everything was conducted by water, with all ages moving around the harbor in dugout canoes not unlike the cayucos of the San Blas. Some had powerful outboards and others paddled. While cruising between the islands, we sometimes came across these little splinters, loaded to the gunwale, slicing along in the open sea.

Utila Cays was as far out a settlement as we could imagine, but beyond it, isolated little hunks of sand and coral, some with one cottage tucked among the palm trees, invited beachcombing and snorkeling. They were strewn about a bank encircled by reefs that kept the water smooth, and each one looked like the perfect dream of island escape. Roatan, with a harbor every couple of miles along its southern shores, has several towns. These are all shrimping ports, and whole fleets of the white, high-bowed vessels were rafted along the waterfronts of Coxen Hole, French Harbour, and Oak Ridge, since this was the off-season for shrimping. These towns look well settled from a harbor vantage, but, in walking through them, they reveal themselves as quiet, scruffy little backwaters, with shanties for houses, dusty streets, and the simplest kind of shops and markets. Roads on Roatan are not well developed, and dust blows across much of it when cars and trucks move about.

At the eastern end of Roatan, a big, reef-enclosed spread of water known as Port Royal was a major pirate hangout in the seventeenth and eighteenth centuries. The remains of a fort put up by Henry Morgan to protect his base can still be seen on a little island to starboard of the pass through the reef. Pirate wrecks dot the fringing reefs, and diving expeditions have spent much time searching for them and working them over. One of the diving boats became a wreck itself, still visible on top of the reef, in one of the infrequent hurricanes that hit the Bay Islands. Port Royal is a wonderful cruising stop, reminiscent of Gorda Sound on Virgin Gorda, with many places for a boat to drop the hook.

Roatan's north coast has one big reef all along it, with only a couple of entrances, Anthony's Cay being the best. In winter, when northers sweep down from the North American plains across the Gulf of Mexico bringing rain squalls and cold winds, Roatan's north coast is not a good place to be, but the south coast offers good protection.

In this spread of little-known and little-developed islands, perhaps the most atmospheric of all of them are the Cochinos, set by themselves in the open sea halfway to the mainland. They were once owned by a wealthy Honduran who seldom visited them and left them to his Scottish caretaker. He and his family, who control most of them, have been enjoying their own little empire for many years now, living quietly and watching the world gradually come to them. Three or four good-sized islands, one with a little grass airstrip for light planes, make up the bulk of the archipelago, and many more islets and cays sit on the reefs that fan out from the Cochinos. There are a few houses, and some fishermen's huts, but most of the land is untouched.

We had a swift, spray-flinging reach across the trades to get there from Oak Ridge, making the 21 miles in under three hours as the curving profile of the Cochinos gradually darkened and took separate shape against the background of the massive mainland mountains. With the hook down in a bight of the biggest Cochinos off the substantial houses of the owner's family, we swam, snorkeled, sailed the dink, and explored ashore in an idyllic setting. Climbing a hilly pasture back of the beach, we had a sweeping view of the pattern of nearby islands set off against reefs. In the foreground, hillsides were lushly green and thick with vegetation. Farther out in the Cochinos, smaller, palm-topped cays became dark dots on the sea, and deep in the distance, afternoon clouds on the mainland peaks were a guide to the faint loom of purple, misty and indistinct, of the mountains themselves. Below us, *Basilisk*, miniaturized by distance in the wide harbor, was the only visiting boat as she rode serenely on her hook, and I was struck with the thought that here again was a scene that would not be duplicated much longer as the world moved in on another of its forgotten corners.

Roche Harbor in the San Juan Islands.

11 · The Pacific Coast

*T*here is great contrast between the offshore islands of America's Atlantic and Pacific coasts. From Panama to Alaska the Pacific sweeps in, almost unimpeded by offshore barriers, while off the shores of New England, Florida, and Central America islands abound. Island magic in the Pacific is more distant in the vast reaches of the central and southern regions. There are coastal islands close to shore in the Gulf of California, Puget Sound, and the Inside Passage to Alaska. But only a few dots of land in the Gulf of Panama and a string of lonely outposts along the southern California coast convey the feeling of being alone at sea, encircled by empty water.

There are a few almost unknown spots like Clipperton, a vestige of French imperial interest, 1200 miles off Costa Rica; Costa Rica's own lush, seldom-visited Cocos; Islas Revillagigedo and Guadaloupe, dots in the sea off Mexico; and the rocky pinnacles of the Farallons standing guard outside San Francisco Bay. But all these hold little allure for visitors and seldom have any.

On the other hand, many have been to Catalina, the island off Los Angeles that singlehandedly combines for Californians what Monhegan, Nantucket, Block Island, and the Bahamas do for the east coast. It is one of the Santa Barbara islands that string along well offshore of the southernmost 200 miles of the California coast, but the only one open to general visiting and even that on a restricted basis. All the other Santa Barbara islands are privately owned or off-limits for military reasons. North of them, except for the uninhabited Farallons, there is not another truly offshore island all the way to Alaska. One must look inside the few bays and sounds of the seldom-indented Pacific coast to find the kind of island world so readily available on the Atlantic side.

· *THE NORTHWEST* ·

"The sunny San Juans are different," everyone told me when we were about to embark on a family cruise on Puget Sound. "When it's rainy or foggy everywhere else, the San Juans will be clear," the sales talk continued. Not when we went there. The San Juans are lovely, forested, gracefully contoured pieces of land that almost fill the waters between Washington state and Vancouver Island, leaving only narrow channels through them for navigation. This is the area where the Canadian and United States border zigzags down the waterways after crossing the northwest all the way from Minnesota on the Forty-ninth Parallel. It was raining here, though, just the way it had been everywhere else in Puget Sound, when we threaded our way into West Sound on Orcas Island, one of the largest San Juans.

This was in early July, and there was a distinct north-woods feeling to the rocky shores, thick growth of evergreens, and lingering gray twilight well into mid-evening, but the rain was a disappointment. We berthed at the private pier of a friend's summer cottage and our daughters perked up when they saw local youngsters getting out water skis. Despite the gloomy weather, there would be something to do. Their enthusiasm dampened perceptibly, however, when they watched the next move: donning a wet suit before taking off. The water temperature was in the low 50 degrees Fahrenheit, adding a strong emphasis to that north-woods feeling.

The islands are on the north side of the Strait of Juan de Fuca—Juan being the sixteenth-century Spanish sailor who was the first European to see it—which is the main channel from the Pacific into Puget Sound. They were the last bit of the continental United States to be taken over from the British. They were disputed by the two nations until 1872, when arbitration by the German emperor assigned the islands to the United States. This put a westward zig in the border, sending it toward Vancouver Island before zagging southward in Haro Strait and turning due west again in the middle of Juan de Fuca. The San Juans were also known as the Haro Islands and their names reveal an interesting mix of Spanish and English exploration and Indian lore: San Juan, Orcas, Shaw, Lopez, Blakely, and so on. Getting there we had experienced names like Utsaladdy, Swinomish, Deception, and Rosario.

Despite the dampness, we had an evening clambake on the rocky shore of West Sound, with enough driftwood strewn along the rocks to light a fire every night of the summer. The water skiers kept at it until after nine o'clock, looking like seals in their shiny suits as they came dripping out of the water to join the feast.

To do the San Juans justice, they were sunny when we went through them on our way back to Puget Sound at the end of the cruise. It was explained that the weather comes through the Strait, funneled by the Olympic mountains on the south and Vancouver Island to the north, and then follows the main waterways south into Puget Sound and north toward the city of Vancouver. This leaves the San Juans in the middle of the split and often free of the clouds that follow these routes.

We had been at Victoria, the capital of British Columbia on the south end of Vancouver Island, a city that takes advantage of the old-world atmosphere implied by its name with double-decker London buses, bagpipers that meet visitors arriving on the ferry from Seattle, a wax museum, turreted, gabled buildings of gray stone, and a big, dark, high-ceilinged hotel, The Empress, facing the yacht docks at the harbor. Dinner there, amid heavy carpets, dark panelling, a string quartet playing dinner music behind ferns, and heavy linen tablecloths and napkins, was marvelously atmospheric, although a seagull sitting on the window sill next to us, watching us eat with baleful eye, was a reminder of another world outside.

When we left Victoria to return to the San Juans, there was, in truth, one patch of blue up ahead, right over them. To starboard the Olympics were in impressive snow-capped array on the horizon, now visible and then hidden in alternate swirls of clouds. Rain clouds hovered over Vancouver's rugged outline to port, and the far shore behind the San Juans was shrouded in gloom. But the bright patch lured us on, and the weather was summery as we entered the deep indentation of Roche Harbor at the northwest tip of San Juan Island. There was a big marina here, with an old-fashioned hotel surrounded by well-tended gardens at the land's end, and some sight-seeing to do. In the fuss over who owned the San Juans, there was one confrontation—in 1859—that threatened to escalate into something more serious. An American army detachment commanded by George Pickett occupied San Juan island, which promptly brought British gunboats to the scene. No shots were fired, however, because General Winfield Scott, the old Mexican War hero, offered the British a compromise—joint occupation of the island—that cooled matters. Some campsites and military relics remain from that past event. History remembers the young commander better as the leader of "Pickett's Charge," a suicidal Confederate infantry action at Gettysburg, in the American Civil War.

This is a United States customs port, where we entered formally into the United States, and it was an arresting sight in the evening to watch a ceremony on the roof of the long shed housing the customs office. Led by a uniformed customs officer, while the loudspeaker blared a martial tune, three dock boys from the marina in T-shirts and khaki pants marched into the sunset to the flagpole silhouetted against flaming skies in the west, and held a snappy evening color drill. Given the dual heritage of the area, it was perhaps appropriate that the tune booming from the loudspeaker as the Stars and Stripes were lowered was Britain's "Colonel Bogey March."

The islands themselves are gracefully atmospheric and a handsome background to the waterways that wind through them. Some of them are quite hilly. Mount Constitution on Orcas rises to 2,400 feet and the contours of hills and bluffs, endlessly crowned with evergreens, blend in everchanging perspectives and degrees of depth perception, with a vividly alive dark green in the foreground and mistier shades in the middle distance. Beautifully appointed camps and cottages can be glimpsed in coves on points set among protective trees, with glossy powerboats, or even seaplanes, poised at piers and floats in front of them. Once a perky steam launch puffed her way serenely past us.

An eye caught with the beauty of a nearby point, the symmetry of a cove, or the rise of a bluff over the steely blue of the water could be satisfied, even satiated, with nearby scenery, but far off, at the limits of visibility, a great peak, such as Mt. Baker hovers like a cloud in the east. The snow-capped Olympics form a sawtoothed frieze of interrelated peaks topped by the 7,954 feet of Mount Olympus.

These were amazing enough to our eastern eyes, but the climax came on our return to Tacoma, Washington. We had left it in rain and drizzle, with a horizon not far over the bow, but coming back we were in bright sunshine as we followed the narrow cut back of Vashon Island that runs most of the way from Seattle to Tacoma, almost filling the Sound. It ends at Commencement Bay, an open body of water off Tacoma.

We had been awed by Mount Rainier's great, 14,000-foot bulk glowing in the last of the late sunset as we flew into Seattle-Tacoma to start our cruise, but we had not seen it since. It was blocked out by rain when we left, and now our horizon was limited to the wooded western shore of Vashon, close above us. Then, as we came around the last point of Vashon onto the wider waters of Commencement Bay, the first sight in the foreground was a fleet of racing sailboats drifting along under multicolored spinnakers. For a moment this was enough of a treat for the eye, but then, adjusting to greater distance, I was suddenly aware of a streaked white mass rising out of a fringe of haze and low-lying clouds far behind the spinnakers. Almost disembodied above them across the bay, the massive dome of Rainier glinted in the sunlight, a breathtaking backdrop to an island world far different from the sandy bluffs and dunes of home, and an awesome, unforgettable sight.

· SAN FRANCISCO BAY ·

Inside San Francisco Bay, practically the only major indentation in more than 400 miles of California coastline, islands play an important role in the flow of bay weather and in the fabric of life in the area. First there is Alcatraz, a gaunt fortress now abandoned, but still "the Rock," perhaps the grimmest of United States Federal prisons because of its isolation amid the beckoning freedom of its setting.

In an ironic juxtaposition of names, Angel Island is next to Alcatraz, a friendly looking, hilly affair of trees and meadows and a favorite spot for a boating rendezvous. Not only is Angel a marked change from the forbidding loom of Alcatraz; it is also an agent in an amazing weather change that takes place behind it. On the Golden Gate side, the wind whistling in from the cold waters of the open Pacific is often raw and cutting, and usually freighted with fog, an impelling reminder of the forces at work just beyond the big red bridge that spans its tricky tides. Sailors huddle into foul-weather gear and hunch down in their collars against the damp knife of wind. Spray flies over the rail and rigging sings with strain. Air temperature is perhaps around 50 degrees Fahrenheit and navigation must always be precise, allowing for almost instantaneous envelopment in fog.

Just on the other side, however, a narrow passage between Angel Island and Marin County called Raccoon Strait has protected coves and the hint of kinder weather. As soon as you move out of Raccoon Strait to the east, with Angel Island as a buffer astern, the temperature rises to 70 degrees Fahrenheit. Oilskins and shirts come off in the bright sunshine and the bay smiles placidly under a gentle breeze. In less than a mile you have gone through a transition in weather that would be similar to March-to-August weather patterns in other parts of the country.

The Bay Area also has an island that stands for a very special kind of escape. This is a marshy tract of land well up the Delta of the Sacramento River, inland from the head of the bay, an island only by courtesy of narrow sloughs, lined with graceful reeds called tules, that cut through Delta country. This is Tinsley Island, owned by the St. Francis Yacht Club, the major one in San Francisco, and it is used as a focal point for weekend cruises, junior sailing camps, and various special affairs. Its main building is a former lighthouse now converted to clubrooms. Tinsley is active in this way for much of the year, but once a year in the early fall it plays host to a unique gathering known as the Stag Cruise.

This is not what might be assumed from its name. It is a completely male affair for four days, but the "stag" tag that ordinarily conjures up images of dancing girls emerging from large cakes, wild drinking, and bouts of locker-room humor, is inaccurate. There is a great deal of drinking, and even more eating, as each meal consists of an overwhelming oversupply of whatever would be normal for breakfast, lunch, or dinner, but it is on a generally decorous level of gentlemanly behavior and good fellowship. Anyone who lets drink take over and reels out of control or becomes crude and boisterous is quietly but firmly escorted off the island and told not to come back. No women are in evidence, although there have been rumors that a houseboat staffed by professional ladies has on occasion been moored not too far down the river from Tinsley—nothing official, of course. Evidently a four-day stag party is too long for some males.

The weekend starts on a Thursday morning at the main clubhouse on the Golden Gate in San Francisco with a rather special breakfast. It is really a big cocktail party, with screwdrivers, Bloody Marys, or whatever you want flowing freely, and a Dixieland band whooping up the tempo of activity. Scrambled eggs are an incidental before everyone boards yachts at the marina, and the fleet heads up bay and into the Sacramento River for the half-day trip to Tinsley. The Delta, crisscrossed with canals and sloughs, is a patchwork of islands that attracts Bay Area boats for leisurely cruising. The only sense of space is of vistas across the low, flat lands, often below the waterways that are held in place by dikes and levees, to the hills of the uplands in the distance. The river flows deep and strong, but not very wide, and the other waterways are narrow and pent in by tules and isolated stands of eucalyptus.

This is cruising at its most landbound and rural. The boats wend their way through the sloughs, and an ocean-going freighter in the channel of the main river looms grotesquely over the levees like a lost elephant. Her superstructure glides by with no hint that it is part of a waterborne vessel. Once at Tinsley, that wonderful euphoria of escape takes over. The assemblage of several hundred males begins to relax in earnest. There are formal programs of stage shows, singalongs, and panel discussions by prominent yachtsmen, naval architects, sailmakers, and other experts, but each man sets his own pace and does what he wants, existing in an atmosphere of disembodied freedom for the long weekend.

Everyone bunks on his respective boat, and the day starts with a mind-boggling bang. At the earliest sunup, when the marshes should be lying quiet under morning mists, silent except for bird calls and the faint gurgle of water in the sloughs, the Dixieland band is herded aboard an open launch and circulates through the mooring area, serenading the groaning, moaning awakeners with "When the Saints Come Marching In," "South Rampart Street Parade," and similar "lullabies." It is much better just to hear the songs than to look at the musicians' dour, doughy, dawn-lit faces, on which every line and furrow screams mortification at having to perform at this unprofessional hour. Somehow it is all so ludicrous that you come awake with a laugh, and the first thing you know a Ramos fizz is shoved in your hand, even before you have brushed your teeth. Another day of jollity and good fellowship has begun.

All this could only seem logical in an island atmosphere, and Tinsley, deep among the tules, manages it perfectly.

· CATALINA ·

Californians, despite pretensions to a free and easy life-style, are actually highly organized and regimented in almost everything they do, especially in the realm of recreation. You just cannot find an isolated bit of woods beside a stream for a picnic, or cruise along the coast and drop anchor in a likely looking cove. Areas are specifically designated for all activities of this sort, and Catalina is the designated island, with a capital I, for offshore escape. Actually, that is about all there is. The other islands of the group are restricted in some way, and they hardly have any usable harbors.

Catalina is actually Santa Catalina, discovered in 1524 by Juan Cabrillo, the Portuguese navigator sailing for Spain who gave many of the Spanish names to Pacific coast sites, but it was not named until 1602 when Sebastian Vizcaino rediscovered it on the eve of the feast of St. Catherine and named it for her. It was part of Mexico until 1848 when the end of the Mexican War gave it to California. It is 25 miles off the densely populated stretch of coast that runs south of Los Angeles harbor. It is 22 miles long, varying in width from eight miles to a few hundred yards at the narrow waist known as The Isthmus.

Although Catalina is open to visitors, and attracts hundreds of thousands each year—mostly to Avalon, its only town—it has been owned by a corporation controlled by the Wrigley family, of chewing-gum fame, since 1919. All access is by permission of the Catalina Company, and many areas are leased to private control by special groups, so you cannot just go to Catalina, drop the hook, and walk ashore at will, or take an excursion steamer or plane there and wander over its hilly terrain as the spirit moves. Everything is highly organized.

There is only one harbor protected in all directions, and it is on the south, or ocean side, at The Isthmus. All other anchorages are merely open coves. Most of them are on the north side, facing Catalina Channel and the mainland, protected from the open Pacific swells and from the prevailing west wind. There are about a dozen good coves, all controlled by the company, and they are filled with long strings of moorings. Some are leased to individuals on a yearly basis; possessing a Catalina mooring lease is like having a season box at a race track or ball park. Some are even passed on by inheritance. Other coves are leased to mainland yacht clubs and are reserved for members under control of the club. Although the weather is pleasant most of the year, major activity is confined to summer weekends, when the boats swarming across the Channel to north shore coves resemble the Dunkirk evacuation, followed by a reverse operation on Sunday afternoons. Then it would be impossible to squeeze another kayak into a Catalina cove and privacy is as remote as the Himalayas. Sounds of revelry echo through the coves far into the night, a blend of cassette recordings, radio music, the tinkle of ice in glasses, and high-pitched shrieks of merriment. Off-season and midweeks are quieter and less crowded, but the controls are still on as to who uses the moorings and can land on the shores of the coves.

All is well along Catalina's north shore when the weather behaves normally, with the afternoon sea breeze humming in nicely from the west, but the picture changes dramatically in a santana. This is a hot, gusty, east wind, actually a Santa Ana but shortened to one word, that blows down across the coastal basin of southern California from the desert under certain conditions. It can blast close to hurricane strength on rare occasions, sometimes hits over 50 knots, and is rough enough even in the more usual 20- to 30-knot range, making the coves completely untenable. It also brings desertlike temperatures up to 90 degrees Fahrenheit, and there is a nightmare quality to the onslaught of a santana as it hurls short, steep waves into the open coves. One can hit with little or no warning, and when it chooses a busy weekend to start its mischief, the result is chaos on the mooring strings as boats fight their way out of the cul-de-sac to open water, often colliding with each other in the confusion of smashing seas and hot, suffocating wind.

In my first few visits to southern California, I refused to believe that Catalina existed. There was either sea fog or the local curse of smog whenever I went, and Catalina was an invisible, offshore myth. Finally, however, I got a chance to go to it on a midweek April cruise with Bill and Peg Lapworth on a Cal 2-46 cruising sloop designed by Bill, who is one of the top yacht designers in the United States. Conditions were a bit unusual. A fresh northwester had been blowing for two days and there was not a hint of smog in the Los Angeles basin. The *Los Angeles Times* actually had a picture of the city's skyline on its front pages to illustrate how strangely clear the weather was. There was Catalina, highly visible as a series of purple humps, topped by 2,100-foot Mount Orizaba on the seaward horizon.

As we approached it, the hills showed verdantly, flecked with gold on the higher slopes by the afternoon sun. The Lapworths said that they had never seen Catalina so green. It had been a rainy winter, and the normally dun-colored hills were covered in new vegetation and spring flowers. We explored several of the coves, all deserted on an April midweek day, their strings of buoys bobbing emptily in neat, white patterns over the blue of the coves, and picked up a mooring in late afternoon at Howland's Cove, one of the bigger ones controlled by a yacht club. We were close to the shore, and between us and the small curve of beach at the head of the cove we could see great beds of tan, rubbery kelp lying just under the surface. Here we were far removed from the touristic attractions of Avalon. Except for Avalon and some orange groves, and here and there a summer camp for children, most of Catalina is wild and untouched, with Wrigley-imported buffalo roaming the hills.

Hiking inland was allowed from our cove, and we headed up a dry riverbed into the hills. The fresh grass of the fields was dotted with wild-flowers, odd clumps of cactus, and buffalo dung, although we met no buffalo face to face. As we went higher, stands of Australian pine and eucalyptus grew thicker. Eventually we were out of sight of the sea in a hushed woodland setting.

On the way down we paused atop a grassy hill, out from under the trees, with an uninterrupted view across the deep blue of Catalina Channel to the mainland. The northwester was still blowing fresh and had routed the last hint of smog from the vast panorama spreading before us. Clean, slanting light from the late afternoon sun glinted on the buildings, tiny in the distance, and in the background, snow-capped mountains, with a fresh, clear brilliance, all the more startling in this capital of smog. In one sweep of the eye, from the limits of visibility at Santa Barbara on the left to Dana Point way off to the right, was a stretch of coast holding more than ten million people. Standing on this lonely hillside, I could understand why careful control and organization is the only way Californians can have one Catalina as an escape valve, no matter how regimented the escape.

· LAS PERLAS ·

On the same trip that took us to the San Blas Islands, we had a vivid example of Atlantic-Pacific contrast when we visited Taboga and Las Perlas (Pearl) Islands in the Gulf of Panama on the Pacific side. Most noticeable is the difference in tides. In the Caribbean there is almost no rise and fall. Except for wind-driven deviations, there is little more than a foot of tidal range in the San Blas. If there were more, these tiny low cays would not even exist, as they are only a few feet above sea level. I remember going through Panama during my Navy days and noticing the extreme difference between the two sides of the Isthmus. As skipper of a 110-foot subchaser, I was fortunate to have a chief boatswain who had done duty in Panama before, and when we came in to berth at the Navy piers in Balboa after transiting the Canal, he suggested that we let the other vessels in our group tie up first so that we could raft outside them. By this ploy they had to tend their docklines continuously through a 30- to 40-foot tide change, while we got a free ride up and down on the outside.

Remembering this, it was still a shock to see the effect when we went out to Taboga, ten miles from the Pacific entrance to the Panama Canal, to spend the day. We arrived at high tide and could step off the launch directly onto the surface of the pier. Alongside it was a sandy beach with a small rim of gold between the water and palm trees fringing it. After a day of sightseeing and exploring Taboga's old houses and forts, and some time spent at the beach, the beach had turned into a great, wide strand sloping down to water far below, and the boat was at the bottom of a long, long ladder. The phenomenon of a body of water with a wide mouth and narrower inner end, as in the Bay of Fundy or English Channel, is part of the explanation for such enormous tidal range.

We were guests of the Panama tourist authorities on this trip, and they wanted us to see Las Perlas as an example of development that was then (1971) just beginning. For years this archipelago in the Gulf of Panama had remained virtually untouched. It strings along for almost 50 miles with islands as large as 30-mile-long San Miguel, and countless islets and small cays. Except for pirates in times past and fishermen who based there temporarily, there had been little attention paid to them, although it is a prime sport-fishing area for marlin and wahoo. They were privately owned and almost totally natural, a lovely complex of bays, coves, curving white beaches, and hilly, thoroughly tropical islands lush in vegetation. Jane and our daughter Alice and I were flown out there in a light plane for New Year's Eve, and did not see one boat in all the islands as we made a circuit of them. The plane then left us to our own devices at a small resort settlement that was just getting started on Contadora, one of the medium-sized Perlas (which later gained attention as a temporary haven for the Shah of Iran in exile). The airstrip was new and well paved, and a dozen mobile homes, moved there after being used for housing when Panama played host to the Pan American games, lined it. Some were privately owned by Panamanian families building vacation homes in the new development. Others were used for visitors by the tourist office. A new clubhouse with bar and restaurant stood on a small rise above a gorgeous scimitar of beach, but it was not yet open for business.

There was to be a private party at the finished but unopened club to celebrate the holiday that night, and we were invited. Our mobile home was nicely air conditioned and well appointed, and everybody was most hospitable in welcoming us to the island. There was just one problem. No arrangements had been made for food. There was no store on the island, and the restaurant was not yet serving. We had been met by a young Panamanian who was to be in charge of the marina when it opened. (Later he took us fishing in a Bertram 25, and I caught a 50-pound wahoo.) He had delivered us to our trailer but had left before we realized there was not a bite of food in it, so I wandered around the premises until I found him again, and explained our situation. He solved it by bringing us a hot stew in a dinner pail for supper. For breakfast I ranged along the mobile homes, palm and empty cup out, begging enough supplies for our first breakfast of the new year. Everyone thought our plight very amusing. It was not exactly Robinson Crusoe style, but it was a form of roughing it on a not-so-desert isle.

Fish nets on Tahaa, French Polynesia.

12 · *Hawaii and the South Pacific*

*T*he Pacific Ocean makes up for its lack of coastal islands off the Americas with an oversupply in its expansive middle reaches, especially south of ten degrees North Latitude. There are a few islands in the northeastern Pacific, but generally it is a mammoth, watery wasteland for thousands of square miles. In the lower section though, from the Galapagos through the Marquesas, Tuamotus, and Iles sous le Vent, on to archipelagos galore—the Gilberts, Marshalls, Solomons, New Hebrides, Carolines, and Philippines, to name a few—the big blue map of Oceania is freckled with island groupings that could occupy a lifetime of exploration. They take up very few square miles in land area, but they make an eternal progression of island hopping out of the tremendous distances of mid-Pacific.

Many of them were unknown to all but geography experts and a few traders and missionaries until World War II made household words out of such as Tarawa, Saipan, and Eniwetok, and the atom bomb test made Bikini forever famous. Now many of them have relapsed into isolation and anonymity, easily forgotten by a world that knew them through the head-lines in 1942–45. There is not always the same peaceful acceptance of the world around them that marked life before the civilized world descended on the area with bombs, artillery, landing craft, tanks, fighter planes, flame throwers, and great gray ships. An awareness of the modern world has caused inevitable disruptions and dislocations in the ancient island ways.

· *OAHU* ·

Hawaii, or, more specifically, Oahu and its Waikiki Beach, is the ultimate commercialization of the island dream. It is a lurid example of what happens when a natural attraction of exceptional beauty becomes open to uncontrolled development, a problem now faced by the Catalinas, Martha's Vineyards, Mount Deserts, Mackinacs, Tortolas, and other such threatened islands around the world. Oahu was well on its way to full exploitation in the days of steamer travel, and the jet age really opened the gates. Today the beauty is still there, dimly glimpsed between the high rises and fast-food outlets, and very much alive in most of the other, less accessible islands, but the epithet "Miami Beach with mountains," is sadly well deserved for the Waikiki section that was originally the symbol of the beauty of Hawaii.

In 1962, on my way home from Australia and knowing that I was to come back with my family, I spent a few hours at Honolulu between planes looking at likely hotels for our visit. I wanted to be near Ale Wai Yacht Harbor, as I would be covering the finish of the ocean race from Los Angeles, and I wanted to be on or near Waikiki so that my daughters could surf. A perfect solution seemed to be a hotel called the Waikikian, right near the harbor and fronting on one end of the beach, an attractive layout of low units set on paths winding through a tropical garden. It had a lovely, secluded atmosphere removed from the din and bustle of the city around it. I made reservations and built it up with glowing advance notice to the family, only to find, on arrival the next year, that a 25-story hotel had been erected immediately outside the garden, completely overshadowing it in the intervening time. It was not quite finished, and each morning at 7:30 we were awakened by the clatter, whirr, and roar of pneumatic drills, cement mixers, hammers, tractors, and trucks. Progress!

All this did not prevent enjoyment of what modern Hawaii has to offer. The girls loved the beach and their initiation into surfing (and Jane and I got as close to surfing as we wanted in an outrigger canoe ride through the waves). There is no denying the symmetry and power of Diamond Head standing sentinel at the opposite end of Waikiki's lovely white curve. A drive into the interior of the island better conformed to our expectations, with great fields of undulating sugar cane, endless rows of pineapples, and the play of cloud shadow and sun over Oahu's mountains—a Hawaii that exists away from the glitter of Waikiki.

There is a grandeur and a boldness to the steep faces and starkly outlined crests of many Pacific island mountains. Hawaii's great volcanic heights are among the most dramatic examples. The "Big Island," Hawaii itself, almost as big as Connecticut, has the great volcanos of Mauna Kea and Mauna Loa that rise more than 13,000 feet. Kauai and Maui, luxuriant in jungle growth, also have tall volcanic peaks, and Molokai and Lanai are the quietest and least developed. Molokai holds the memory of Father Damien and his leper colony at Kalaupapa, and Maui's Lahaina, an old whaling port, still retains the atmosphere of one through the help of restoration.

In addition to pineapples, which are grown on every island but Hawaii, coffee, sugar, macadamia nuts, cattle, and orchids are Hawaiian products that flourish in this climate, and fishing for dolphin (*mahi-mahi*), mullet, billfish, and many local reef varieties is excellent. Surfing, of course, started in the Hawaiian Islands, where it has been a sport for centuries, and modern catamarans, double-hulled sailboats that can achieve great speeds, are descended from the prehistoric craft of Polynesian voyagers from Hawaii.

Honolulu, a busy, modern city and still a Navy town, with the memory of Pearl Harbor ever-present in the monument fashioned out of the sunken battleship *Arizona*, is one of the world's great racial melting pots, bringing together ethnic strains from all over the world, with an emphasis on the Oriental. In it, the Polynesian heritage has been watered down to insignificance, and one must get away to the striking countryside of the islands to gain a sense of this fascinating background.

· THE SOCIETY ISLANDS ·

The name Society Islands was given to this group by Captain James Cook, the great explorer whose remarkable voyages opened much of the Pacific, in honor of the Royal Society that sponsored his expeditions. My first view of one of the distinctive peaks of Polynesia, of which the Society Islands are a part, was that of Bora Bora. Perpendicularly faced, and flat on top with a cleft, it emerged in full outline on the distant horizon at the end of a 23-day convoy from Panama in June, 1943. Suddenly in a noonday sun there it was, the South Pacific exemplified. The crew of 25 men and two other officers of the 110-foot subchaser I commanded was on deck, eagerly awaiting the expected landfall when it leapt into view. We had skirted the Galapagos and Tuamotus, tantalizingly beyond the horizon, and had seen nothing but blue Pacific for more than three weeks. A current of excitement electrified all of us at the sight of Bora Bora.

As we drew closer, and curving white beaches fringed in palms began to show behind the great explosions of surf on the outer reef, the excitement grew to audible cries and murmurs. It was picture-book material come to life—only two in the crew were over thirty years old and many were in their teens, away from home for the first time—and the picture was filled in further as we rolled through the pass on the gradually subsiding surge of Pacific combers. An outrigger sailing canoe skimmed toward us across the pale green waters of the lagoon, with an honest-to-God Polynesian maiden in a *pareu* standing by the mast, waving and smiling gaily.

When we arrived ashore and found that the United States Army had been established there for 18 months and that most of the Polynesian "maidens" had already had one child and were perhaps pregnant again, courtesy of the worthy warriors, it took a bit of the bloom off the romantic image. Still, the villagers did keep as much as possible to traditional ways, and it was a rare experience to visit with them in their houses, talk about our families at home in answer to their questions, eat raw fish "cooked" in lime juice, and trade for necklaces, canoe models, and sea shells. Money helped, but the most prized item for Bora Bora's flat-footed, callous-soled belles was a pair of GI shoes. They could be cut out at the toes and used for sandals for going to church, the only time anyone would consider wearing shoes in a 100-percent barefoot community.

It was a shock, too, to see victims of elephantiasis slowly clumping along on grotesquely distorted legs or holding a mammoth, swollen arm in a sling. Polynesia was not all mountain peaks and palm-lined lagoons. The real-life Dorothy Lamour image was pregnant without benefit of clergy and very lucky not to have elephantiasis. The realities of South Sea island life were an eye-opener.

Tahiti, where the jet was headed 20 years after the trip to Bora Bora, provided another inspiring spectacle in the golden dawn, but the reality of Papeete dispelled much of the magic. Tahiti is still one of the world's most beautiful pieces of land with its peaks soaring over 7,000 feet above the gentle curves of its reef-lined shore, but the city of Papeete is a modern-day mess. Not only has the jet age brought a flood of tourism, turning the natural, free and easy life-style into conscious posing, but it is also a military base for France's atomic tests on a remote off-lying atoll, and the combination has been ruinous to the atmosphere. We had to spend a night there before we could go on to Moorea, and memories of Tahiti are of disappointment and disenchantment. The French military strutting through the town took away any semblance of South Sea island languor, the hotel was not very good and quite expensive, taxis were overpriced, and, as a special touch of disillusion, the Gauguin Museum did not have a single original Gauguin in it. Present-day Tahiti was symbolized for us by the girls and boys who performed native dances in the hotel floor show. As soon as they finished, they replaced their grass skirts with blue jeans and leather jackets, did a few American dances, mingling with the guests with cigarettes hanging out of the corners of their mouths, then roared off into the night on motorcycles.

After our stay in Moorea (see Chapter 14) our final touch of Tahiti was in the one night spent there before making connections westward. It was our twenty-fifth wedding anniversary, and I inquired about the best restaurant for a special dinner. The one recommended was well up in the hills above Papeete, an excellent French restaurant with Polynesian overtones, and the dinner was indeed fine. There was only one problem. In trying to order a martini, in French to a Polynesian waitress for whom it was even more of a second language than for me, we somehow ended up with sweet Vermouth on the rocks. With all those blue jeans and motorcycles, I thought they would at least know about martinis.

• *SAMOA AND FIJI* •

Westward from Tahiti, my wartime hegira took me to Samoa and the Fijis, while our jet from Tahiti this time went nonstop to New Zealand, erasing half of our anniversary on the International Date Line. Samoa proved how right Somerset Maugham was to call his saga of Sadie Thompson *Rain*. There was not a two-hour period in the week our convoy spent there that there was not a downpour. We were berthed in Pago Pago Harbor (and surely all the world knows by now that it is pronounced Pango Pango), and there is something about a rain cloud that really loves the shape of this long, narrow slit between hills that rise steeply, lush and brilliant green with jungle growth, to a cap of trade-wind clouds. The shape of the harbor, the height of the peaks, and the direction of the prevailing wind all combine in this steady production of wet. Samoa's hills, reefs, and brilliant water-colors are a treat to the eye—if you can manage to get the moisture out of it.

Fiji is a name that has always conjured images of primitive savagery and faraway mystery to me, and it was full of surprises. In two brief visits it has risen to the top of my list of places I want to visit again. Somehow it is especially intriguing to find a "sea" in an unexpected place, and I really did not imagine a separate one in the middle of the Pacific. But there is one surrounded by the Fijis—the Koro Sea, over 100 miles wide. This containment by a ring of utterly remote islands and reefs seems to set it off as a world by itself, a secret never-never land removed from all outside influences, and it had that feeling for me as our wartime convoy slipped through the reefs at Nanuku Passage, guarded by Wailangilala Island, in the growing light of a pale, purpled dawn. The names themselves have such a wonderful ring, and soon there were others: Ovalau, Ngau, Taveuni, Moala, and Totoya. They shone golden brown in the sunlight as we crossed the Koro Sea's whitecaps, and later in the day the great land masses of Vanau Levu to the north and Viti Levu on the west began to bulk on the horizon. These are big islands. Vanau Levu is 117 miles long, and Viti Levu is 95 by 67 miles, with mountains as high as 4,000 feet.

There are 250 islands in the Fijis, all but 80 uninhabited, and the possibilities for exploration are obviously endless. Yet, there, at the end of the Koro Sea passage, is Suva, a modern, cosmopolitan city with heavy overtones of British colonialism—now departed—in its public buildings. And on the west coast of Viti Levu on a long stretch of coast lined with idyllic beaches near the great crossroad airport of Nandi there are plush modern resorts. Fiji has gained a troubled independence from the British, many of whom have remained in the jobs they held before, but there is a difficult split to reconcile between the native Fijians and East Indians. The East Indians were imported during British rule to do much of the work and have all but taken over business life and economic control.

Fiji is the easternmost outpost of Melanesia, thrusting into Micronesia on the north and Polynesia on the east, where natives are light skinned and coppery tan. Melanesians are pure black, and the Fijians are magnificent physical specimens, tall, robust, handsome, and gracefully athletic. They are also genuinely friendly (although cannibalism existed into the twentieth century in some remote areas), and a visitor is greeted with a booming "boola," for "hello." In combat in World War II, the Fijians proved extremely courageous and resourceful, but they have never been attracted to hard physical labor, and as a result they now share their land with the East Indians on an almost equal population, but not economic, basis.

I was so taken with Fiji in the wartime glimpse of the Koro Sea and Suva that I arranged a stop there in 1962 on my way home from Australia, chartering an Eight-Meter sloop at the Royal Suva Yacht Club. It was really just a long weekend, taking advantage of the extra day to be gained on the Date Line between Fiji and Hawaii. Unfortunately, it was not quite the end of the rainy season. This was mid-March and perhaps the last week of it before dry easterlies would set in for six months. The weather was not the greatest, but it was a successful interlude despite it. The boat's owner was a tall, sandy-haired New Zealander, raw-boned and freckled, with a booming voice. He was the professional secretary of the Suva service club, a social organization of war veterans and British civil servants, and he had a crew of two shy, ever-smiling and efficient Fijians as deck hands and galley operators. As a back-up, in case the strange American proved difficult, he brought a Kiwi friend who had just finished 15 years on a banana plantation in the far uplands of Viti Levu. He had been virtually out of touch with civilization for most of that time, yet seemed a completely urbane man and was a delightful shipmate.

We had a great sail out to a pass in the reef ringing Viti Levu, where a little island called Nukulau, round as a dollar and about a mile in circumference, sat just inside the pass. It was privately owned, with one vacation camp under tall palms and a white ring of sand all the way around it. To windward the surf pounded in on the reef, with a string of islands on the horizon beyond it, and the Koro Sea stretched out to the east. Behind us Viti Levu's peaks were in and out of great cloud curtains that gradually moved toward us, covering the sun, and catching us in the frothy frontal line of a squall just when we were preparing to anchor at Nukulau. We rode it out under jib, reaching back and forth in the pass with the rail down in a great welter of spray and rain, and then came in to anchor when the squall front passed, leaving a humid calm behind, scented with the flowers and wet earth of Nukulau.

It was a quiet night at anchor as we yarned in the cabin over uniced pink gins, listening to the steady fall of rain on deck. It turned out we had all done New Guinea duty in the war, and there were many notes to compare and tall tales to top.

Radio Suva was not encouraging about the next day, and it was so right. Rain came and went in great shrouds, with no wind at all, as vistas of Viti Levu would open up through the showers showing large, purple clouds pouring rain onto its peaks, only to be blotted from sight again as new downpours enveloped us. In nothing but a bathing suit, with the rain warm on my skin, I did a beachcombing circuit of Nukulau, picking up attractive shells, such as gleaming "cat's eyes" on the side facing the pass, and poking along in the shallows. A clearing period at sunset revealed great banks of clouds in tumbling tiers over the mountains, shot through with shafts of red and gold, and the next day saw clearing and a brisk sail back across the edge of the Koro Sea to Suva, where freighters from many countries were being worked at the pier.

The rainy day happened to have been St. Patrick's Day, and, in addition to giving its gloomy weather reports, Radio Suva wafted Irish melodies our way for most of the day. I think I must be the only person for whom "Danny Boy" acts as a reminder of the Fiji Islands.

· *TONGA AND SAMOA* ·

Somehow, I had never thought to see Samoa again after our wartime stop, but back we were in 1980, not for Samoa itself but as a transfer point on the way to a charter cruise in Tonga, the remote island group 2,600 miles southwest of Hawaii, whose very name seems to ring with the essence of the South Pacific. The only way to get there is to jet to Samoa from California and then take a little STOL plane the 300 miles southward from Pago Pago, and we had two nights and a day to nurse our jet lag in the Sadie Thompson (what else?) Bar of the Rainmaker Hotel and to see what 37 years had done to the place made famous by Somerset Maugham.

The rain had not changed at all. For our entire stay, the mountains around the harbor, now jam-packed with Japanese tuna boats rather than U.S. Navy ships on their way to war, were draped in heavy clouds, and curtains of rain swept continuously across the scene. The hotel is named for the highest mountain, and the setting on the point at the harbor entrance is dramatic, if damp. The main building, a giant, round Polynesian *fale*, with reception, bar and dining room, is on the end of the point, and two-story wings of bedrooms extend back from this building in a V on each side of the point. A month before our visit, a Navy plane taking part in an air show ran into the wires of a cable car that crossed the harbor to the top of Rainmaker Mountain and crashed on the southern wing of the hotel, burning it out.

Under the steady rain, this burned-out wreckage made a desolate sight, and Pago Pago itself had an overall air of seedy clutter. Trash, empty bottles, cans, and all sorts of litter were everywhere in the streets and around the houses, and an air of neglect and decay was pervasive. Dodging through the rain squalls, we walked the streets and took a look at the many yachts at out-of-season moorings in the harbor, and most of them looked as run-down and neglected as the town. The only "local color" was an enormous bingo game, with hundreds of players squatting cross-legged on the dirt , floor of a big open-sided market building on the waterfront, stolidly listening to the numbers being called and tending their boards. Samoan natives did not seem to have that jolly *joie de vivre* for which Polynesian people are noted, as the game was a very solemn affair. We also noticed that every Samoan we saw in the Sadie Thompson Bar, and they were 90 percent of the clientele, was smoking continuously. Beer was far and away the most popular drink.

Tonga was a fantastic contrast in every way. It is unique in that it is the only independent kingdom in the Pacific and has been for centuries, long before the coming of the white man, although it was a British Protectorate for many years. It is made up of three separate groups of islands strung out on a northeast-southwest axis over 200 miles of ocean. The capital is at Tongatapu in the south. In the center is the Ha'pai Group, and we were headed for the Vava'u Group in the north, where charter yachts are based.

We left the rain behind in Pago as our plane winged into the dawn from an 0600 departure, and we dropped a day in the flight, as the International Dateline runs between Samoa and Tonga. It was clear and surprisingly cool in Tonga (18° South Latitude) in early June, the dead of winter there, a bracing climate in the 70s, and we only had a couple of rain squalls in eight days.

The Vava'u Group is reminiscent of the Virgin Islands in scope and lay of the land, although the hills are not quite as high. About 600 feet is the highest elevation, but the contours are graceful, and bold cliffs and hills dropping steeply to sheltered coves provide lovely scenery.

The group covers about 100 square miles, and there were 45 numbered anchorages on the crusing chart provided by the charter service, which meant an anchorage almost every few hundred yards. The island of Vava'u is about eight miles across and has the major hills, and the rest of the islands, varying from a mile or two long to tiny dots of sand, string off to the southward in close order. Names like Foeata, Mananita, Pulepelekai, Fonga Unga, Kenutu, Ovaka, Ofu, and Taunga stir images of golden beaches, waving palms, and surf-lashed reefs, and the images all come to life in idyllic reality in sailing through the channels (called *avas*) that wind through the islands.

Jane and I had a native guide with us named Safeliti Taufa, a shy but engaging man of about 40, stocky and well-built with strong features, one of 12 children and father of nine himself, who was a great help in steering us to the best anchorages and in telling us about the life of the islands. The Tongans are a proud, disciplined people, conscientious when there is work to be done, but happy-go-lucky and laughing while they do it, and religion plays an important part in their lives. The country is almost entirely Christian, with Catholics, Mormons, and Methodists as the major sects, and Sunday "blue laws" of no fishing, swimming, or playing games are strictly observed. In contrast to Samoa's unlovely clutter (and Tongans and Samoans hate each other like Hatfields and McCoys), the towns and villages are scrupulously neat. As an example and contrast, empty bottles are saved and used, upended into the dirt, as borders for garden plots that surround the houses.

Safeliti took us to a village on Ofu where we had a glimpse of Tongan life. Mormons were playing a spirited game of volleyball, men were working on fishing boats on the white curve of beach along which the town's one sandy lane of a street ran, women were in the water up to their thighs stripping stems of plants to make grass skirts, children ran everywhere, following us with wide-eyed curiosity, and dogs, pigs, and chickens wandered freely. Between the houses, the grass was cropped in park-like neatness under towering, widely spaced palms. It was a happy, self-sufficient seeming place. No doubt there are cares and problems, but those of the rest of the world seemed far, far away.

Our anchorages varied between sheltered ones in deeply indented coves, and lunch-time stops at a succession of tiny cays and islets, ringed with picture-book beaches. Each had a particular charm, and exploring and beachcoming was always a delight, but one that stands out was Mananita, farthest out from the big islands on the fringing reef to the eastward. We lazed to it on a day of near calm, easing over water protected from the long Pacific rollers by the reef. It could be seen as a line of white near the horizon, and the waves rearing up to crash on it seemed almost disembodied in the clear air as they heaved into the sun for the last time before thundering to destruction in a smother of white. The distant thunder of their demise throbbed faintly in the air.

Safeliti guided us through an intricate set of reefs to a pool of calm just off Mananita's pale beach. The anchor shot down to clean sand through the crystal clarity of the water, while small sets of surging waves leaped and foamed over reef tops showing greenish brown just a few feet away on all sides.

Aside from its beautiful beach, which all the islands have, Mananita is unusual in its stand of puko trees, tall, smooth barked and heavily leafed. From a distance, they look like an impenetrable tangle of forest, but the ground beneath them is free of underbrush because the thickness of their cover keeps the sun from shining through. We walked from the brilliant glare of the beach into the dim green stillness of the trees, and the ground, softly carpeted in leaves, was as clear for walking as the aisles of a church. There was, in fact, a cathedral-like feeling under the great vault of the trees, with here and there just a thin beam of light slanting through to glance off Jane's hair or dance on the little mounds of leaves underfoot. Even the rush and roar of the surf was all but stilled in the verdant silence, and it was not until we worked our way the several hundred feet across to the ocean side of the cay that we began to hear water noises again.

Suddenly, we were out of the cover and standing on the windward beach, back in the world of southeast trade wind, brilliant sun on brightly hued waters, and the rush and rumble of surf across a reef. Tonga was a fascinating, out-of-this-world experience, and Mananita will always stand in my memory as the symbol of it.

A working junk at Hong Kong.

13 · The Southwest and Far Pacific

The Southwest Pacific is as full of islands as the Northeast Pacific is devoid of them. From New Zealand through New Caledonia, Australia, New Guinea, Indonesia, and the Philippines, great insular land masses take up large amounts of space all the way to the Asian mainland, and then there are, of course, Taiwan and Japan as part of the island world of the Far Pacific. The interlocking masses of land could almost be called another continent, a maritime one cut through with seas and straits.

Although New Zealand and Australia are too big to be treated in the same insular league with Block Island, Tortola, or Tahiti, the Kiwis and Aussies have long lived with a geographic chip on their shoulders. Because of their far-off, isolated station of the globe, they have always felt, even if only subconsciously, out of the mainstream and ignored by the rest of the world. This has led to a bravura, boastful manner in many of the people that seeks to cover up for this imagined neglect, aggravated, too, by the old business of the convict background of early settlers. It is still an insulting gag to ask an Aussie if you can have a look at his wrists, checking for manacle scars.

World War II and its global mixing of military forces helped to overcome this sense of isolation, and the jet age has increased ease of communication tremendously. In the days of steamer travel, it was truly a journey to the end of the earth to get to the Antipodes, but now the time factor has been nearly eliminated.

• *NEW ZEALAND* •

After our flight across the International Date Line from Tahiti, which wiped out half of the actual date of our twenty-fifth wedding anniversary, Jane and I spent two days in Auckland, in the subtropical northern part of New Zealand. We did not see the impressive mountain and lake scenery to the south, and Auckland, except for its harbor, is not exceptionally scenic. It does, however, have a magnificent harbor, and as a yachtsman I was astounded at the great number of pleasure boats. I would venture a guess that New Zealand has more boats per capita than any other area of the world, and they are used constantly.

Just north of Auckland is a beautiful area for cruising known as the Bay of Islands, which is very popular with Kiwi sailors who head there as often as they have the chance. The climate is mild and pleasant all year and there is a great choice of harbors, coves, and small islands for exploration.

In Auckland we were intrigued by a peculiar paradox of New Zealand life. Politically it is very advanced into socialism, but the actual social life seems almost a throwback to Victorian times. Women are supposed to take their place as homemakers, and, for example, the Royal New Zealand Yacht Squadron is strictly stag for all but one night of the year, the annual ball. Jane had to sit in our hotel room and do the laundry while I went to the club to be the speaker at a meeting. There were over 600 men present for my after-dinner speech in the main hall of the big old clubhouse, and, by way of starting the program, the Commodore announced that, since it was a very warm night, he was removing his coat and all present could do the same.

Seeing this, I could not resist starting my talk by saying, "You don't know how frightening it is to a lone Yank, who spent some time down this way during the war, to see hundreds of you taking off your coats at the same time." During the war it was not uncommon for American and Anzac troops to end up in brawls, usually over women, which meant taking off jackets, and understanding guffaws greeted my remark.

There were no brawls this time, and the hospitality was overwhelming. One facet of the concern with being so far out of the mainstream is a sincere effort to put a best foot forward in entertaining visitors, and we had the full benefit, short of Jane getting inside R.N.Z.Y.S., of course.

Before taking the plane to Australia we were driven to the highest point on the hills behind Auckland for a panoramic view of the whole harbor, the islands stretching off to the north, and the graceful green ones where New Zealanders go when they seek a change. Even people who live on big islands like to escape to smaller ones.

· NEW CALEDONIA ·

My visits to New Caledonia and New Guinea were under the sponsorship of the United States Navy in World War II, when there were other things on the mind besides the fascination of escaping to an island. There was little of that sort of feeling; rather one of exile and banishment. There was a basic underlying question of "What on earth am I doing here, and why?" Preoccupation with enemy action, or, if not that, just plain boredom, fostered a hopeless feeling that the war would go on forever in these never-never lands that none of us had ever heard of two years before. In 1943, seeing a minesweeper with the motto GOLDEN GATE IN '48 painted on her stack seemed disturbingly prophetic in the Southwest Pacific.

Everyone was preoccupied with orders home, especially commanding officers who had brought subchasers all the way out from the States and knew that their execs were qualified to take over. A new administrative officer for the subchaser squadron arrived in Milne Bay, New Guinea, in the spring of 1944 and was immediately besieged with requests for transfer home by officers reporting that their execs were ready. He knew, but we did not, that the big Hollandia operation was in the wind, and there were not going to be many transfers back while preparations for it were under-way. Trying to jolly his petitioners along, he used the tack, "Why don't you relax and enjoy the magnificent scenery out here. In peacetime people would pay thousands of dollars to see places like this." If lynching were allowed in the Navy he would have been a candidate after that remark, and the logic of his argument was totally wasted. Scenery had a different meaning when there was no choice but to admire it because we were imprisoned.

Even in this frame of mind, though, I can remember thinking that New Caledonia could well become a tourist attraction in the air age that would obviously follow the war. It is equally south of the equator as Cuba is north of it—about 21 degrees—and, although smaller, about 200 miles long to Cuba's 600 miles, it is reminiscent of Cuba in climate and landscape.

My ship was undergoing engine repairs there in a small shipyard on Ile Nu, a dry, hilly island that forms the main harbor of Noumea, capital of the French island, and one day when the work was in progess and I had nothing special to do, I took a walk into the hills, finally emerging on a flat summit several hundred feet above the enormous harbor. It was crowded with every kind of Navy vessel, as we were just beginning to gather forces for the next northward push after securing the Solomons. The carrier *Saratoga* bulked largest of all, surrounded by battleships, cruisers, destroyers, and all manner of support craft, but my eye wandered away from the obviously impressive naval display to the fringing reef on the other side of Ile Nu, the deep blue of the Pacific beyond it, the lovely curves of palm-lined beaches scalloping the deep jungle green of the main island's shore, and the mountains bulking the landward horizon. The harbor was far enough below me for its noisy bustle to have faded to a faint hum, and I was surrounded by silence in the tropical sun.

For a few minutes I appreciated what New Caledonia could be like at another time, when the harbor was not overrun with great, gray ships, and hordes of Navy men on liberty were not swarming through the sleepy little city in the late afternoons, where officers, a seething mass of khaki, would take over the Hotel du Pacific in a frenetic cocktail hour, pushing and shoving for a place at the bar, each man clutching his own glass or beer can, as you had to bring your own utensils to get a drink. From the hilltop on Ile Nu, I had a momentary, wistful vision of another way of life on this beautiful island.

And there was still another wistful vision on a trip into the hills for dinner at a country inn. We were all officers in khaki and there was drinking, singing, and telling of jokes, but it was nevertheless a startling change from the military mess 20 miles away at Noumea. The inn provided dinner in a private room, by reservation, and it was cooked and served by a tiny Indonesian woman. The courses were exotic, and only some large salty oysters were recognizable. It was all excellent, especially in contrast to subchaser food. The inn was actually a private plantation, set on a hill, with a dreamlike view of a stream wandering gracefully through a valley richly planted in coconut palms and bananas. The center section of the house had balconies looking down on a water wheel turning lazily in the stream, and two Ls off the main section formed a courtyard, where small brown children tumbled in play. The whitewashed walls had a French provincial look about them.

During dinner we were greeted by the planter, who had made part of his house into an inn. I remember him as a tall, hearty man with a firm handshake. Now, years later, after I have learned that he was the prototype for Emile deBecque in *Tales of the South Pacific*, I can only visualize him as Ezio Pinza.

• *NEW GUINEA* •

The facetious officer was right in his remark about the impact of New Guinea's scenery. The world's second largest island, at 312,000 square miles, it is smaller only than Greenland. It is a land of primitive grandeur, strikingly beautiful here, grim and forbidding there, as untamed and remote in its tremendous mountains (to 16,000 feet), jungle valleys, muddy rivers, and the brilliant waters of its reefs, as anywhere in the world. It was a strange arena for warfare, as far from home as Americans could get in mileage, climate, and atmosphere, and so completely uncivilized and untouched that it seemed an incongruous background for artillery, tanks, fighter planes, and landing craft.

The first sight of it, as hills of brilliant green appeared above the Coral Sea's dark waves, rising toward mountains that were a hazy smudge in the interior, was a stirring one not only because of its raw beauty, but because it was where the tide of war had been turned. All the time I was there, the mix of wartime concerns and the overwhelming physical impact of New Guinea and its heavy, constant heat was a powerful, dominating force. Concentrating on navigating a poorly charted pass in the reefs and taking bearings and checking landmarks, I would suddenly become aware of the brilliance of the water and the strange, distorted loom of the reef through its clarity, not as a factor in navigation, but as an assault on the senses. And the smell of jungle vegetation, earth, flowers, and wood smoke on the pungent night breeze in the lee of a tropical island will forever recall New Guinea to me.

There were many of the satellite islands that were as striking as Bora Bora, Moorea, or Hispaniola, but were just almost anonymous adjuncts of New Guinea's great complex of off-lying islands, reefs, and atolls, that, in more accessible, better-known locations might have been among the most glamorized in the world. Goodenough and Normanby were two of great beauty, but whose charm became somewhat tarnished when troops based on them suffered severely from typhus. I have been forever intrigued by the names of an octet of islets stringing northwest from Madang to the section of the coast where the great, turbulent, brown Sepik River spews effluvium from deep in New Guinea's unexplored interior into the Bismarck Sea in a muddy stain that spreads far offshore. Their names form the wonderful, jabberwockian chant of Blup Blup, Bagabag, Karkar, Bam, Vokeo, Kairuru, Mushu, Manam. Several of them are semiactive volcanos, with wisps of threatening smoke streaming from their peaks.

As military occupiers, we had little contact with the natives of New Guinea. Native canoes would dot the waters away from the combat zone, and some of the men worked at the bases. Sometimes we would drive through a village on a foraging expedition, but for the most part the natives were out of sight. There was a pilot boat in Buna commanded by a young Aussie whose only crew consisted of two natives named Fishface and Lincoln. They were a great help to him in running the boat, a former trading launch, and in their local knowledge of the reefs, but they were as shy as jungle birds.

In Milne Bay, a deep indentation at the tip of the "tail" of the huge bird shape that New Guinea's outline makes on a map, the war had moved on to the north and west. The big Navy base was on the site of a former Australian administrative headquarters, and the bay, deep and well-protected, with mountain chains marching off to the east on both its shores, had been a lonely, isolated spot before the war. The only "civilization" had been the administrator's camp, and a sleepy little town named Samarai on an island in China Strait. This is the entrance to the bay from the Coral Sea and a main trading route between Australia and the islands to the northwest, all the way to China. By the time we arrived, despite the disruption of the base, native life had settled fairly well back to normal, with the settlements hidden up a creek at the head of the bay, the Maiwara River. It was a favorite expedition, when we were back in Milne Bay for repairs or reassignment, to take our outboard-powered rubber dinghy and head up the Maiwara into the jungle.

As soon as the open bay, with its big ships at anchor and its towering mountains, had disappeared astern after the first bend in the river, we would find ourselves in a world apart. Dense growth came right to the water's edge, with vines lacing the dark, thickly clustered trees in brilliant bloom, and only a shaft of sunlight here and there penetrated to the water. Birds of many bright colors flitted through the trees, as strange cries and chitterings filled the air. Away from the breeze of the bay, the heat closed around us in an aromatic humidity rich in the scent of trees, wildflowers, and damp earth. With little or no advance warning, we would round a bend and come upon a native village in a clearing on the bank, with canoes pulled up in the mud, and houses standing on stilts in a dapple of sunshine. Naked children played along the water's edge and under the trees, while men and women went about tasks in the houses or in small garden patches near the huts. They were short, squat, and heavily wrinkled, and would look at us in not unfriendly shyness, answering a wave if we gave one and sometimes smiling. Clothing was at a minimum, consisting of loincloths and cloth skirts. As soon as we slid by the clearing the jungle would close in again, as densely as before, but the tableau of a Stone Age existence, as close as we ever came to knowing these primitive people, would linger in the mind as a reminder of what an anachronism war was in this faraway island.

· HONG KONG ·

Hong Kong is an island city, that fact being an obvious and an integral part of the atmosphere. Unlike New York, where Manhattan is overwhelmed by the city around it, Venice and its land ties to the mainland, or Copenhagen, where the island of Zealand is big enough to make you forget that it is one, Hong Kong clings to the soaring peaks of its 32-square-mile island just across the harbor from the mainland in a dramatic display of insularity. Ferries are its only link, a constant stream of big, fast ones from its mainland adjunct, Kowloon, plying a harbor that has to be one of the most heavily, and variously, trafficked in the world.

Freighters of all nations and naval vessels are in a mix with big, red-sailed junks that bring food down the river from Canton, smaller fishing boats, yachts, launches, and thousands upon thousands of sampans and junks, rafted in great flotillas in the side coves and bays, that are home to a population of untold thousands who seldom get ashore. Over these examples of a type of vessel that has not changed in thousands of years, large modern skyscrapers, office buildings, and hotels look down, and the incredible bustle of one of the most crowded and busiest cities in the world roars through its daily paces. The city runs along the harbor and scales the peaks to the 1,800-foot summit, where the fanciest residences are, facing north toward Kowloon, and there is more of a feel of open country on the south side, looking off to the South China Sea. It is here, though, that the biggest junk colony of all is located, at a harbor called Aberdeen, which is filled from shore to shore with junks rafted gunwale-to-gunwale in an incredible jumble of masts and rigging.

In a whirlwind tour of Hong Kong, in which Jane and I turned down the opportunity to shop for several hours for the chance to see more of the sights and were told that we were the only tourists in history to come to Hong Kong and not do any shopping, we paused for a restful interlude at the Repulse Bay Hotel on the south shore. This was a wonderful relic of gracious living from the days of glory of the British Empire. We had cocktails and lunch on a flower-bordered terrace overlooking velvet lawns and a view of the smiling, sunlit sea, with the long, rambling hotel building behind us. It has since been torn down.

It was then a vivid change to stroll through the crowded side streets of the city, in an incredible jumble of signs, pushcarts, open-air markets, and swarming humanity. A trip in the cable car to the breathtaking view from the island's peak was a fine climax to a day of varied sights, scenes, and smells. The car was filled beyond capacity, and the cacophony of Oriental sounds, high-pitched, singsong, and completely alien to western ears, as everyone chattered at once, was a symbol of the main impression carried away from Hong Kong—that of people, people, people everywhere, busy and active in a noisy outpouring of vibrant life.

· AUSTRALIA'S BARRIER REEF AND ITS ISLANDS ·

On June 4, 1770, Captain Cook, the first explorer to see the east coast of Australia, was headed north in *Endeavour,* his bluff-bowed 106-foot ship, in the vicinity of 21 degrees South Latitude. For several days he had been in the open sea, hugging the mainland of the world's geologically oldest but most recently discovered continent as the shoreline changed from un-broken cliffs in the southern regions to the capes and deeply indented bays of what is now Queensland.

As he sailed on this first of his epic Pacific voyages, running before the favorable southeast trades on a pale green sea, a string of islands began to appear on what had been an empty eastern horizon. The first were mere dots on the rim, but more came into view ahead, closer to the mainland and closer together, until *Endeavour* was surging along in calm water in a passage that was less than five miles wide. To port were the blue mountains of the continent, and to starboard, a hilly archipelago clustered around a main island about ten miles long, with three distinctive peaks, one at each end. The highest, almost 2,000 feet, appeared as a symmetrical cone in the center of the archipelago. The islands were well wooded, and more than 50 of them lay in a tightly spaced row over a distance of 53 miles.

In the habit of explorers, Cook named the whole string the Cumberland Islands in honor of the Duke of Cumberland, one of the patrons of his sponsor, the Royal Society. And, since it was Whitsunday when they reached the northernmost group, 12 main ones stretched along 20 miles, and cen-tered on the island with three peaks, they were given that name. Whitsun-day is the feast of the Pentecost, the fiftieth day after Easter and one of the major festivals of the Anglican Church. The central island was also named Whitsunday, and a smaller island with a bold, steep face plunging directly to the sea, was dubbed Pentecost. This was, in a way, a British version of the practice so often followed by Columbus in giving names of saints and their days, and other religious allusions, to so many of his dis-coveries.

While he was sailing along the coast, which he named New South Wales (this applied to the whole east coast of Australia until 1859, when Queens-land became a separate state), Cook did not know that one of nature's most incredible phenomena lay just over the horizon to the east, the world's longest barrier reef, some 1,200 miles long. As an experienced seaman, he must have suspected that there was some reason for the calm seas, lacking the rollers and underlying surge of the open ocean all along this great stretch of coast, but he had no visual evidence of it until much further north, where what is now known as the Great Barrier Reef comes to within five miles of the mainland. There, just short of the northern tip of Australia,

Endeavour hit a reef and was only saved by the tremendous hard work of the crew in manning the pumps, with Cook himself pitching in during the desperate emergency.

When she floated free on an 18-foot rise of tide, the hole was patched with an old sail lashed across it that worked well enough to get her into a nearby river, where it took six weeks to make repairs. That river is now called the Endeavour River, and the town on the site is called Cooktown. While there, Cook and Joseph Banks, the ship's young naturalist, had the first chance ever to study the hitherto unknown Australian aborigines, probably the most primitive people in the world. The aborigines had no houses, no agriculture, no tools except spears, no clothes, and a very shy and diffident manner. The Englishmen found them much more difficult to get to know than the Polynesians of the Society Islands. They were so ignorant of possessions that they paid no attention to the usual gifts of beads and cloth. The entire colony of aborigines consisted of twelve men, seven women, and two children.

Today the Whitsunday Islands remain much as Cook saw them in 1770. The whole coast of northern Queensland is still very sparsely settled in comparison with the big population centers of Brisbane, Sydney, and Melbourne to the south, and the islands have been preserved in a virtually uninhabited state. Of the dozen or so major islands in the group, five have modest out-island-type resorts similar to those found in the Bahamas and Caribbean, there is a marine biology station, and everything else is a completely undeveloped national park.

From a distance they have very much the look of the Virgins in the interplay of peaks and hills and the narrow cuts of channels between them. Bays slice deeply into the bigger islands, with one or two, such as Nara Inlet, having the proportions of a small fjord as it narrows down for several miles between rocky escarpments and steep peaks on Hook Island. Closer up, though, the land could not be mistaken for anywhere else in the world, as the vegetation is peculiarly Australian and far from tropical, even though this is well within the Tropic of Capricorn at 20 degrees South Latitude. Towering eucalyptus, with their spindly leaves and rounded tops, predominate, set off by the gaunt profiles of hoop pines, husky trees with clumps of dark-green needles spaced far apart on the branches, like Norfolk pines that have been distorted out of their special symmetry. A great variety of ferns, plants, and the spiky, long-leafed pandanas fill in underneath, and all of it clings to the steepest, rockiest slopes. High in the trees near the top of the hills, flocks of white cockatoos, peculiar only to Australia, circle and perch, filling the air with their raucous cries.

I first saw the Whitsundays on a quick passage inside the Barrier Reef in my subchaser, headed for the war zone in New Guinea in 1943, and they left a lasting memory of graceful beauty as one of my main impressions of the Queensland coast, even though we swept by at our top speed of about 14 knots. We did not return for 36 years, when Jane and I spent a week cruising through them in a bareboat charter yacht, and the old impression was fully confirmed. Especially at such a tropical latitude, these are islands unique in atmosphere and a sense of timeless, unchanging beauty.

It was September, early spring in the southern hemisphere, and for the eight days we were in the area the weather was unbelievably idyllic. There was none of the expected tropical languor in the air, so familiar in a similar northern latitude. Temperatures were about 75 degrees Fahrenheit—or hovering above 21 degrees Celsius as Australia now has it—the sun was brilliant, and the only clouds were the usual afternoon collections of cumulus over the land masses of the islands and the mountains of the mainland. The southeast trade varied from zephyric to semiboisterous, and the air had the fresh, clean, bracing quality of a perfect summer day in an area like Maine. Combined with the nontropical look of the vegetation, with the hoop pines silhouetted against the clear sky along the ridge tops, there was almost a north woods feel in being there. Later on, in full summer, it does get much hotter, with periods of heavy, tropical rain. In January and February it is considered too hot and unstable for pleasant sailing or any other kind of holidaying. Hurricanes, called cyclones here, are rare, but there were two bad ones in the 1970s after years of freedom from them.

Sailing into the dozens of harbors where reef walking, oyster gathering, and bush hiking are the main activities, is to find them as they were in 1770 except for a few chaste antilittering signs, trash barrels, and barbecue pits placed by the National Park Service. In Nara Inlet, if you are adventurous, you can follow a narrow path from the shoreline up through the bush to a cave with aboriginal drawings, and the great tide range, up to 18 feet as Captain Cook discovered, bares vast areas of sand flats and reefs for low-tide exploration. In Macona Inlet we found starfish, sand dollars, and many small shells we were not knowledgeable enough to identify, as well as the almost ubiquitous oysters. When the tide begins to make, its advance across the flats is a visible flow of ripples covering a few feet every minute.

Underway, we were convoyed by porpoises, smaller than the Atlantic species we were used to, and every once in a while, a head would pop out of the water like a scuba diver coming up for air, soon to be identified as sea turtles four or five feet wide and weighing up to several hundred pounds. Of the local fish, we sampled barramundi, john dory, red emperor, and reef fish, all of which were very good, especially reef fish when crumbed. This was the main course at one island resort we visited, South Molle, which from the water is unobtrusive, but is actually rather an extensive spread in the out-island mode, with bedroom units in separate huts along a white sand beach, a central dining and entertainment hall, tennis courts, all water sports, and even an abbreviated golf course. Guests arrive by ferry or helicopter.

It was a time of fun and games as we sat with several couples at dinner and then attended the main entertainment of the evening in the dancing area, a hopping-toad contest. After a strident mistress of ceremonies in outsize harlequin glasses and a violently colored caftan cajoled the crowd into making bets with her jolliest "Strine," the peculiar Aussie slang delivered in a nasal, Cockneylike twang, six toads were released from under a pot in the center of a circle of about 20 feet in diameter, and the first one to hop out of the circle would be the winner. Jane won four dollars by betting on toad number two, named Raquel Squelch, who made it to the edge before any of the others had even moved. Toads are practically a plague in the cane fields of Queensland, so large that they intimidate dogs, and packing a venom that is strong enough to be used in medicine as an anesthetic. A new industry has recently grown up—one that exports cured toad skins to America for use in shoes, belts, and handbags. We gathered that Queensland toads were not an endangered species.

There is a natural compatability between Australians and Americans, and many elements of Australian life are a close match to American ways. We found universal, easygoing friendship and cordiality, and a very real interest in American politics. Except for the Strine accents and the natural confusion in certain words and terms used differently, we felt completely at home and accepted.

The Whitsundays are a tight little world, ideally suited to relaxed cruising, and, as you gaze across an open expanse of calm water, stretching to the far horizon when islands are not in the way, there is a constant awareness that the conditions depend on that great coral barrier off to the east. Charter yachts are not allowed to head there, as it takes expert local knowledge to handle the reef's intricacies, but there is a way to visit it. From the small, dirt Whitsunday airstrip on the mainland, served by STOL planes that connect with jetliners at the city of Mackay 60 miles away, a company with two small, four-seater amphibians runs trips out to the reef when the tide and weather are right. We arranged by ship's radio to be picked up from our boat when we were anchored on the east side of Whitsunday Island off a five-mile stretch of the whitest, squeaky-clean, powdered sand I have ever seen. Low tide was early in the morning that day, and the plane arrived at 6:30, sliding into a landing near the anchored boat. The pilot killed the motor as he approached and then used a canoe paddle to come alongside our dinghy, trailing off astern, to pick us up. It was a little over 30 miles to the northeast over a mirror-flat sea before the first brownish-green reefs appeared below and we banked down to land on a glassy lagoon. The landing was a difficult feat, because it was hard for the pilot to judge our distance above the water. The other plane was already there with more visitors, moored to a stake in the reef-girt lagoon, and we were picked off our plane in a small glass-bottomed boat and taken to the nearby reef, where the tops of lumps of coral were barely sticking out of the water.

It was an eerie setting in the early morning light, a watery platform where we waded ankle-deep through the incredible colors and formations of the coral, surrounded by an unbroken expanse of empty sea in all directions, wide and shining and not marred by so much as one ripple. At low tide the reef can be walked, wearing sneakers of course, but it is well underwater at high tide, when it can only be seen by diving. Coral cannot live out of water for any time, and the whole complex is in delicate ecological balance.

The pilots were also trained naturalists, and they gave us some idea of the fantastic variety of life on the reef as they guided us across it. We were warned against picking up certain mollusks in brown and white shells of graceful contours, as they defend themselves with poison darts, and were shown the delicate-looking tan fronds of fire coral that can cause a painful burn if touched. The most dangerous reef denizen is the stone fish, which camouflages itself on sandy patches and has a strong enough poison in its spikes to kill a human. But it is not often seen. (Shoes provide protection.) We were asked not to step on the brightly colored coral growths as they were alive and could be damaged. The browns and grays of dead coral were the places to walk, and a gray, mushy, soft coral could not be hurt if stepped on.

A catalogue of life forms on the reef could fill pages, and each square foot would be worth a microscopic inspection of hours. The variety of colors in every shading of the basic ones and many odd pastels in lavender, chartreuse, pink, and pale blue was endless, and there was continuous fascination in shifting focus from a broad view of the whole reef to the minute details of a coral underfoot, where tiny polyps could be seen pulsating and extending, changing the look of the surface, as they sought food in the water around them. Brain coral, anemones, clusters of mosslike green, and an endless variation in shapes, forms, and hues became distinct and separate only when examined very closely through the film of water, revealing the full subtlety of their colors and contours. Weirdest of all were the clams, the tridacnids, which include the giant clam that can be as much as four and a half feet wide. We saw none approaching that size, but there were some close to a foot wide with oddly serrated openings lined with "lips" of the brightest hues in greens, blues, reds, oranges, and combinations thereof. One had lips that were blue-and-gold striped. All are deeply imbedded in the coral and seem a permanent part of it. Here and there a sea cucumber, the *bêche-de-mer* or *trepang* so sought after as an Oriental delicacy, would be inert in a sandy spot, although still alive.

All too soon the inexorable cycle of the tides made it time to stop wading, and we were then taken in the glass-bottomed boat along the edge of the reef where it plunged vertically for 20 or 30 feet to the sandy floor of the lagoon. Here the brown branches of stag coral rose to heights of several feet, and the wavering water made odd distortions of the coral heads, large brain corals, sea fans, and anemones that clustered below us. On the reef we had seen a few tiny fish trapped in the tide pools, but here there were clouds of brightly colored ones, big and small, in schools and darting about by themselves. Brilliant parrot fish that actually bite off pieces of coral and feed on it nibbled at the reef walls, and red and white clown fish slid in and out of openings.

Suddenly a long gray shadow broke from under the reef wall, and, with a flick of the tail, was gone from sight. It was the only shark we saw in Australia. Next, a large, yellowish-green turtle moved lazily away as the boat's shadow passed over him. Rays with their long, whip-like tails glided over the bottom, bulky groupers nosed around the heads, and tiny fish of the most vivid striping wheeled and skittered across our view. The water was so calm that we did not need the glass bottom to see the wildlife.

Back in the plane, the last view we had of the lagoon was of water pouring through a break in the reeflike river rapids as the quickest way for the tide to move. The green-brown of the reefs under us soon gave way to the pale slatiness of the open water inside the reef. The Whitsundays, looming up ahead with our boat, appearing as a speck of white off the long curve of the island's beach, brought us back to a more solid sense of reality. Behind us was the otherworldly, dreamlike experience of the isolation of the reef, one of earth's truly remarkable natural features.

Moorea, by dawn's early light.

14 · Moorea

"**W**elcome to Paradise!" A tall, sunburned man in flowered bathing trunks stood on the quay as a launch landed us from the big flying boat that had brought us the few miles from Tahiti, and he greeted each passenger with this cheery phrase while helping them ashore. As often as he had said it, he still seemed to mean it, and the surroundings supported him. This was Moorea, often described as the world's most beautiful island.

Its splendor had been glimpsed in the previous dawn from our inbound jet from California on its approach to Papeete. From the air, with slanting sunlight beginning to burnish its peaks, the impact was overwhelming, a dream-like fantasy. Now, with these same crests soaring above us, there was still a sense of unreality, a reaction that this was just an artist's concept of what a South Sea island should look like. The pinnacles, outcroppings,

223

and perpendicular facades of the peaks, jungle green on the lower slopes and bluish gray rock where they met the sky, seemed like the towers and turrets of a Bavarian castle. Nature seldom puts shapes like these together, and there was an impression that all this was somehow a contrivance. It seemed as though sculptors with giant hammers and chisels must have rigged scaffolds to chip the pinnacles into such symmetry and tumble the piles of rocks into these balanced proportions. It just could not be real. But it is.

In the days we spent on Moorea there was never a moment that lacked awareness of this magnificent scenery, and there were ever-new perspectives on it from the bays, beaches, and coral-stone roads of the island. Glimpsed through a grove of palms bending over a beach, the mountains held a softer light but dominated still, and the sudden confrontation with a new view of one on rounding a road bend or the point of a bay would bring a gasp of astonishment at another facet or contour. From one certain angle in Papetoi Bay, one of the peaks showed a hole through it that again looked as though the hand of man had hollowed it out. Away from the trade wind, Moorea was a fragrant riot of flowers, its air softly freighted with tropical scents, and splashes of color assaulted the eye at every turn.

Moorea has no big towns, just several small villages, and the white-capped channel that separates it from Tahiti has been enough of a barrier to stem the commercialism that sometimes taints that enduring symbol of island perfection. This is not to call Moorea totally unspoiled. There are several small hotels along its shores, and a Club Mediterranée resort operates for part of the year, so visitors are in evidence. One-day tours are run from Tahiti for a luau and native dance show, and the big, lumbering double-decker flying boat that brought us there has given way to an airport and land-plane service.

We found, on a side trip to Raiatea, one of the Iles sous le Vent (Leeward Islands) that string northwestward from Tahiti for over 100 miles, that Raiatea is a better example of how South Sea islanders actually live today. It is almost untouched by tourism, has 10,000 inhabitants, and a busy little city, Uturoa, with considerable commercial activity. There are no through roads around Raiatea, and the copra and food grown in outlying areas are brought in by boat to Uturoa, the marketing and shopping center. Raiatea's mountains are high, and there are interesting reefs, jungle rivers, and prehistoric ruins of Polynesian altars and burial ground, called *maraes*, always built on points, which were considered sacred. Raiatea has traditionally been a center of Polynesian life, but it is a plain Jane of an island in comparison with Moorea's overwhelming beauty.

Life for a visitor on Moorea is one of relaxation and ease, but living and working there has another side. The sunburned host as we disembarked was one of three young Americans who came to Tahiti in an ocean race from California in 1959 and decided to stay. It is not that easy, though, to say, "Here I am," and become a Society Islander. In French Polynesia, there is great concern, dating well back into the nineteenth century, about unwanted vagabonds becoming beachcombers. Permits, not easy to acquire, must be obtained in order to remain, and there must be a guarantee of support or gainful occupation of some sort. The three sailors decided on Moorea as their headquarters and opened a beachfront hotel called the Bali Hai, but for several years they were only operating on six-month visitors' permits. They had to rotate home to California to qualify for reentry, working out a schedule so that at least one of them was always in Moorea to run the business. They eventually obtained permanent permits, married locally, and raised families.

They have worked hard and done well with the Bali Hai, and have opened similar resorts with the same name on Huahine and Raiatea. All three are informal affairs with thatch-roofed cottages as bedroom units and a larger central building for eating and entertainment. All the comforts are offered in a completely informal atmosphere, and the emphasis is naturally on enjoyment of what the islands offer in swimming, fishing, diving, and exploration.

At Moorea it was almost enough to sit in front of our *fale* (house) under palms rustling in the trade wind and look out across the pale, clear inshore waters to the frothy tumble where rollers crashed on the reef. Outside the white line of the reef, the open Pacific was a deep, rich blue, and beyond the clubhouse to our left a long stretch of white sand led to Moorea's two beautiful bays, Cook and Papetoi. In the other direction the red roof and spire of a small church showed through the trees on a point. Behind us, the ever-amazing peaks reared to the clouds. Not normally given to beach-sitting, we enjoyed it in this setting, adding a dip now and then in the warm, transparent lagoon water, but there were other things to do and see.

One day the Bali Hai pickup truck took us into the interior on a rough, dusty road to the farm where much of the food for the dining room is grown, and we walked on from there up a forested slope, climbing ever higher, following the tumble of a stream, until we came to a natural pool in the rock. Shafts of sunlight filtered through the thick cover of boughs, glancing off the water in bursts of sparkling light, and a waterfall splashed down from the rim of a small bluff in a clear cascade. The atmosphere was sultry and heavy with jungle scents, and it was a perfect place for a swim.

Another expedition found us in Bali Hai's recreation vessel, a nearly derelict catamaran raft that had been salvaged from a reef off Papeete, where its owner had abandoned plans for a cruise to Hawaii. Aptly named *Liki-Tiki*, it took us along the shore in a reef-hopping cruise into Papetoi Bay. From the water Moorea's profile opened in new compositions and an ever-shifting panorama as we scudded before the trade under a squaresail that might well have been left behind by Captain Cook. It was easy going downwind, but heading back to windward after a swim and lunch beneath Papetoi's steep cliffs was a tough job for two little Seagull outboards. We made progress in inches, but there could not have been a better coastline to examine slowly.

Captain Cook came to Moorea in 1777 on one of his epic voyages of discovery that opened up so much of the unknown areas of the Pacific. His journal is very detailed on all his activities and on the places he visited, and I read it with interest after we returned home to find what he had said about this island, which could not have failed to impress even such a wide-ranging explorer as Cook. Impressed he might have been, but most of the entry on Moorea is concerned with the problems he faced when the natives stole one of the ship's goats that had been put ashore to pasture. After much politicking and a show of firmness, along with a promise not to take revenge on the guilty natives, the goat was returned without bloodshed, although Cook's native aide, Omai, a Raiatean he had picked up as interpreter and navigational guide, was eager to use the gun he carried to teach the Mooreans a lesson. Cook believed that firmness without bloodshed was the best way of handling long-term relationships with islanders, but the policy failed him a year and a half later, when he met his death in Hawaii as a result of misunderstandings during a confrontation.

Cook, one of the great seamen of all time, and a self-taught scientist who elevated himself from cabin boy on a North Sea collier to command of Royal Society expeditions, did say, before he became involved with goat thieves, that the bay he entered at Moorea was one of the best natural harbors he had found in the Pacific. Ships could sail in and out easily because of its angle to the trades, and there was good anchoring ground, excellent protection, and a fine place to take on water from the mountain streams pouring into the bay. The bay, a twin with Papetoi, is now named for him.

When his ships sailed in, natives crowded aboard and brought him breadfruit, coconuts, and hogs in trade for hatchets, nails, and beads. Because the bay is deep, and ships can move in almost to the trees, Cook thought it would be a good place to rid the ships of the rats that were a perpetual problem, and he moored within 30 yards of the beach. Hawsers were then led to the trees on shore in hope that the rats would find an easy path off the ships, but the experiment did not work well. "I believe we got clear of very few, if any, of the numerous tribe that haunted us," was the comment in his journal.

Moorea at that time was much more heavily populated than today, with many villages around the island. In the evenings, Cook and Omai went ashore to ride horses, visiting the villages and the chief, Maheine, and it was in dealing with Maheine that the return of the goat was eventually arranged. Cook had ordered several canoes broken up as a show of his concern over the goat, but after its return, the natives brought breadfruit and coconuts to his ship, *Discovery,* and the affair ended amicably.

Evenings at Bali Hai, where dressing for dinner consisted of changing from bathing suit to shorts and putting on a sport shirt, were pleasantly easygoing. The usual preliminaries in the bar, with many of the women dressed in *muumuus* or *pareus* they had just bought in one of the villages, gave guests the chance to compare notes on their day's adventures, and there was usually some form of entertainment. One night there was a complete Polynesian feast, with pig roasted in a pit of coals and vegetables served on pandanus leaves for plates, followed by mangoes, bananas, and coconuts. On another, there was a native dance performance that seemed to take in half the population of the island. All ages took part, from preteenagers to grandmothers, who were directing traffic and supervising costumes. These were fresh and colorful, the dancing was good, not the perfunctory type often passed off in Hawaii or Tahiti, and the drums throbbed and resounded under the palms.

As we walked back to our *fale* along the beach, with the soft hiss of waves at our feet and the profile of the peaks outlined against the stars above the trees, the drift of cool air from the mountain slopes carried that special mix of flowers, damp earth, and wood smoke that can only come from a tropical island at night, a blending of all the elements of sensuous beauty and savagery, and I still seemed to feel the drums throbbing through the trees.

In the morning, it was time to leave, and the next evening in Tahiti, where we awaited our connections west, Moorea's now-familiar and unforgettable profile stood against the sunset in sharp relief above the shimmering path of light on the water. I could now fully believe its claim: the world's most beautiful island.